3

"Be Proud"
Hertfordshire and the Great War.

Private Adams (Bedfordshire Regiment)
whose gravestone is depicted on the cover of this book was of St. Albans.
His parents lived in Offa-road, and he was employed before the war by
Viscount Grimston, Grimston Tyres Ltd.

For over forty years, John Cox has been working as a professional Librarian, Archivist and Information Researcher. From 1969-73 he was editor of *RICS Abstracts and Reviews*. As editor of the *Alban Link* for the Fraternity of the Friends of St. Albans Abbey he organised the publication of the reprint of the St.Albans section of the *Victoria History for Hertfordshire* and in 1990-94 edited volume 11 of *Hertfordshire Archaeology*.

In partnership with Sheila, his wife, they established Eddington Press, St. Albans and have published local histories: *St. Albans-news of 1889; St.Albans and West Herts-news of 1890;* three cookery books; and a children's story for Wren Publications.

Future projects include a biography of Field Marshal, the 10th Earl of Cavan and an anthology on Frederic George Kitton, 1856-1904.

"Be Proud"

Hertfordshire and the Great War.

An anthology, compiled
by John G.E.Cox

Eddington Press, St. Albans. 2002.

ISBN: 1 872067 07 7

Designed by Eddington Press,

104 Lancaster Road, St. Albans AL1 4ES

© John G.E. Cox

Cover by Simon Beer, graphic designer.

Set in Book Antiqua,

Printed by Cavalry Creative Service, Hatfield.

Contents

Entries are arranged in years, by date. Each year, from 1914 until 1919 has an individual contents page, which lists the precise page no, subject content and the title of the entry. A composite contents page is provided for 1920-1925.

Photographs

Harry Carrington (*page vi*) and Edward Warner, VC (*page 47*)
All other photographs are found in whole pages, at intervals throughout the anthology.

Harry Carrington
Chief Reporter and Editor of the
Herfordshire Advertiser and St. Albans Times, 1896-1947,
a photograph taken on his last day
before retirement in 1947.

Harry Carrington [1872-1951]

Hertfordshire is very fortunate in having a number of local newspaper titles which have had a healthy history in reporting news. The *Herts. Advertiser and St. Albans Times* began life in 1855 and continues to be published as a weekly newspaper. Until comparatively recently, it served a readership throughout central Hertfordshire from Hitchin in the north and Watford and Elstree in the south, whilst at its heart lay the city of St. Albans.

Harry Carrington arrived in St. Albans in 1896 from Staffordshire to become Chief Reporter on the paper. He had been born in Ipswich and had been an apprentice-compositor on the *Ipswich Journal* before turning to journalism. From 1916 until 1947 he was Editor of the *Herts. Advertiser* and it is largely due to his efforts that the letters written by soldiers during the Great War, 1914-1918 were published in its news columns. His daughter, Beryl Carrington, herself a long-serving member of the newspaper staff, told the compiler that she believes that her father "helped his friend Canon George Glossop in preparing the lists for the street memorials which were erected in the St. Albans Abbey Parish" and she has no doubt that "he called on most of the families of the war-dead, but that he never mentioned this at their home, then in Carlisle Avenue. "The 1914-1918 war was a dreadful secret which was not talked about as it was so painful!".

Mr Carrington, was, as newspaper editor, a leader of the community in St. Albans. A founder member of St. Albans Rotary Club, he sang in the choir at St. Peter's Church where he became a sidesman and later churchwarden. At. Bricket House, which after the war became the St. Albans and District Nursing Association Hospital he was Hon.Treasurer, a position he held until the arrival of the National Health Service, in 1948. During the General Strike, 1926 he alone produced his newspaper for two weeks and as a result was sacked from the *National Union of Journalists*.
Source: *Beryl Carrington.*

Introduction.

In 1990 I was unwrapping parcels which contained the business papers of Viscount Grimston, later 4th Earl of Verulam. Having been stored for many years in a farm building they were full of grain. Among them was a collection of letters written to Lord Grimston, of Grimston Tyres Ltd from employees who were serving in various army regiments during the Great War.

Three years later when I became the School Librarian at *Stanborough School, Welwyn Garden City* a teacher in the History Department asked for "resources on trench warfare" and I remembered these documents. Later evaluating the effectiveness of the available resources I began to query how they related to Hertfordshire and Welwyn Garden City. How many students had grandparents who had served in that war? Were there any useful Hertfordshire archive resources?

To answer these questions, I began looking at the *Herts. Advertiser and St. Albans Times*, which in 1914-18 had circulated throughout central Hertfordshire. As Hon.Archivist for the *City and District Council of St. Albans*, the staff of *St. Albans Museums Service* lent me the newspaper volumes relating to that time. From these I was able to build up files from which I began to put together extracts for use in a possible anthology. Miss Carrington, who has been a good friend for forty years told me of her father's involvement.

Between 1995 and 2000 we made three visits to some of the battlefields in France, Flanders and northern Italy which gave me the context of some of the letters I had read. Not content to use only one resource, I used the *Hertfordshire Record Office,* visited other libraries and institutions to build up a picture of all the theatres of the war, where Hertfordshire men and women had been involved.

We went to Poperinghe, Ypres, Hill 60, Arras; Peronne and the *Historial de la Grande Guerre,* to Corbie, Albert, the *Thiepval memorial* and the Somme battlefield; to Vimy Ridge, Loos and Boulogne to find the grave of Julian Grenfell.

In *La Neuville British Cemetery*, Corbie, beneath the south wall of this small, isolated cemetery, just north of a line of poplar trees, lies the grave of Private W. Waldock, 2nd Battalion, *Bedfordshire Regiment* who died on 3rd July 1916. Had he been wounded on the first day of the Battle of the Somme?

On another visit we found the village near St. Omer where the *Hertfordshire Regiment* trained in preparation for their part in the battle on the 31st July 1917; visited Talbot House, Poperinghe and saw the newly re-opened inter-active exhibition *In Flanders Fields* in the Cloth Hall, Ypres. In Italy we visited the British Church in Venice which has a memorial to those British soldiers who died in Italy in 1917-18 as well as driving up the specially created road up onto the Asiago plateau where much of the fighting took place.

This anthology has been selected from a number of different sources in addition to the *Herts. Advertiser*. Many reports have been précised and some have had the tense changed. Addresses are shown as reported, thus Harley-street, not Harley Street. (Harley-street was later to be named Mount Pleasant), Some items show amazing co-incidences. For example, Julian Grenfell's brother Billy, became Staff Captain to Lord Cavan in August 1915. Earlier in that year, Ernest Brabazon, brother of Violet, wife of Viscount Grimston, held the same rank. Both died in 1915.

Local newspapers are not copyright, but if I have failed to obtain copyright clearance of other items, I apologise and will rectify this in any future edition. Though every effort has been made to make this anthology accurate in every detail, any errors are mine and mine alone.

John Cox

Acknowledgements.

St.Albans Cemetery superintendent Barbara Thompson and her predecessor, Jim Hamilton; Ann Wheeler, Chris Saunders, Sam Mullins formerly of St. Albans Museums Service; Vivienne Prowse (retired) and the staff of St. Albans Central Library; Paul Underhill, Dean's Verger, St. Albans Abbey; Hertfordshire Local Studies and Archives; Bedfordshire Record Office; Luton Museum janitors who enabled me to view the V.C.s of Private Edward Warner when that Museum gallery was being reorganised; St. Saviour's Church, St. Albans; Gorhambury collection; Librarian and staff at the Imperial War Museum, London; Keeper of Public Records and staff in the Search Rooms at the Public Record Office; Toc H Headquarters, Wendover; the Curator of Talbot House, Poperinghe, Flanders, Mr John Burgess of Hatfield; Miss Dorothy "Dottie" Owen; Derrick Brunt, Plaistows Farm, Chiswell Green for providing some information about flying activities at London Colney; Lady Elizabeth Longman and Lady Joanna Stourton for information on Field Marshal, the 10th Earl of Cavan; Rod. Higham and the Revd. Pauline Higham; Brian Moody; David Kelsall; John Manning, *Herts Advertiser* and Beryl Carrington for information and loan of photographs. Paddy Storrie, Andy Barnes, Martin Learmonth, Paul Simon, Sophia Davison, Jed Whelan and Kathryn Hodgkinson of Stanborough School, Welwyn Garden City; Ron and Mollie Upton, Hatfield formerly owners of R.U. Litho, Hatfield, Charlie McKay, owner of Cavalry Creative Services, Hatfield; copyright holders of material included.

Winifred Stobbart, my mother-in-law, now aged 98 years, corrected pages of the original draft; my wife, Sheila for putting up with this project for so long and who has read and commented on all the drafts, who has been my driver and made so many helpful suggestions. St. Albans District Councillor Gordon Myland, who at one time worked for *Gibbs and Bamforth*, the former publishers of the *Herts. Advertiser*, and who has read and commented on the entire text.

JGEC, October 2002.

They may not have had the education
that our children receive today, but many
wrote home to their families, employers and friends
and described their circumstances in the war,
which is the base of this anthology.
Some died in the service of their King and country.
Some were disabled and required permanent care.
Many returned home in the hope of a better life.

This book is dedicated to all
who were part of the Great War.

They were staunch to the end against odds uncounted.
Laurence Binyon.

Noble deeds of noble men (and women)
Canon Frederick Scott, Quebec.

We think that we gave in vain. The world was not renewed.
There was hope in the homestead and anger in the streets
But the old world was restored and we returned
To the dreary field and workshop, and the immemorial feud.
Herbert Read.

Contents: 1914

War breaks out.

Austria declared war on Serbia on Tuesday. Belgrade was taken by the Austrians on Thursday. The Serbians suffered a defeat in Bosnia losing 800 men whilst the Austrians lost 200 men. Russia is mobilising troops and Germany is preparing in feverish haste. German nationals are being recalled from foreign countries and Russians are leaving Germany in large numbers. ...

Food prices are rising at panic rates throughout Europe and there have been a number of business failures. In the House of Commons, the Prime Minister - Mr. Asquith said, that the outlook was grave.

The British Fleet has been moved and all leave has been stopped and those men on leave are being recalled to duty. Troops are being moved although these measures are stated to be precautionary only.
Source: *Herts. Advertiser and St.Albans Times, Saturday, 1st August 1914.*
Throughout, this weekly newspaper is referred to as the "Herts. Advertiser".

Newspaper Editor witnesses chaos in France.
Extracts from a feature article, penned by Mr. A.E.Gibbs, Editor of the Herts Advertiser on his return from France at the beginning of the war.
By a stroke of ill-luck, I happened to be caught in Lyons when hostilities between France and Germany were just commencing. ... Things were looking very black and ominous signs were in the air, but just before leaving London on Thursday of last week, I was advised by those who ought to be well informed on such matters, that the journey need not be abandoned, and that the risk of inconvenience was small.

So on the evening of that day, I found myself in Paris. Early next morning I made my way to the *Gare de Lyons*, and took the place which had been reserved for me on the 09.15 *rapide*. It was not until I ordered a place for luncheon in the restaurant car that anything at all unusual happened. The attendant, before giving me my ticket asked if I had the money to pay for it as notes could not be taken. In conversation with him I learned that paper money, either French or English was not being accepted and that only hard cash would avail me. Fortunately, I had a few hundred francs in gold, more than enough to carry me through my subsequent adventures, in which respect I was very much more fortunate than many other people. Scores of travellers, especially Americans, were stranded for want of money although they were carrying drafts for large amounts, but which they were unable to cash. They had difficulties in purchasing the bare necessities of life.

Lyons was gaily decorated for the Exhibition. The illuminations in the streets were very fine and the city presented a joyful appearance, little in harmony with the sad times that were to come. I decided to postpone my visit to the Exhibition to the next day, although the hotel porter advised me to go that evening to see the illuminations.

Alas! the next morning the great show closed its gates and came to an untimely end. After dinner I went for a stroll in the streets and found great crowds of people thronging the central streets, which were still gay with thousands of coloured lights on the triumphal arches. Pressing towards the thickest parts of the crowd which surrounded a newspaper office, I found the latest telegrams concerning the crisis were being read by an excited throng.

During the night I was awakened by noises of movement going on in adjoining rooms, where heavy luggage was apparently being dragged about, and when I went downstairs in the morning, I seemed to be the only visitor left in the hotel. Everybody had cleared out!

I was told that an ultimatum had been received from Germany, and that the railway had been taken over by the Government and that no more trains would run to Paris. Here was a dilemma - I was held up in the middle of France with no means of getting home and with a limited supply of money, and that principally in unnegotiable paper.

What was there to be done? I decided to go, at once, to the British Consul and ask his advice. After some trouble I found the Consulate which was not yet opened. I awaited the arrival of the representative of my native country, who received me very kindly. He advised me to go to the station and wait till a train was going somewhere, preferably to Paris, but if I could not go there, to try to get to Bordeaux or some other seaport where I would stand a chance of getting a boat to England. He gave me a written message to take to the Stationmaster asking him to help me in any way he could. He thought I should be wise to encumber myself with as little luggage as possible, and advised me to abandon my baggage at the hotel, kindly promising to look after it and send it on to me when happier days arrived. So resolving to be guided by him, I put a few necessities in a small handbag and left everything else with the hotel keeper.

When I reached the station, I was informed that an effort was being made to get unfortunate people like myself back to the *Metropolis* [Paris] by a circuitous route through a more western district than was served by the main line, and that a train would leave at 12.20 p.m. There being more than an hour to spare, I sent a cab-driver with my card to the hotel to reclaim my luggage which was thus in a short time restored to me and I managed to bring it home without loss. ...

To cut a long story short - after several changes, innumerable stoppages, struggles for food at buffets denuded of almost everything eatable. I arrived in Paris between two or three in the morning and eventually reached England and St.Albans safely.
Source: *Herts. Advertiser, 8th August 1914.*

British Red Cross Voluntary Aid Detachment

Active preparations for dealing with the wounded in the case of war are being made by the *British Red Cross (St.Albans) Voluntary Aid Detachment* which has been, for some time, at full strength - thirty in all including nurses. They are in a state of complete efficiency for their work. Other ladies who are qualified for work have volunteered to help as supernumeraries.

Arrangements have been made, in case of necessity, to fit *Bricket House, Bricket Road, St.Albans* as a temporary hospital. The residence is a large

one and offers extensive accommodation, but should this prove inadequate, the detachment has power to requisition other buildings.
Source: *Herts. Advertiser, 8th August 1914.*

Hertfordshire hears that war has been declared.

Readers of local newspapers, at the beginning of August, learned of the steps being taken by the British government to limit the actions being taken in Europe. Yet at the same time, members of the nobility and gentry - their sons and relatives were either asked to make ready for evacuation to a war zone or were expecting orders to report for duty. For example, four *St. Albans City Police Constables* rejoined their regiments, P.C. Atkins to Dunbar to rejoin the *1st King's Dragoons;* P.C. Edwards to Bedford to *1st Battalion, Bedfordshire Regiment;* P.C. Thorpe to Chelsea Barracks to the *Coldstream Guards;* and P.C. Bass to Woolwich to the *Royal Army Service Corps.*

Troops arrive in St. Albans

Within days the population of St. Albans, like other Hertfordshire towns, increased rapidly as troops arrived, until such time as they were required elsewhere.

The goods sidings at *St. Albans Midland Railway Station* were converted to unload horses, guns and other stores; the railways were taken over by the Government and the majority of cheap and excursion tickets were cancelled. This resulted in many, who normally took their holidays at this time of the year, to make alternative and somewhat unsatisfactory re-arrangements. The August Bank-Holiday was extended by Order of the *Privy Council* in London for a further three days, until Friday, 7th August.

Proclamations calling up Reservists and the Territorial Forces were posted on various buildings in the city centre.
Source: *Herts. Advertiser, 8th August 1914.*

Food hoarded.

Grocers experienced at first hand the consequences of the war immediately. Refined sugar could not be obtained and this resulted in panic buying for other goods. Three-quarters of our bacon supplies come from the continent of Europe - the major part comes from Denmark.

No eggs are being exported from Russia, Austria and Hungary who are our chief suppliers. The Manager of one local Grocer reported: *that those who usually* spent a sovereign, had given orders for up to five pounds or even more. ... One gentleman, took away in his motor car, a dozen tins of tongue, two dozen tins of milk, two dozen tins of corned beef, a half-a-side of bacon, two hams, a hundredweight of flour and other provisions. ...

Source: *Herts Advertiser, 8th August 1914.*

Horses commandeered.

Local landowners and tradesmen voluntarily gave horses to the war effort. The Marquess of Salisbury at *Hatfield* indicated that many of his horses would be available. Mr. Joel at *Childwickbury* offered any of his horses that were suitable and the Master of the *Hertfordshire Hounds*, the Earl of Cavan, gave 17 kennel horses to the regular cavalry. Messrs. *Adey and White*, the St. Albans Brewers gave two pairs of horse vans, two carts and three horses, whilst another Brewer, Messrs. *Thomas Kent and Son* gave a good deal more.

Some individuals were not so accommodating. A lady driving in the neighbourhood was stopped by the military. She told her coachman to "drive on". "No, you won't", said the officer, "we shall require your horse". Another lady observed the action from a distance and directed her coachman to double-back and drive as smartly as he could in another directions!

Source: *Herts. Advertiser, 8th August 1914.*

Troops billeted in St.Albans.

About 1,350 officers and men of the *1st, 2nd and 3rd Batteries of the Hertfordshire Battery, Royal Field Artillery* [R.F.A], together with the *4th London Brigade* and the *Lancashire Brigade* were in Northumberland on their annual training when news was received, ordering them to return immediately. Two days later they arrived in St. Albans and by the following weekend, they had left on a route-march towards Brentwood. Some of the men, by then, had not had their clothes off for the best part of a week. Fifty new recruits were enrolled between Wednesday and Saturday. Many more volunteered, so a selection was possible. Only the best of the men were chosen.

Local schools were taken over as billets for the troops and it soon became common to see shirts and socks being hung in large numbers from the windows of schools and other public buildings. Local ladies arranged to have soldiers' washing done by local people at fixed rates and official notices were posted telling soldiers where they could get their shirts mended and washed.

St. Albans City Council's Urban Committee put in work to extend the sewerage system as some cesspools filled so quickly because of the unusual amount of water being used for baths etc. The St. Albans *Medical Officer of Health* had to arrange for a daily collection of house refuse from all buildings where soldiers were stationed in any numbers.

The *St. Albans Public Library's* opening hours were extended to include Sunday, which was open from 2.00 until 9.30 p.m. for the exclusive use of soldiers in uniform. The Mayor of St.Albans supplied the stationery required for letter writing.

Pageant House, at the corner of Victoria Street and Upper Marlborough Road was turned into a social club for the military. The *St. Albans Gas Company* provided the gas supply free of charge and a local builder, Mr. Ezra Dunham fitted the building out with a cloakroom and lavatory accommodation in the basement. On the ground floor, a

refreshment room and bar were provided, whilst two rooms on the first floor were made available for non-commissioned officers and rooms on the top-floor were turned into an entertainments and concerts' room.
Source: *Herts. Advertiser, 8th August 1914.*

Housing the troops.

Major Caldwell Smith, *Royal Army Medical Corps*, Chief Sanitary Officer of the *2nd London Brigade* called on me and officially informed me that 8,000 Territorial Forces would be billeted in St. Albans within a few days.

Early on in the following week, billeting officers arrived and nearly all public buildings, schools and empty houses were commandeered by the Military authorities. In most of these buildings, the means for the disposal of sewage was quite inadequate, and in order to protect the health of the civil population, and to keep the city in a sanitary condition, arrangements, which necessitated the expenditure of public money, had to be made at once.

Towards the end of September and the beginning of October most of the elementary schools were vacated by the Military authorities as the Territorial Forces were billeted in private houses.
Source: *Hertfordshire Record Office: St. Albans City Archives.*
Medical Officer of Health's Annual Report, 1914.

Hertfordshire Yeomanry.

About eighty troopers of 'C' squadron of the *Hertfordshire Yeomanry* were billeted in St. Albans for three nights, quarters having been secured for them at various houses and inns in the city. The purchase of mounts was made, horses were commandeered and some excellent animals were procured. The squadron leaves for Hertford today to join other squadrons.
Source: *Herts. Advertiser, 8th August 1914.*

Hertfordshire Regiment.

Next day found me in camp with the *First Battalion* of the *Hertfordshire Regiment*, a territorial unit, in which I was a junior Major. We were at Ashridge, the beautiful home of Lord Brownlow. ... I had only been there a day or so when the storm broke over Europe. Austria, France, Germany and Russia all-in, but England, where did she stand?

Almost every day after training, I rushed up to the House of Parliament (I am a Member of Parliament) to hear the news in the House of Commons. There was no decision and whilst precious hours passed, and hours became days before the dramatic declaration was made. Back I sped through the night to Ashridge, and my boats were burnt in a day, for I had ceased to be a politician except in name; and thenceforth a soldier's work called.

The camp broke up and units returned to their native towns and villages. We knew that the mobilization of the Territorial Army was but a matter of days, and what days they were! The settlement of our business affairs, our domestic concerns, all the planning perhaps for a year or more was rushed into those few hours. Of all the population, none had less time to square their accounts than the serving citizen soldier.

Mobilization followed speedily and I found myself back in my native town of Ware where I greeted a hundred lads of my old company, everyone known to me personally. Old hands who had retired were pressing round the Drill Hall to ask if they could enlist and serve with me.

That day I had to turn away fifty men because we were up to strength. We were a unit of the *East Anglian Division*, and marched in stages to Bury St. Edmunds, as part of the East Coast Defence. Previously we had been declared fit for active service, a fact of which we were proud, but day after day we sweated to improve.
Source: *Croft, Henry Page. My Life of Strife.*

10

Standing Orders - 5th London Infantry Brigade
extract on Marches

9. Order of March
Brigade Headquarters; Brigade Staff; O.C. Signal Section; Orderlies and Horse holders to above; Brigade M.M.P.; No.3, Section Signal Company; Brigade Headquarters Transport will march in the above order.

10. Starting Point
The rate of march of Units from billets or quarters to the Starting Point, will always be reckoned as 100 yards a minute.

11. Halts
When on the Continent, men, horses, and vehicles will be packed to the *right* of the road when halted.

12. Pace
The regulation pace (3 miles per hour including halts) will be maintained. Units in rear are responsible for keeping closed up to those in front. If the pace is too fast for any Unit in rear, that Unit must at once send a message to the head of the Brigade.

13. Flank Men
At each halt, the left-hand man (if on the Continent the right-hand man) of each four will be changed over to the opposite flank of the four.

14. Discipline
(a) The strictest March Discipline is to be maintained **at all times**.
(b) When troops or trains are coming into quarters, no Units are to send parties, horses, watercarts, or other vehicles along the road, on which troops, etc., are moving, without leave from the Brigade staff.

15. Smoking
No smoking is to be allowed on the march, except pipes and cigars.
Source: *Hertfordshire Libraries. St. Albans Central Library. Local Studies Pamphlet Collection.*

Bedfordshire Regiment.

The 4th August found 'C' Company of the *1st Battalion, Bedfordshire Regiment* guarding the *Marconi Wireless Station* near the village of Clifden, Galway on the north-west coast of Ireland. We heard the news that England was at war with Germany almost as it was declared in London, and in accordance with orders received from Battalion H.Q., we returned to Mulligar to mobilize.

The next few days were very busy. Reservists arrived daily from the depot in Bedford. Each company was made up to establishment. All reservists were put through a short but hard course of musketry and field training, special attention being paid to open order drill and movement.

On the 10th August we got final orders and on the 13th, the entraining and embarkation orders were received in detail. During the afternoon the whole Battalion was entrained in the siding near Mulligar station. Many people gathered at the station and cheered tremendously as the train moved out of the station.

We arrived at Belfast the following morning and marched through the town to the decks and went straight on board ship. Here we met the remainder of the *15th Infantry Brigade* which included the *1st Battalion, Cheshire Regiment; 1st Battalion, Dorset Regiment; 1st Battalion, Norfolk Regiment and the 13th, 14th and 15th Field Ambulances of the Royal Army Medical Corps.*

The men were finally heartened for the fray by a ringing message from The King, which was read out:

You are leaving home to fight for the safety and honour of my Empire. Belgium, whose country we are pledged to defend has been attacked, and France is about to be invaded by the same powerful force. I have implicit confidence in you my soldiers. Duty is your watchword, and I know your duty will be nobly done. I shall follow your every movement with deepest interest, and mark with eager satisfaction your daily progress. Your welfare

12

will never be absent from my thoughts. I pray to God to bless you and guard you and bring you back victorious.

9th August 1914   **George R.I.**

In addition, every man received this message from Lord Kitchener, *Secretary of State for War*, which he was instructed to preserve in his Active Service Paybook:

You are ordered abroad as a soldier of the King to help our French comrades against the invasion of a common enemy. You have to perform a task which will need all your courage, your energy and your patience. Remember that the honour of the British Army depends on your individual conduct. It will be your duty not only to set an example of discipline and perfect steadiness under fire, but also to maintain the most friendly relations with those whom you are helping in their struggle.

The operations in which you are engaged will, for the most part, take place in a friendly country, and you can do your own country no better service than showing yourselves in France and Belgium in the true character of British soldiers. Be invariably courteous, considerate and kind; never do anything likely to injure or destroy property and always look upon looting as a disloyal act. You are sure to meet with a welcome and to be trusted. Your duty cannot be done unless your health is sound, so keep constantly on your guard, against any excess. In this new experience you may meet temptations, both in wine and women. You must resist both temptations. Whilst treating all women with perfect courtesy you should avoid any intimacy.

Kitchener, *Field Marshal.*

On 16th August, we arrived in France and were the first Battalion to disembark. We formed up independently and march off to Camp No.8, six miles in the hills above Le Havre. It had been pouring with rain for two days so the ground was in a bad condition.

The following day we were very comfortably settled down with the

13

expectation of another night there, but shortly after noon we got orders that we were to move off by train that evening. We eventually marched off at 11 p.m. arriving at the station in Le Havre just after midnight. The train did not leave until 4 a.m. We were packed like sardines, but during the day many men climbed out on top of the carriages and some even rode on the footboards, although it was contrary to orders. At Rouen we stopped for an hour's rest for coffee, and again at Amiens. We arrived at Le Cateau at 4 p.m. and marched off to Pommereuil, a little village ten miles away, where we were billeted.

Source: *Bedfordshire Record Office. War Diary. 1st Battalion, Bedfordshire Regiment, 1914-1919.*

Stragglers.

21st August. - Stragglers were many. Each Battalion was the same as we passed. Many on the side of the roads belonged to Battalions who were in front of us. Most of them were reservists who had not carried a pack for years. They had every intention of keeping up but simply could not. I talked to several in my platoon and urged them to keep up, but the answer was invariably the same. "Oh, I'll get along alright after a few minutes rest".

Truly I shall not forget the marching we did on this and the days to come. Beside my own pack and rifle, I carried Private Talbot's pack for several miles. One of our platoon, Private Newsome was always happy and would sing when everyone was tired. He earned for himself the nickname "blinder".

Source: *Bedfordshire Record Office. War Diary, Bedfordshire Regiment .*

Billeting the troops in St. Albans.

For some days past, billeting officers have been working busily in St. Albans and preparations have been made for accommodation of any troops that may be stationed here. Nearly every public building has been taken, and many private residents have been called upon. The experience has been quite a new one for the people of St. Albans who

14

at first were inclined to view the enquiries of the billeting officers as an interference with the sanctity of the home. As the work has proceeded however, people have come to realise that the cause for which our soldiers are fighting is their own cause.

A few amusing stories relative to billeting operations are current. A dutiful housewife, in accordance with the instructions of her husband informed the billeting officer, when he arrived that they could not take any of the soldiers. "Book three here," said the officer curtly. Another lady informed her military caller that the only accommodation she had was the door-mat! "Very well, we'll book two for that," was the order.
Source: *Herts. Advertiser, 15th August 1914.*

Spy?

There was considerable excitement in Fishpool Street, St. Albans on Thursday arising from a report that a foreign spy was abroad. A man was found by the military quartered in the district obtaining certain information and taking notes. He was, however, identified by people residing in the district as a St. Albans man and was eventually released!
Source: *Herts. Advertiser, 22nd August 1914.*

Visiting Day.

Sunday was the visiting day for friends of the soldiers quartered in St. Albans. Passengers from London came by 'buses of the *London General Omnibus Company*, were numbered by their thousands. The "tommies" awaited their arrival in large numbers and took a wholesome delight in showing them around the city. Many of the married men were joined by wives and children, and it was a pleasant sight to see them carefully tending to their little ones. When the time arrived for the return of their friends, there was a long queue, often extending quite halfway up St.Peter's Street, and alongside was a queue of khaki-clad men taking farewell of their mothers, wives or sweethearts.
Source: *Herts. Advertiser, 5th September 1914.*

Caught in the act!

It has been necessary, on account of alleged attempts to cause army horses to stampede, to put out special pickets. Last week in Bishops Stortford, where several horses were killed in two such stampedes. On Wednesday night in Whitwell, troops caught a man in the act of stampeding their horses.

Source: *Herts Advertiser, 5th September 1914.*

The 10th Earl of Cavan joins the war.

On 8th September, whilst marching from Bisley to Clandon Park, Surrey, Lord Cavan, in command of the *2nd London Brigade Territorial Force* was handed a telegram by a despatch rider. "You are appointed to command the 4th Guards Brigade, vice General Scott Kerr, wounded. Report War Office immediately!"

Cavan, who had been born in Hertfordshire in 1865 was 49 years old. From 1885 until 1912 he had served in the *Grenadier Guards,* and was, at the time of his retirement, Colonel of the 1st Battalion.

He arrived in France on 17th September 1914 with the rank of Brigadier-General and reporting to the commander of the 2nd Division he was told "Your Brigade is on that hill, see that they stick to it." On carrying out a reconnaissance, he himself narrowly missed being injured. In October his Brigade was moved to Flanders and fought in the *First Battle of Ypres,* where heavy fighting depleted the men under his command. It was, by co-incidence, that his troops were joined in early November by the *First Battalion, Hertfordshire Regiment,* one of the first territorial units to be sent from England to serve on the Western front.

Source: *Cavan's Memoirs. [unpublished].*

Hertfordshire Yeomanry receive their orders.

The Hertfordshire Yeomanry were informed on Monday that they would sail for Egypt shortly. Given twenty-four hours leave enabling

Food being supplied
to troops billeted
in St. Albans, 1914.

The photographs on
this page were
re-photographed
from a copy of
the *Herts. Advertiser.*

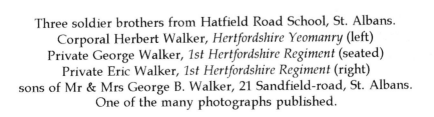

Three soldier brothers from Hatfield Road School, St. Albans.
Corporal Herbert Walker, *Hertfordshire Yeomanry* (left)
Private George Walker, *1st Hertfordshire Regiment* (seated)
Private Eric Walker, *1st Hertfordshire Regiment* (right)
sons of Mr & Mrs George B. Walker, 21 Sandfield-road, St. Albans.
One of the many photographs published.

Voluntary Aid Detachment Nurses at Bricket House Hospital
with Mrs A.N.Boycott, Commandant.

Red Cross V.A.D. Nurses with patients at a social gathering
held at Marlborough House, St. Albans.

them to say *au-revoir* to relatives and friends, those attached to 'C' Company came home from Bury St. Edmunds, to St. Albans. All looked remarkedly fit and well. The regiment has been supplied with special clothing and equipment suitable to the climate and conditions of life in the East. Long bayonets have been served out, suitable for the Yeomanry carbines.

Source: *Herts. Advertiser, 5th September 1914.*

A deserter is executed.

This morning we had an unpleasant task. A firing party was detailed to execute a deserter belonging to the *13th Infantry Brigade.* I saw this man march to the appointed place, and although he was to be executed for desertion, he marched like a British soldier!

Source: *Bedfordshire Record Office. War Diary. Bedfordshire Regiment.*

The King and Lord Kitchener review the troops.

His Majesty paid a visit to St. Albans on Friday, 18th September to review the troops. At the entrance to Gorhambury he took up a position on the right hand side of the carriage drive. The troops then marched past in column of route.

On Tuesday, Field Marshal Lord Kitchener came to review the troops. He and his staff were mounted. The scene was a very brilliant one and will long be remembered by the thousands of people who witnessed it.

Source: *Watford and St. Albans Illustrated, 3rd October 1914.*

Standard Test.

Mr. Philip Kingham serving with the 1st Battalion, Hertfordshire Regiment writes:
St. Albans 'B' Company were sent to Sudbury to fire the *Standard Test.* They accomplished some of the best shooting ever seen on the range. One old member of the St. Albans School Officer Training Corps scored of 91 out of 97. In rapid fire, he scored 7 bulls out of eight shots.

Source: *Herts. Advertiser, 31st October 1914.*

"Fit for active service"

Three years before war was declared, the *1st Battalion, Hertfordshire Regiment* was reported as *fit for active service*. We could afford to smile at those who asked why we wasted our precious holidays in training. Had not the regular soldiers declared us worthy to fight with them?

Hints for wives.

What do you do with your husband's contribution card and insurance book if he has left them behind. The Army or Navy authorities will pay contributions for your husband during service. It is quite unnecessary for you to stamp a card for him.

You should write *called-up* or *enlisted* across it and send it either (a) to his approved Society, if he is a member of a Society; or (b) to the Insurance Commissioners, if he is not a member of a Society.

A special printed, addressed envelope, in which to post the card to the Commissioners can be obtained at any Post Office. You should keep his Insurance Book as you may want it, if you claim Maternity Benefit.

Maternity Benefits

You will be entitled to the full maternity benefit in respect of your husband's insurance whether you are married on the strength or not. The only condition is that your husband should already have been in Insurance for at least 26 weeks and should have paid 26 weekly contributions towards all the contributions paid during service (see above).

Source: *Herts Advertiser, 19th September 1914.*

Hertfordshire Regiment at First Battle of Ypres.

On Wednesday, 4th November 1914, the *1st Battalion, Hertfordshire Regiment* marched through Bury St. Edmunds in the early hours of the morning and arrived at the station just as day dawned. As the sun rose a band played and we entrained for the great adventure.

We arrived on the 5th November at Le Havre and disembarked, marching through the streets as an incessant stream of *Red Cross* cars wended its way past us with their gruesome passengers to the docks.

On our first night in France at a rest camp, we experienced rain and mud so frequently to be our companions thereafter. The following night we were given sudden orders to entrain on a tedious journey with great discomfort to St.Omer. The distant boom of guns could be heard. We had one day of attack practice before the Headquarters staff and the next, feverishly digging a line in front of St. Omer. With hardly any warning, buses arrived to take us to Ypres where we were to join the *4th Guards Brigade*, under Lord Cavan.

We arrived at Poperinghe in the dark, very weary after marching, and an apparently endless bus ride in rain. The second in command went sick with a bad attack of rheumatism, and I became second in command, but remained in command of a Company.

Now we were marching through Ypres. It was a still night with a ghostly moon and the unearthly din of gunfire seemingly to the front, and on both flanks, the flashes all the time lighting up the sky. Just past the Cloth Hall, which is still intact, and looks magnificient, there is a frightful explosion over the head of my Company. Our first enemy shell - three men drop but we march on. More shells and at last when nearly played out, we reach a wood with a few trees and many stumps of what were once trees. Three companies doss down in damp holes and my Company goes into the luxury of farm buildings on the *Menin Road*. The Officers sleep in the stables.

This was our first night of war. We were the second territorial battalion to arrive at the front and the only one at the [*First*] *Battle of Ypres*. During the German attack the previous day, the divisional reserves were two platoons with nothing else between the firing line and the Channel ports. Tonight there is a whole battalion in support with nearly a thousand men of the '*Herts Guards*'. A quarter of a million Germans face what remains of three regular British divisions and our lads of the villages behind. What a grim joke. What if the Boche knew too? Had they spent their efforts? Would they make one final supreme effort to throw the *Contempibles* back into the sea?

Source: *Croft, Henry Page. My life of strife.*

Frank O. Salisbury's experience.

On the fourth of August we were at war with Germany. It was probably the experience of every artist that all his work was stopped and all commissions cancelled. My rates and expenses almost doubled, and we were faced with a grave domestic situation. We economized to avoid disaster and came to the conclusion that the next thing to go was the telephone. But every tide turns. One afternoon the telephone rang and a lady asked if I could paint her with her children. It was settled in two minutes and solved our problem for six months. The telephone was not cut off.

It turned out that the artists were soon wanted again, for war was leaving gaps in many houses. Lord Bethell's eldest son was among the fallen, and from small snapshots, and with the help of his sister, I was able to paint a full-length portrait. In the first August also I painted the poet Colwyn Philipps, Lord St. David's son. The dear fellow had a premonition that he would not return, and he never did. He fell in 1915, waving his cap and shouting "Come on, boys" as they attacked the German trenches, and one of his fellow-officers said he was the bravest man he had ever met. The tragic toll of war was something our generation had not experienced before. Three of Mr. Gandar Dower's sons were called up and all sat for me. The eldest gave me a whole day when he went on leave. Within a week of his return he was killed.

Source: *Salisbury, Frank O. Portrait and Pageant.*

St.Albans welcomes wounded Belgian soldiers.

Eight wounded Belgian soldiers who are now convalescing at Little Berkhamstead were brought in two motor cars to St. Albans. As they drew up in Chequer Street, the uniforms of the occupants attracted attention, and it was not before long that a considerable crowd collected. Soldiers who were about the streets lost no time in making the acquaintance of those valiant comrades direct from the battlefield and the fraternal spirit rapidly developed. Despite linguistic difficulties they soon understood one another.

Source: *Herts. Advertiser, 7th November 1914.*

London Scottish losses.

The *London Scottish* whose men were, until recently, billeted between St.Albans and Watford have suffered very heavy losses recently.

Source: *Herts. Advertiser, 7th November 1914.*

Game of chance.

Private Frank West, 1st Battalion, Norfolk Regiment and formerly of St.Albans Midland Station staff, describes his experiences:

I am writing this in the trenches. We are having a hot time. I have been in all the engagements from [*the Battle of*] Mons onwards. I expect you saw in the papers that we lost roughly 270 men; but it is all a game of chance. I have not had a change of clothes since I left St. Albans and we are only able to get a wash sometimes. None of us in the firing line have seen a blanket yet. All letters are censored, so I cannot tell you any of my experiences.

I have just been watching [the Germans] fire forty-five rounds of shrapnel at one of our aeroplanes, but they did not hit it. I shall be glad when it is all over, but I cannot see any prospect of a finish for some time yet.

Source: *Herts. Advertiser, 14th November 1914.*

'Coal boxes'

Gunner J.W. Smith, 2nd Siege Battery, Royal Garrison Artillery, British Expeditionary Force, writes to Viscount Grimston (his former employer), Grimston Tyres Ltd, St.Albans:

7th November 1914. - Sir, I hope you will excuse me in writing to you but no doubt my letter will be welcome. We are all having not too bad a time of it. We get a little march now and again of about thirty miles at a stretch, but we are getting used to it. We have to make ourselves as comfortable as we can. We manage to get a barn to sleep in and we think we are doing fine.

We have been under heavy fire of late. The shells have been coming around us. We call them *coal boxes* as they are big, but nothing to compare with ours. We have very good officers in our battery, which has been highly praised for the good work we have done.

I shall be pleased when all is over and I get back to my work and home. It is pitiful to see the houses and churches that are ruined. Women and children walking miles to seek shelter, having to leave their homes and everything behind to be scattered and blown up.

Source: *Gorhambury Collection. Business Correspondence. 4th Earl of Verulam.*

Appalling noise in the trenches.

Lieutenant 'Billy' Grenfell of Taplow, Buckinghamshire and Panshanger, near Hertford writes to his parents, Lord and Lady Desborough:

It's our first morning of snow today. It has been raining a lot lately and the roads and fields and even the insides of the houses are two inches deep in slush, whilst the trenches are just muck-heaps. We've been doing all trench work lately, and it's horrible. You just lie there, all hunched up and all day long the shells burst just outside the trench if you're lucky, and just inside if you're unlucky. Anyhow, the noise is appalling and one's head is rocking with it by the end of the day. They generally start about 8.0 a.m. and go on till 4.30 p.m.

Source: *Hertfordshire Record Office. Panshanger Collection D/Erv C1135/688.*

Lieut. Grenfell goes sniping.

From a letter of Lieut. Billy Grenfell, dated 18th November 1914:

These last days we had a different kind of trench in a dripping, sodden wood, with the German trenches in some places only 40 yards ahead, too close for them to shell us. Dead Germans lie along the front. Most of the fir trees have been cut down by bullets and shrapnel is piled along the ground.

We have been awfully worried by their sniping, and I asked to go out and have a try myself. On Tuesday, 16th November I was given leave. They told me to take a section with me and I said that I would rather cut my own throat and have done with it. So they let me go out alone. Off I crawled, through the sodden clay and branches (which were sticking up over the ground), going a yard a minute, listening and looking as I thought it was not possible to look and listen.

I went out to the right of our lines, where the '10th were, and where the Germans were nearest. I took 30 minutes to do 30 yards. Then I saw the 'Hun' trench and I waited a long time, but could see or hear nothing. It was about 10 yards from me. Then I heard some Germans talking and saw one put his head up over some bushes about 10 yards behind the trench. I could not get a shot at him as I was too low down, and of course I couldn't get up. So I crawled on very slowly to the parapet of their trench. It was very exciting. I was not sure if there might not have been somewhere there, or a little further along the trench. I peered through their loophole and saw nobody in the trench. Then the German put his head up again. He was laughing and talking. I saw his teeth glisten against my foresight, and then I pulled the trigger very steadily. He just gave a grunt and crumpled up. The others got up and whispered to each other. I don't know who was more frightened, them or me. I think there were four or five of them. They couldn't place the shot. I was flattened behind their parapet and hidden. I just had the nerve not to move a muscle and stay there. My heart was fully hammering. They did not come forward, and I could not see them as they were behind some bushes and trees. So I crept back inch by inch.

I went out again in the afternoon in front of our bit of the line. Almost 60 yards off I found their trench again but it was empty. I waited there for an hour but saw nobody. Then I went because I did not want to get inside. I reported that the trench was empty.

Just before dawn on the next day I crawled out there again and the trench was empty. Then a single German came through the wood towards the trench. I saw him 50 yards off. He was coming along upright, quite carelessly making a great noise. I heard him before I saw him. I let him get to within 25 yards and shot him through the heart. He never made a sound. Nothing then for 10 minutes, and then there was noise and talking and a lot of them came through the wood behind the trench about 40 yards from me. I counted 20 and there were more coming. They halted in front and I picked the one I thought was the officer or sergeant. He stood facing the other way and I had a steady shot at him behind the shoulders. He went down and that was all I saw.

I went back at a galloping crawl to our lines and sent a message to the '*10th*, that the Germans were moving up their way in numbers. Half an hour afterwards they attacked the '*10th,* and to our right in massed formation, advancing to within 10 yards of the trenches. We simply mowed them down. It was rather horrible. I was to far to the left. They did not attack our part of the line, but the '*10th* told me in the evening that they counted 200 dead in a little bit of the line.

They have made quite a ridiculous fuss about my stalking and getting the message through. I believe they are going to send me up to our General.

It is only up to someone to do it, instead of leaving it all to the Germans and losing two officers a day through snipers.

All our men have started it now. It is a popular amusement.
Source: Hertfordshire Record Office. Panshanger Collection.

Pageant House, St. Albans
Rules for Lady Visitors

Lady friends of soldiers will be admitted to the Recreation Rooms from 2.30 p.m. until 6.30 p.m. on Sundays under the following conditions:-

[1] The upper floor will be reserved during these hours on Sundays for soldiers accompanied by a lady friend. No soldier unaccompanied by a lady friend will be admitted to those rooms, and no lady unattended by a soldier will be admitted to any part of the Club (except, of course, the ladies who are kindly helping in the canteen);

[2] It will be understood that only lady visitors from a distance should be invited and not residents in the city, who have their own homes at hand, and who, if they came to the Club, would crowd out those who really required these rooms as a place for rest and refreshment;

[3] The rooms reserved will be the large room upstairs, the adjoining card room which can be used as a cloakroom or for the children, and the lavatories which will be reserved for ladies only;

[4] Arrangements will be made to serve refreshments upstairs from the main canteen.

Soldiers will, no doubt, recognise that these regulations are made for the comfort and convenience of themselves and their lady friends and relations, and will remember that though rules are necessary, it is their own co-operation that will make this arrangement a success, and prevent any possibility of its being abused.
Source: *Herts. Advertiser, 21st November 1914.*

At the 'pictures'.

Excellent audiences continued to patronise the St.Albans Cinema House. Topical film showing the entry by the Germans into Ghent, which was taken by the operator at great personal risk, aroused great interest.

On Thursday, Friday and Saturday evenings a film depicting the German occupation of Louvain is being shown.
Source: *Herts. Advertiser, 21st November 1914.*

Children collect chocolate for the troops.

56lbs. of chocolate and cigarettes were made up in parcels for transport by a St. Albans company, *Messrs. Horace Slade Ltd.*, is to be taken by transport to Southampton and then shipped to the continent for the soldiers in France and Belgium from Hertfordshire. The collection was made at schools in the city. St. Albans Town Hall which was visited by the children, bringing their gifts of chocolate and cigarettes, which were accompanied with messages written by the children themselves - *"good luck to the tommy what gets this"*, and *"with love, from a soldier's daughter"*.
Source: *Herts. Advertiser, 21st November 1914.*

In the trenches and under fire for the first time.

From a letter of Private Percy Ives, dated 15th November:
We've been here just over a week and it seems like years. I'm still unhurt but cannot say how long it will last as we are right in the firing line now. We were twenty-three hours in the train, and then we stayed in a place about two and a half miles from one of our bases. I got on finely with some farm people and was having a good time, when we were suddenly rushed off on motor 'buses to within miles of where we are now. We walked the last part of the journey through a town which the Germans were shelling, and it gave is a good start - the first time we were under fire.

Then we stayed in a farm shed for two nights and shells and *'coal-boxes'* were bursting all around us especially for half-an-hour before we left. You can hear the things coming for quite a long time, and you can get under cover from them.

Last night we shifted up into the reserve trenches, where the shells went right over us. I am at present on guard, and twice during the night heard terrific firing from our trenches - presumably an attack. We get no news and can't tell what is happening. It is bitterly cold and has been raining and snowing all day with a heavy wind blowing. It is really marvellous how well the majority of us are, considering the weather and the queer grub we get.

Source: *Herts. Advertiser, 28th November 1914.*

Meeting 'Jack Johnson'.

From a letter of Lance Corporal Cyril Paul, dated November 1914:
A few nights ago our great adventure came. We had orders to relieve some troops and marched off for about four miles and were shelled to pieces. When we got to our destination, we found we had to go into the trenches. We were in them for twenty-four hours, and then we were relieved by other companies in our battalion, whilst we remained in reserve.

We were there also for twenty-four hours and then we were all relieved and marched back to our barn and the wood. The artillery fire the next day was terrific. *Jack Johnsons* came over by the dozen, but none of them fell more than 150 yards away, so we were safe. The weather was terrible and bitterly cold. At first it was mud, rain and slush, which afterwards turned to snow and frost. An inch of snow fell whilst we were in the trenches and many of our fellows were knocked up.

The Germans went through this place about a month ago, and the beggars pinched all the chocolate and candles as well. That is why your supplies of chocolate are so awfully welcome.

Source: *Herts. Advertiser, 28th November 1914.*

A Sergeant's story.

A sergeant, on leave in St. Albans with his wife for a weekend, recalls what he has seen in the supply column of the Army Service Corps:
We first saw fighting at Mons in a village near the town where the rations were left by the Supply Column at the roadside for the troops to pick up as they retired from the front. Between Alney and Mons they brought in the first lot of wounded numbering eighteen in all. These they left at the hospital in Landrecies.

The fighting at the *Battle of Mons* was very severe. We could see it from the field where I was. This was my first experience of actual battle and I have been very interested in watching the shells bursting. I was sent from Boue to Landrecies the morning they took Landrecies. Our guns were firing just I was there. After that we were travelling night and day in the direction of Paris: I didn't see much of the actual fighting or the retreat. When we had started to advance we saw all the dead horses lying along the road. The Germans had buried their dead in rough graves along the roadside. There was a lot of equipment lying about with motor lorries left behind. Some of this we commandeered and used ourselves.

The *Battle of Aisne*, when seen from a distance was a grand sight. For miles the shells were bursting, and looked like a grand display of fireworks. We were then at Pont-Arcy. We unloaded supplies at a farm house used as a hospital. It was in a hollow so no one could see us. Behind us were *sixty pounders*. The German artillery found us there at last, and started to drop *Jack Johnsons'* near us. They were bursting all along the ridge, but they didn't hit anyone, although some burst as near as twenty yards from us. The ground being soft, the shells were buried to such a depth when they fell that they practically lost all their force. They showered about 150 shells all around us, and there was not a man killed!

I saw an ambulance blown up at Pont-Arcy. The chaplain seemed rather angry about it, but the doctor said that he did not think it was done intentionally. It was strange, however, that they always seem to fire as someone was going over the bridge, and some of us were inclined to suspect that they were receiving a signal from some unknown quarter. One shell fell in the midst of eight horses and we could only see one half of one afterwards. Another shell fell on top of a house, drop through a mattress, through the floor and then destroyed the entire house.

About three weeks ago we made our headquarters at Ypres and moved down to Poperinghe. The Germans dropped a few shells around us and the last one hit the side of the church portal, perforating the door with bullet holes.

As we proceeded around the country we found every place looted. Bayonets had been used to force open the doors of the houses and the contents of dwellings scattered about. Drawers and cupboards had been ransacked, and clothing and other things were littered about in all directions. At one house they had blown up the safe and torn up a lot of paper which could be of no possible value. Beside the road we found quite a number of bottles from wine-cellars which had been looted and at Rebais there were ruins of a house which they had burnt down because the inhabitants would not respond to their demands.

I saw a good many Germans prisoners and I gathered that they were pretty sanguine that they would win. They freely admitted that the British infantry work was very good. I don't think the Germàns stand very much chance; I don't see how they can win. Once they know of the every small force that held them back at Ypres, they will be surprised.

Source: *Herts. Advertiser, 28th November 1914.*

Living underground, in trenches and holes.

Major Montague Jones, 'B' Company Commander, 1st Battalion, Hertfordshire Regiment, talks to boys at St.Albans School:
We held the trenches with half a battalion for three days. The Germans attacked several times and they shelled the trenches and blew some of them out with high explosive shells, but their attacks were repulsed.

It is much to the credit of the men that not one of them left his trench. They stood it like bricks and the Germans were driven back every time. We were faced with both day and night attacks. In some attacks the Germans out-numbered the British by ten-to-one, and they generally concentrated on different points.

We were relieved and went back. We started to march at eleven o'clock at night and marched for twelve hours in a hard frost. The roads on some of our marches were dreadful. We were sometimes up to our knees in mud, and in the first lot of trenches we were up to our knees in water. We could not take our boots off for ten days, and we had to lie out in the cold and snow, rain and slush, without blankets, which are not allowed in the firing line. It is a very trying time. For ten days we practically lived underground in holes and trenches so that we could not light fires.

We could not get hot food and lived on *bully beef and biscuits*. Tobacco and cigarettes are now served out with the rations. The things that are really wanted are candles, matches, chocolates, socks, clean shirts and little khaki handerkerchiefs.

The men have had to keep their socks on for twelve days and then they are not fit to wear again. In the early days of the war, tobacco and cigarettes were much needed, but recently the *Hertfordshire Regiment* has had more cigarettes than can be smoked, although that does not apply to all units.

Source: *Herts. Advertiser, 6th December 1914.*

Lord Cavan welcomes the Hertfordshire men.

The Brigadier [General], the Earl of Cavan would like to take this opportunity of welcoming the *Herts. Battalion* to the *4th [Guards] Brigade*. Being a Hertfordshire man himself, he knows the desire of all Herts. men to do their utmost for the King and country: and from what he has already seen in the trenches, and on the march, he is certain that the Battalion will play a noble part in this Great War. They have

already had a hard week and lost some good comrades, but they left Ypres with their line intact, which was an achievement.
Source: *Herts. Advertiser, 6th December 1914.*

Hertfordshire men thank St.Albans for chocolate.

Lance Corporal Evans, 'F' Company, 1st Hertfordshire Regiment writes to the babies at Bernard Street Infants School:
This is to let you know that the chocolate you so kindly sent us has reached us quite safely. Where we are now staying, we cannot go into a shop and buy any chocolate because the Germans have been here and stolen it all.

Colour Sergeant E.G. Crawley, 'A' Company, 1st Hertfordshire Regiment writes to the Mayor of St. Albans:
On behalf of the non-commissioned officers and men of 'A' Company *(Hertford and Hatfield)*, I beg to thank the citizens of St.Albans for our share of the splendid gift of chocolate made by them to the Regiment. I would particularly ask you to thank the children who contributed. We are very much touched by their little gifts of single bars, and only wish that it were possible for us to thank them individually.

Sergeant A.J. Green, 'B' Company, 1st Hertfordshire Regiment writes to Mr. Day (hat manufacturer), Marlborough Road, St.Albans:
We had a surprise on Friday from St.Albans for some chocolate which arrived out here with about ½lb. to ¾lb. per man, which I think was very good considering there are 1,220 of us from different parts of the county.
Source: *Herts. Advertiser, 20th December 1914.*

The Prince of Wales marches with Herts. men.

We were ordered to march to Bethune on 22nd December 1914. In the early hours the *4th [Guards] Brigade* assembled for the long march of nineteen miles. To the *"Hertfordshires"* was given the honour of leading, and this put the Battalion on their mettle.

For a considerable part of the march, the Prince of Wales marched at the head of the Regiment with our Colonel. When we arrived at the outskirts of Bethune it was already dark and we lay down on the banks of the canal waiting for orders as to billeting. It was a very quiet night and a well-known songster in our Battalion stood by the side of the canal and began to sing, the chorus being taken up by the whole brigade. The Battalion marched through the town as if they had come two miles instead of nineteen and the inhabitants, hearing our marching songs, turned out to welcome us.
Source: *Croft, Henry Page. Twenty-two months under fire.*

Christmas Day, 1914.

Christmas in the trenches was celebrated at dawn by rapid fire and the festival was lively. It was a cold sharp day, and we received various gifts which friends at home had sent us and many a charcoal fire was busy cooking wonderful dishes along the trench. That night both sides sang carols and the firing ended.
Source: *Croft, Henry Page. Twenty-two months under fire.*

On Christmas Day, about 1,000 of the *1st Surrey Rifles* took their Christmas dinner in the seed warehouse of Messrs. Ryder & Sons, Holywell Hill, St. Albans. They did ample justice to 100 turkeys and 500lbs. of roast pork which had so generously been provided.
Source: *Herts Advertiser, 2nd January 1915.*

Private R. Rolph, 'B' Company, 1st Hertfordshire Regiment writes to Mr. Gray and friends at Slater's, St.Albans:
I expect you would like to know how we spent Christmas. We went into the trenches at 6 o'clock on Christmas morning. For breakfast we had a little bit of bacon and a loaf between two of us and a drop of tea. For dinner we got a tin of beef and vegetable rations and a bit of the *Daily Mail and Leader* plum pudding.

Well we went through the week all right; the Germans didn't worry us much, but they made an attack on our right about ten minutes to twelve on New Year's Eve, so we saw New Year in, in the trenches.

Water came over the tops of our boots and we had to get on top of the trenches to bale it out. The Germans were doing the same thing but they didn't fire on us, and we didn't fire on them.
Source: *Herts Advertiser, 9th January 1915.*

Getting lost and becoming wounded.

A Sergeant in the 3rd South Wales Borderer's recounts life under attack, getting lost and being wounded, in a letter to Mr. E.L. Snowden, President of the St. Albans Trades' Council. It is written from a hospital in Bristol.

On the 19th October our company was told to attack a village occupied by the enemy two miles away. We were told to advance by platoons. We went out and extended, then advanced, but by jingo we were soon shelled but we kept advancing under terrible fire until we reached some outbuildings. We were then 700 or 800 yards from the enemy. We found a number of Belgians and French behind, in these buildings but they were getting shelled and many were dead. lying in heaps. As soon as we got there we found the French were retiring, which somewhat disheartened us, but we kept on and lined an old ditch just in front of the buildings. Those who could not get into the ditch were lying flat in the mangold field, but poor fellows, their number was soon up.

We had a terrible time for about three hours: my men were dropping around me and I had some narrow escapes, as I had to keep getting up to supply them with the ammunition, the ditch being so small. I had my cap shot off my head, my greatcoat and pack pierced, but still escaped. Messages were passed and re-passed. We had our work cut out to keep them back. I sent for the officer and heard that he had been killed hours ago. When I sent the next time for orders, the message got no farther than the fourth man, as he found no one was on his right. I told those that were left to retire.

The following day I was put on guard with six men. I had not been mounted long when we were ordered to stand to. I got the men of my platoon together. We had to fix bayonets and lie quite flat in the open just behind the trenches as we were expecting a charge. The ground

33

was wet and and there we lay for hours, cold, uncomfortable, yet on the alert, hoping that the attack would be given.

The artillery was playing for time, then suddenly shells burst close to us, coming from behind, wounding one of our men, as the shells kept dropping short. I called to the officer as the men were getting desperate. It was extremely trying to lie there and be in danger of being shelled by our own artillery, so I said to the officer "would it not be well to send back to headquarters at once". He concurred and he sent me back. I ran for all I was worth. It was 1½ miles to the rear. I had to go through a wood, stumbled over ditches and bushes as it was nearly dark, was shot at by snipers on the way, but I got there and reported. A wire was sent to the battery at once and the fire rectified. Now I was in a difficulty to get back to my regiment as I had only been that way, the once. I was lost with not a soul to be seen, with bullets whizzing by my head.

Eventually I found some French soldiers entrenched as supports. I knew then that I had gone too far to the left. One officer tried to prevail upon me to wait until daylight as I had lost my bearings and he could not direct me; I refused and I turned and shortly afterwards met another group who had been relieved from some part of the line and asked them the way, but they did not know. Just then there came heavy fire from the right, and I knew by the sound that an attack was on. I met some six or so men and saw that one of them was a man from my own regiment. He said that they had been for water and were trying to get back as soon as possible, but that they could not be sure of the way. So I set off and found the wood that I had to pass through, but alas I got my *cough-drop*! I was shot!

I did not know whether it was a bullet or shrapnel at the time, as the fire from both was like hail, but down I went and managed to crawl into a wet trench. I lay there for hours until the fire abated. I bound myself up and started to worm myself towards where I guessed the dressing station stood.

When I came into the open I was sniped at, and expected at every minute, to be taken prisoner, but I suppose they were afraid of my rifle which I had stuck to, in spite of my wound, though I threw my pack off. I must have been crawling for hours.

At last I heard voices and recognising English, I chanced it and shouted out, but got no reply. I drew myself along the place where the sound was coming from and there loomed a dressing station before me. One of the men there came to my assistance and he helped me into the building and laid me down on an old mattress. He told me that this building was had been evacuated and that he and his men had to move off at once. I lay there in great pain and expected to be buried at any minute as shells from the Germans were bursting all round the building.

Later he was helped by a General who arranged for stretcher-bearers to come and pick him up. He was taken to Ypres and on to Boulogne, Rouen and Le Havre. He returned to England by hospital ship and arrived in Bristol.
Source: Herts Advertiser, 9th January 1915.

continued on page 36

Contents 1915

Burying the dead.

2nd January 1915 - Six days rest. ... It rained incessantly so that we shivered at the idea of going back to our next trenches, which were in front of Richebourg where we now experienced the full powers of the Flanders mud. We found that what had been trenches were now nothing but rivers and only a few posts held in front of the firing line. Troops are now being quartered in the *Rue de Bois*. On either side of the road are some substantial brick cottages which give good cover from the weather and these we proceeded to fortify. The brigade moved up to the Guinchy area, the *3rd Coldstream* and *Irish Guards* into the line with the *Herts.* in close support, and the *2nd Grenadiers* and the *2nd Coldstream* in reserve.

During the first few nights we were busily engaged in burying the dead who were lying about from previous fighting and the brigadier was most particular that all British and German soldiers should be carried out of the line and buried in cemeteries in the rear. It was dangerous work and trying to young hands, but we carried over a hundred dead back and gave them a decent burial.

The temptation is to bury on the spot, but the disadvantages are so great that an effort is always made, if the enemy's guns permit, to carry the dead on stretchers to selected cemeteries, where great trouble is taken to make and preserve the graves of the fallen.
Source: *Croft, Henry Page. Twenty-two months under fire.*

Off East Africa, on board H.M.S.Chatham.

Stoker Fred Kent, one of the five sons of Mr. Thomas Kent, head gardener of the Countess of Caledon, Tyttenhanger Park, St.Albans reports from H.M.S.Chatham which blew up the German ship, Konisburg off East Africa:
Whilst we were at Aden, we heard that the *Konisburg* had fired on the *Pegasus* whilst lying at anchor, cleaning boilers and repairing engines at Zanzibar. We had to proceed here at once to seek and destroy her. When we got to Zanzibar we found the place overrun with Germans so the first thing the Captain did, was to go ashore and have them all

placed under arrest, as it was evident how the news was spread that the *Pegasus* was in such a helpless condition. The German ship hid seven thousand yards away for the greater part of night behind a lighthouse and as soon as it was light they started firing on them, whilst they were asleep in their hammocks. She answered the fire, but being a very old ship with a very old pattern gun, the shells dropped two thousand yards short. Thirty eight of the *Pegasus* were killed and eighty were wounded. We have the rest on board here.

When we got down the German East Africa coast, we found that they were using a code of signals to signal the "all clear". During the night she came out. We had a look round and located her up a creek, well out of range of our guns, so we went very slowly and kept sinking, with rifle fire, what we took to be mines, but when we picked them up, we found that they were long, empty, cartridge drums put there as dummies.

We have got one of them on board and have made a real mine of it, loading it with 320lbs. of gun-cotton. It will be fine to blow her up with a mine made out of one of her own cartridge cases. An officer has volunteered to lay the "mine" up the creek where she is, and I have volunteered to take the motor boat we have, to take him and the mine there ...
Source: *Herts. Advertiser, 30th January 1915.*

Billeting conditions in St. Albans.

Men located in private houses very much appreciate the change from cheerlessness and discomfort of life in public buildings. Payment is made for beds at the rate of 9d. per night or 5s 3d. per week. In many instances there are three, four and five men in a house and in a few instances, seven men. Billeting money is generally paid monthly and when it arrives, it amounts to quite a substantial sum.

In most of the billets, cooking is done for the men even though this can lead to lots of inconvenience where there are lots of inmates including young children.

There is invariably a roll-call at about seven o'clock in the morning after which the men return to the billets for breakfast. Overnight a distribution has been made of tea, sugar and one slice of bacon per man. After breakfast the troops are off on a morning of drill, route-marching, field operations or range firing. If they go for the day a bread-and-cheese ration is served out to each man.

The real comfort of the private billet is experienced when, on their return home, the beef or mutton and potatoes ration is awaiting them, nicely cooked. This makes a happy change from the stew provided by army cooks. For tea there is a liberal supply of jam with butter served out of 1lb. tins and for supper, bread and cheese. There is ample supply of food and the quality is excellent. In many working-class homes, the presence of soldiers is a source of assistance to the household.
Source: *Herts. Advertiser, 6th February 1915.*

Captain Julian Grenfell asks for supplies.

Capt. Grenfell, 1st Royal Dragoons writes to his parents, Lord & Lady Desborough:
I have been asked by the Brigade to get hold of some fishing reels to be used by snipers. When they go out of the trench, they take the line with them and tie it up at a place about 50 yards out. Then, when they want to come back, they jerk the end of the line and that clicks the reel and warns the sentry in the trench that they are coming back, and he tells the others not to shoot. Do you think you could get me a couple of reels with a good length of line on them? If you send me the bill, I will recover the costs.

8th March - Can you please send me two footballs for the men? Please send two extra bladders for the footballs. Can you send me a box of relief nibs, a large block of writing paper and envelopes.

14th March - The men have had very few cigarettes since Christmas and what they had were Government issue. No cakes, pies etc. have arrived at all, only pipe lighters, vests and pants so far.

The Colt Automatic 380 pistol arrived quite safely. Can you send me a big foolscap size notebook, shaving soap, toothpaste in a tube, soap, two towels, nails for the soles of boots, good maps of the Eastern and Western Fronts, matches, an old kitbag to hold my spare stuff, labels and methylated spirits. Please stop the *Daily Telegraph*. (We get newspapers now).

20th March - Thank you awfully for your letter, two footballs and extra bladders, two large blocks of writing paper and heaps of envelopes, relief nibs, cakes and two very good bottles of port, which were awfully good.

The only thing that has not arrived is the 3,000 cigarettes. Did you send them to me?
Source: *Hertfordshire Record Office. Panshanger Collection D/Erv C1135/701, 702,704, 705.*

Bedfordshire Regiment gets a heavy bombardment.

6th April - It was 6 a.m. before we returned to our cellars. After a strenuous night we hoped to sleep all day, but we had only been asleep for a few minutes when the Germans opened a very heavy bombardment on the town. The artillery estimated the number to be six hundred of all calibres. The whole town was shelled with the town centre and the Cloth Hall receiving the greatest number of shells. The bombardment lasted just over two hours, but the shelling continued, intermittently, all day. Much damage was done with many houses around the Barracks and the Cloth Hall were totally demolished. Several were set on fire and burned furiously for a long time.

During the afternoon we received news that the 'Battalion was moving that evening. We left Ypres by companies and formed up on the road to Vlamertinghe. We marched to Reninhelst, situated five miles south-east of Poperinghe. Here we were billeted in hutments and canvas tents. The country here and to the north is very flat and about three miles to the south is the French-Belgian frontier. We remained here until 10th April. During these few days we saw many Regiments marching northwards. It was a steady stream of men and guns moving forward day and night at a regular pace. Never once for three days was the column broken. Some were old troops who had been relieved from somewhere south, others were new units who had not yet been into action, but old and new marched, singing gaily as they passed along.

A heavy bombardment was in progress about and to the north of Ypres. Some of it was our own guns replying to German fire, but reports from the front line stated that our trenches were being very heavily shelled.

Source: *Bedfordshire Record Office. War Diary, Bedfordshire Regiment.*

Bedfordshire Regiment moves to Hill 60.

10th April - At 6 p.m. we received orders to move at once. It did not take long. Our equipment was ready and so all we had to do was to put it on and we were ready to move to any part of the front where we were needed.

The Battalion pushed on to Ypres where an extra day's ration and ammunition was issued. From here we marched along the railway from Ypres towards Menin and to trenches opposite to *Hill 60* where we relieved the *Queen Victoria Rifles,* a territorial division. It was well after midnight before the relief was completed. We had not been in this position scarcely more than an hour when we sustained our first casualty - Private Stainer, who was hit and killed.

11th April - We had a troublesome night with bursts of rifle fire and at intervals some shelling which hampered us considerably. It was daylight before we settled down and could get the men evenly distributed to the condition of the trenches. In places our trenches were quite close to the Germans, so close we could hear them talking. One day a letter was thrown into our trench, addressed to "Dear Comrades". The letter stated that the war had gone on long enough and it was time it was over. The letter was answered by the best means available, by a shower of rifle grenades and we sent over as many as could be spared for such an occasion. The result was a retaliation by the German artillery. However, the grenades answered the letter for we were not troubled again.

Hill 60 is the highest point south of Ypres and is a place of observation of the town to the north. During April and early May 1915, Hill 60 was mined and counter mined by allied and enemy forces. Even now, the grave of many soldiers whose remains have never been recovered. When I went there in May 1995, I was struck by the silence on top of the hilll and the lack of birdsong.

The mining company of the 'Engineers had been busy for over a month preparing mines with charges of guncotton and powder. The Germans too were mining and they were known to have galleries within a few feet of ours. It really was a race.

15th April - The weather was lovely. The trenches were now in a much better conditions as many improvements had been made since we had been in the line. Several strong shelters had been built up and these provided good cover against light shells but they were not much use against the heavy shells which could pierce almost anything. In the morning, a strong working party came up from the *14th Brigade* to assist in preparing the assembly trenches and deepening the communication trenches. Other fatigue parties were busy blowing up the saphead, all the mines having been laid with electric cable ready to blow up the hill. The Battalion headquarters were situated in the shelters in the railway cutting near the mound.

'A' and 'B' Companies were left in the line, one company on each side of the troops who were to attack. They were to remain in the front line. Their orders were to assist the attacking troops by opening a heavy rifle on the flank of the attack. The attack was timed for 7 p.m. and at that time six large clouds rose from the hill and a few seconds later, a yellow flame lit up the countryside for miles around. This was followed by three explosions. The earth was shaken for miles and we were thrown to the ground. Every gun within range opened fire and the noise was simply deafening. The flash of so many guns almost blinded one.

The explosion of the mines had killed the Germans who were on the hill and the first rush of our infantry caught the Germans unprepared and there was practically no resistance. Our men gained the hill with its three craters, but at midnight the enemy attacked with strong forces and regained a large part of the hill. Fierce fighting continued all night. 'A' and 'B' Companies had four men killed and many were wounded. Several men had arms broken by falling debris.

18th April - The German bombardment continued all night and at daylight our Battery and back areas were heavily shelled. One of the heavy guns was hit by a large shell and blown up. Luckily the crew were not at the gun.

About mid-day we were ordered forward to the shelters in Larch Wood in the railway cutting. We had a nasty time getting to this position as the enemy kept up a heavy bombardment the whole time and there were many casualties. On arriving at Larch Wood, the two companies were distributed outwards from the railway and took what cover they could in odd trenches and cubby holes that had been dug in the wood and a bank running northwards.

19th April - We found it very difficult to relieve troops on the hill. It is bad enough when there is a regular line of trenches, but here on the hill when there are only posts containing a few men, with no officers and very few NCOs it was very trying. No one appeared to know where the next post on the right or left was and to make matters worse, the enemy kept making small bombing attacks all along the line. After struggling through the craters, over dead and wounded men, and along pieces of trench, we eventually managed to relieve the *West Ridings*. Then we begun the hard work. We made a more or less continuous line of fire trenches and to dig a communications trench from the top of the hill to our front line. Before we could do this we had to get away a large number of wounded men who were scattered about everywhere.

Every man worked hard all night and although we frequently had to stop work to repel a bombing attack, we managed, by dawn, to make some sort of trench which afforded a little cover and from which we could fire our rifles. The bombardment never ceased and at about 5 a.m. it increased in intensity and the German infantry made a very powerful attack. After a hard struggle with some fierce hand-to-hand fighting in which the bayonet was freely used, the attack was repulsed. Both sides suffered heavily.

24th April - Ypres was again the centre of interest. The Germans began to concentrate the artillery on the town. They brought up a new seventeen inch gun and with this weapon of destruction, they systematically shelled the town. The craters caused by the shells were enormous. When the shells exploded whole blocks of houses on each side of the road simply disappeared with fragments of debris being blown 600-800 yards by the force of the explosion.

When inhabitants that were in the town began to stream back through Vlamertinge carrying bundles of household goods and their best clothing, it became clear that the shelling of these last two days was too much for them. It was a pitiable sight to see all these poor creatures being driven from their homes, losing all they possessed except for a few personal belongings that they could manage to carry with them.
Source: *Bedfordshire Record Office. War Diary. Bedfordshire Regiment.*

Private Edward Warner is gassed.

1st May - All was quiet until 6 o'clock in the evening when the enemy suddenly made a strong attack on the trenches to our right with gas and gas shells. After a time the company on our right became involved in the fight and felt the effects of gas. Most of the men were violently sick. Over twenty were admitted to hospital and two died shortly afterwards.

The *Dorset Regiment,* who held *Hill 60* got the full effects of the gas and many were seen out of action. The situation was very serious. The trenches on our right and on Hill 60 were practically defenceless but luckily the Germans did not press their advantage, and it became apparent that they were afraid of their own gas!

Splendid work was done by some of the company, of whom a number suffered from the effects of gas and were unprotected by masks as they moved along the deserted trenches where the gas was still thick.

Private Edward Warner of 'B' Company, though badly gassed, voluntarily entered and held a position in a deserted trench where the gas was thickest and remained there using his rifle with deadly effect until he was finally overcome by the gas and collapsed. For this act of gallantry he was awarded the Victoria Cross. He was removed from the trenches, but I regret to say he died the following day.
Source: *Bedfordshire Record Office. War Diary. Bedfordshire Regiment.*

I saw Private Warner buried.

Private C. Ives, 'B' Company, 1st Bedfordshire Regiment wrote to his sister -
We are still hard at it out here. We were occupying a trench opposite Hill 60 when it was blown up on Saturday night at seven o'clock. Of course we had been given the tip that it was going up, so we were prepared. The noise that followed was awful as hundreds of big guns opened fire.

On the evening of the 20th April we were in dugouts about 200 yards. in the rear of the firing line, and nine men and I were occupying one of these holes. The Germans started sending big shells over. One hit our dug-out and came right in, wounding seven men, five of them so severely that they died shortly afterwards. One young man sitting next to me had his leg blown completely off. The force of the explosion numbed my left leg, so that I lost all use of it for a while.

I daresay you have read the account of how poor Ted Warner held a trench on his own and won the V.C. He belonged to 'B' Company. His platoon occupied a part of the trench about 50 yds. on our right when

46

they caught more of the gas than we did. It is a pity he did not survive to wear his 'Cross. He was liked by everybody. I saw him laid to rest. He is the first one up to now to receive the Victoria Cross.
Source: *Herts Advertiser, 24th July 1915.*

Private Edward Warner, V.C. 1st Battalion, Bedfordshire Regiment.
For most conspicuous bravery near Hill 60 on 1st May 1915. After trench 46 had been vacated by our troops, consequent on a gas attack, Private Warner entered it single-handed in order to prevent the enemy taking possession. Reinforcements were sent to Private Warner, but could not reach him owing to the gas. He then came back and brought up more men, by which time he was completely exhausted, but the trench was held until the enemy's attack ceased. This gallant soldier died shortly afterwards from the effect of gas poisoning.
Source: *London Gazette, 29th June 1915.*

A view of Ypres from Hill 60.

Hill 60, where Private Edward Warner won his VC
and where he was buried, although none was later found,
hence his listing on the Menin Gate memorial, Ypres.

Of Private Warner and his family.

In 1914 when the war broke out, Edward Warner was working for the *Post Office Telephones Department*. As a reservist in the *Bedfordshire Regiment*, he had ten months of service remaining, which would have been completed at the end of May 1915. He was the son of Mr and Mrs Mårk Warner. His father, who died in 1913, was a labourer. His mother, now a widow, lived in Cannon Street, St. Albans with Miss Maud Burton, who worked in a factory. Maud Burton and Edward Warner were engaged to be married. Edward also had a married sister who was living in Watford. He had attended Hatfield Road School.

Since the beginning of the Great War he had served in all major battles since the *Battle of Mons*, with the exception of *Messines*, when he had a poisoned hand. In all other engagements, he had not received as much as a scratch from the enemy. In his last letter home, from *Hill 60* he had written "you will see from the papers that we have been in a very tight corner. I think it is the hottest place I have ever been in, but, thank the Lord, I have been spared to get through all right. We have lost a lot - killed and wounded. It was a proper death-trap. The dirty pigs could not blow us to pieces fast enough, so they tried to blind us, but I am pleased to say I am safe".

Writing to his mother, his platoon Sergeant said: "He faced his untimely end with courage and endurance, and I am extremely proud of him as one of the men in my platoon".

As his dependant, his mother had been sent 3s 6d of his army pay and the War Office provided a further 2s 10d. At the time of his death she was living on her Old Age Pension of 5s 0d plus 6s 4d, from which she paid out 7s 3d per week in rent. In July 1915, the Poly Picture Palace, St.Albans held a special matinee for his dependants.

His Victoria Cross was received by his mother, from King George V at Buckingham Palace at a private audience. The Mayor of St.Albans and her Member of Parliament went with her to the Palace.
Source: *Herts. Advertiser, November 1916.*

Increased Separation Allowances for the War are now given to the wives and children of married soldiers and to the dependants of unmarried men and widowers.

WIVES AND CHILDREN OF MARRIED MEN.

The New Weekly Rates are as follows:—

	Private and Corporal.	Sergeant.	Company Quartermaster-Sergeant.	Warrant Officer, Class II.	Warrant Officer, Class I.
	s. d.	s. d.	s. d.	s. d.	s. d.
Wife	12 6	15 0	16 6	22 0	23 0
Wife and child ...	17 6	20 0	21 6	27 0	28 0
Wife and 2 children	21 0	23 6	25 0	30 6	31 6

With 2s. extra for each additional child.

These rates include the usual allotment of 3s. 6d. a week for privates and corporals, and 5s. 10d. for other ranks, which is deducted from the married soldier's pay.

Adopted children are admitted. The ordinary limit of age for children is now 16; and the allowance is continued up to 21 in certain cases (for higher education, apprenticeship on a nominal wage, or physical or mental infirmity). Soldiers marrying AFTER enlistment are now eligible.

An extra 3s. 6d. a week is paid in the case of soldiers living in the London postal area at the time of enlistment if the families continue to live there.

Forms of Application for Separation Allowance can be filled in at the Recruiting Office.

MOTHERLESS CHILDREN.

5s. a week clear for each child.

Last to leave Hill 60.

In 1919, the Yorkshire Post published an account of the achievements of Captain George Upton Robins, who died on the 5th May in the Field Ambulance, the sole survivor of a Company of the Duke of Wellington's West Riding Regiment.

Captain Robins was born at Delaport, near Wheathamstead, and before the war had been Assistant Secretary of the Hertfordshire Hunt.

5th May - He was in command of his Company on Hill 60 when a gas attack took place. Apart from himself and his orderly, the entire Company was wiped out. They managed to crawl down the hill at the end of the attack to report. His last words, spoken slowly and in a gasping voice were: "The have gassed the *Duke's*. I believe I was the last man to leave the hill. The men up there are all dead. They were splendid".

His brother, later spoke to Capt. Robins' orderly who told him: "Captain Robins came down from the advanced trenches directly after the attack began. He came for reinforcements. He was gassed then, not so badly as he was afterwards, but quite badly enough to have gone sick. He would have been alive now if he had, but he would go back to his men. It was terrible getting back to the Hill. He had to climb up the railway cutting, and there was no outlet for the gas. We were being shelled all the time. He would go back. He was a brave man".

George Robins had already published a short book of poems *Lays of the Hertfordshire Hunt* ... A second edition, published in 1916 contained a preface by Lord Cavan:

"He was the last to leave Hill 60. Only those members of the 'Hunt who have served and suffered in this War, will perhaps fully appreciate what that short sentence means. To me, it means absolute self-sacrifice, splendid courage and an undying example. History will not forget those who fought that great fight of the 5th May, 1915".

Source: *Robins, George Upton. Lays of Hertfordshire Hunt, 2nd edn., 1916.*

Letters to the Editor.
Recruits required.

Major Henry Page Croft, Commanding Officer, 1st Battalion, Hertfordshire Regiment writes:

13th April - Sir, I am writing to ask you to bring before your readers some reasons why the young men of the county should join the County Territorial Regiment.

In the first place, those who join the *1st Hertfordshire Regiment* know they are joining a corps which is entirely composed of the men of the county, and, in consequence, they will fight beside their own friends, and will share the fortunes and hardships of war with men, who from the first, will regard them as comrades.

Secondly, the *Hertfordshire Regiment*, was one of the first Territorial Regiments in the whole country to be selected for foreign service, and was the second territorial regiment which ever went into the firing line on behalf of "King and Country".

Thirdly, we believe that we have justified the choice which the War Office made in sending us to the Front at a time when troops were badly needed. ... It is because we have now been fighting since the first week of November that I appeal to my neighbours in Hertfordshire to send us men. Hardly a day goes by in which we do not lose one or two and often more of our men. ...

This Regiment possesses a fine fighting spirit and that the men who have been through so many trials cheerfully, deserve all the support which the county can give. ... It is the bounded duty of every eligible young man in Hertfordshire, who still lags behind, to join our ranks.
Source: *Herts. Advertiser, 23rd April 1915.*

News from Captain Grenfell.

We've had boiling hot weather lately and no snow at all. It's rather trying weather with winter clothes and no outlet for one's energy.

We had a boxing show on Saturday and a Private Hay volunteered to fight me. We went into the ring and stripped in silence. A loud voice suddenly came from the back of the room from one of his friends, "pore old 'ay". It was rather a good omen for me, and I landed him a terrific thump with my second punch which shook him up so that I outed him in the second round. The same voice came across "oo's the next?" I wish I could find out who it was: he would make a very good man to hire to give me moral support when I fight.
Source: *Hertfordshire Record Office. Panshanger Collection. D/Erv C1135/708.*

15th April - We have just moved billets again but only a little way into a good little village, but off the hill where we were before. I am billeted with a lovely girl (and her mother), and we sit solemnly for hours (with the mother), kicking each other under the table.
Source: *Hertfordshire Record Office. Panshanger Collection. D/Erv C1135/709.*

30th April - I went to Paris for four days. Then we have been up to assist at the fighting with the *5th Brigade*, which has meant lying in the fields all day with the horses in the most wonderful hot summer sun. The '*Greys* had taken their horses and were in a field next to us with a few men (the rest being in the trenches). Three or four shells suddenly came from the blue into the middle of them. They stampeded and the few '*Greys* men helped by us got them away, riding one horse and leading four through the pandemonium. Only two men were hit and two horses.

We also had an aeroplane bomb in our garden that day which got two Canadian men. It was a funny mixture in that house just off the big road - Canadians, doctors, refugees, the '*Greys*, the Yeomanry and all our officers, crammed together anyhow and mucking together.

The road was a wonderful sight; wonderful in the ambulances going back, wounded walking back (Turcos, Zouaves, Indians, Canadians, French and our men). There were supplies going up and

51

reinforcements, doctors, generals and ambulances to and fro'; and the constant stream of refugees - old women and old men and young children carrying all they could in little carts and trolleys, pulled by themselves and their dogs. The road was shelled intermittently.

I was asleep in the sun when they started a bit of shelling and they ragged me terribly because I slept through the first three shells that fell. I don't believe I did. When I got up, a man staggered into me - very white and gibbering, saying he had been hit in the legs. I carried him to a doctor; I have never heard what happened to him.

We were turned out quickly that night to go to a gap but after half and hour we got a message to say that things were better and we were not wanted. The next day we marched back the six miles to our horses.

I went into one of the forward dressing stations - a tiny hovel of a farm with five doctors and the bad cases coming in and going out on stretchers. Everything was choc-a-bloc. How marvellously brave and cheerful is the wounded English Tommy!
Source: *Hertfordshire Record Office. Panshanger Collection D/ERv C1135/710.*

Prayer for those on the staff.

Fighting in mud, we turn to thee,
In these dread time of battle, Lord,
To keep us safe, if so it be,
From shrapnel, snipers, steel and sword.

Yet, not on us (for we'ave men
Of meaner clay, who fight in clay)
But on the staff, the Upper Ten,
Depends the issue of the day.

The staff is working with its brains,
While we are sitting in the trench;
The staff knows what verse ordains
Subject to thee and General French.   .../

52

God, help the staff - especially
The young ones, many of them sprung
From our high aristocracy;
Their task is hard, and they are young.

Julian Grenfell.

Source: *Hertfordshire Record Office. Panshanger Collection D/Ex 789 F23.*

"I stopped a 'Jack Johnson' with my head".

10th May - Too cold to sleep. Germans shells not very close. Made dugouts for ourselves in the morning in case of shell fire. Head of the unsuccessful attack by the French at *Arras* and our unsuccessful attack at *Aubers Ridge*. Our troops at Ypres going back, but holding the Hun. Five Hun attacks yesterday. Aeroplanes all day.

Source: *Hertfordshire Record Office. Panshanger Collection D/Ex 780 F23.*

14th May - We are practically wiped out, but we charged and took the Hun trenches yesterday. I stopped a 'Jack Johnson' with my head, and my skull is slightly cracked. But I'm getting on splendidly. I did awfully well! Today I go down to *Wimereux* to hospital. Shall we see you there. All my love, Julian of the 'ard 'ead.

Source: *Hertfordshire Record Office. Panshanger Collection D/ERv C1135/712.*

War Office to Lord Desborough.
16th May - Regret that Capt. Hon. J.H.F.Grenfell, *1st Royal Dragoons* was wounded on 12th May. Nature and degree not stated. Secretary of War. Official.

Source: *Hertfordshire Record Office. Panshanger Collection, D/Erv C2681/1.*

Lord Desborough to Lord Kitchener {Secretary of State for War]
28th May - Dear Julian is to be buried today: his end was peaceful and he looked happy. He had everything done for him that could be done. The Doctors and Nurses were so good to him and loved him and said "he was the harvest of the brave".

The most trying thing was that we were told not to let him talk, and he was longing to talk. There was some particular piece of work he was very pleased about, but I never heard what it was. He was so glad to let me tell him about your enquiries. I did let him know you had asked after him often, which pleased him much.

His soul was in the war and he loved the fighting, and everyone tells me how grandly he was doing, and we shall always think of him with joy and affection and great pride. Etti [Lady Desborough] sends her love: she was with him night and morning.
Source: *Hertfordshire Record Office. Panshanger Collection. D/ERv C1170/2.*

War Office to Lord Desborough - 13th October:
Captain Julian Grenfell was awarded, posthumously, the Distinguished Service Order [D.S.O] in recognition of his service with the Expeditionary Force in France.
Source: *Hertfordshire Record Office. Panshanger Collection. D/ERc C2681/3.*

Julian Grenfell lies among the graves in Boulogne (Eastern) Cemetery outside the town centre. Here the gravestones are laid flat because there is a risk of subsidence.

50th Northumbrian Division

In May 1915, Lord Cavan was given command of the *50th Northumbrian Division,* which was a recognition of the work he had achieved with the *4th Guards Brigade,* since September 1914.

Henry Page Croft, *1st Battalion, Hertfordshire Regiment* said of him:
"He is one of the exceptional personalities who gives confidence from the first moment you see him, but unlike the most famous Generals and Admirals, makes you feel his friendship at once and you realise you are dealing with a very humane man. Short in stature (he was five feet, four inches tall), very strongly built with a somewhat large head, he meets you with a merry twinkle in his eyes, and you find a rather unusual type of soldier, master of hounds, statesman, leader and friend, all rolled into one".
Source: *Croft, Henry Page. Twenty-two months under fire; Cavan's Memoirs ...*

Germans caught laying gas.

Private Smith to Mrs. F. Smith, Hart Road, St. Albans from 'somewhere in France':
The Germans were caught the other morning laying some asphyxiating gas fumes in front of our trenches. They were nabbed red-handed and shot.
Source: *Herts. Advertiser, 15th May 1915.*

Indian coolness in the face of danger.

Private Colmore, 17th Battalion, London Regiment, of Bow, writes of his rescue to the Revd. C.P.Heywood, St.Albans. [He had been billeted in St. Albans]:
I was buried in a trench by the fall of a shrapnel shell, a portion of which blew away a piece of the back of my leg. I would, inevitably, have lost my life but for the daring of an Indian, who despite the danger to himself, dug me out.

Finding that he could manage to carry him himself, the Indian walked some distance, all in the fire zone and brought back another Indian and a door. The first Indian placed a cigarette in my mouth, lit it, and then placed me on the door and they marched me off to hospital and safety.
Source: *Herts. Advertiser, 15th May 1915.*

Private Wilson loses an eye.

Private Wilson, 13th County of London Regiment, younger son of Mr.A.Wilson, baker of Holywell Hill, St.Albans. [Before the war, Wilson had been employed by Messrs Thomas Cook & Son, Ludgate Circus, London E.C.].
I was on a bayonet charge against the *Prussian Guard.* A bullet, after grazing the skin off the bridge of my nose, cut out my right eye, and came out at the temple, missing my brain by only a hair's breath. I had a miraculous escape from death. In spite of my injury, I never lost consciousness and remained, unattended in the trenches between the German and British lines for eighteen hours after being wounded, shells and bullets continuing to fly all round me. I was taken to the base hospital, then to the hospital ship and on to the Royal Victoria Hospital, Netley.
Source: *Herts. Advertiser, 22nd May 1915.*

55

"Short of cocoa and sugar".

Private E.A.Groom, 1st Bedfordshire Regiment writes to old colleagues at St. Albans (Midland) Station, where he was a porter:

We are just about to be relieved from the trenches for a few days. We are doing well, but cannot get a chance to get any of our clothes off; in fact, I have not had a wash for a week.

Old chums, could you send some cocoa and sugar. I should be glad of a common piece of cake, but I cannot expect too much of you.
Source: *Herts. Advertiser, 22nd May 1915.*

Life in the firing line.

Private Alexander M. Clark, 20th Battalion, County of London Regiment writes to his parents:

Am writing this on the loveliest of sunny days with a cool gentle breeze running down the trenches and my back supported by a traverse. A British aeroplane is flying overhead and the Germans are sending futile shrapnel after it, but it eludes them and cheekily sails further over their lines.

I was talking to a fellow in a "butt" as the trenches here are called. He showed me his hat into which he had put a box of matches, and whilst taking a look over the parapet, a bullet entered in the front, smashed through the match box and out of the middle of the crown, without touching a hair.

In front of our line runs an old communications trench that has, I believe, been vacated owing to water, which was deep enough to make it untenable. Well, some of our fellows swear they have seen stray Germans creeping up it at times, and seeing that it is near where most of our casualties occur, it seems quite possible. We are beginning to settle down to trench life and from now on will be doing four days in and four days out. You can imagine how spruce we look with no facilities for washing and shaving, and living in our boots.
Source: *Herts. Advertiser, 29th May 1915.*

Ordinary enlistments at St. Albans.

There has been a very busy week at the recruitment offices in St. Albans. Ordinary enlistments have been better than usual, and in addition, there have been 157 re-enlistments of Mechanical Transport men in the Territorial Army and in the regular Army. They have now left for France. A total of 179 men have been added to the previous total of 1,138 recruits received since the outbreak of the war. This makes a grand total of 1,257 recruits.

Source: *Herts. Advertiser, 29th May 1915.*

Hertfordshire Volunteers Service Regiment.

The Platoon Commander (Harpenden) tells of making an "attack":
Whit Monday, 24th May - We parade at the Gymnasium at 10.45 a.m. The men's uniforms have not arrived though the officers are in possession of theirs.

I walk, somewhat self-consciously, part of a group of the *North and South Staffordshire Territorials,* and find that there are at least two opinions among them about the compliments to be paid to a "Sam Browne" belt. belt. With an uneasy recollection of *Punch's Sergeant,* who was hauled over the coals for acknowledging the salute of a recruit. I cheerfully return the salute of the police and avoid the rest.

Having fallen in we are marched off by Lieut-Col. Braithwaite, our Commandant with Cyclist Scouts at the head and make good time to Wheathamsted where we await the Hatfield detachment who are our comrades in the operations against the two St. Albans companies.

The general idea is to learn of the intention of the St. Albans commander in attacking Wheathamstead. We are to advance and check him at *No-Mans Land,* from which, it is his job to eject us.

We cooled our heels in Wheathamsted and then lost no time in sending the cyclists on to spy out the land. We followed at a good five miles an hour which tried the wind of the veterans. Previous examination of the proposed field of battle had given us a good idea of its danger spots and we avoid the mouth of the Wheathamsted to St. Albans road by filing through a gap in the hedge and hugging its friendly cover, till we get in the rear of the gorse and so the back of the cottages, in front of which, our positions of defence have been selected. A cyclist meets us with the welcome news that no enemy is as yet in sight, but we double forward, crouching, in case his 'eagle eye' watches us from some secure retreat. We conceal ourselves in the gorse. We watch anxiously, until against the skyline opposite, small groups can be seen. ...

The whole scheme was most instructive for all concerned. The St. Albans Companies advanced through the gorse in extended manner, which was complimented by the umpire, Colonel Harland Bowden.

In the afternoon Colonel Rumball and Major Steel carried out Battalion drill and after tea, the various companies marched to their respective headquarters.
Source: *Herts. Advertiser, 29th May 1915.*

Joining up with no time to say goodbye.
Private R.H.Latchford, 'A' Company, Army Service Corps, 'C' Camp, Aldershot to his former employer, Viscount Grimston, Grimston Tyres Ltd., St. Albans:
26th May - Dear Sir, You will see by this that I am now in the Army. I had to report on Tuesday morning at the Recruiting Office, St. Albans. I thought of coming down to explain to you after I had been there, but instead, I was provided with an escort to the station for Aldershot. I hope you will accept my apology for this apparent act of discourtesy. Dear Sir, would you please send my money and Insurance Card to my mother, and dear Sir, I hope I shall be able to come back to you.
Source: *Gorhambury Collection. Business correspondence, 4th Earl of Verulam.*

Major Croft leads the charge. .
Company Sergeant-Major Langford, No.4 Company, Hertfordshire Regiment writes:
Major Croft gave the order to advance and led the charge himself.

58

With a moment's hesitation, No.1 Company (Hertford, Hoddesden and Waltham Cross men) were over the parapet in a twinkling and started their charge. They immediately came under maximum gun and rifle fire and their casualties were rather heavy, but they continued as though it was an everyday occurrence, and they attained their object.

I was at one of the dressing stations when some of the wounded came in, and although some of them had nasty wounds, they were all cheerful and the first thing they asked for was a drink and a cigarette. The arrangements for getting the wounded away were excellent, and I don't think that any man was more than ten minutes after being 'dressed', before he was off to the General Hospital by motor car.

Last Monday, the Battalion was inspected by the Major-General commanding the division. He spoke very highly of the work the Battalion had done and said he considered we were as good as any line regiment.

Today we had a Battalion drill. It was the first time that Major Croft had had the opportunity to address the men and he said that he was proud to command the *1st Hertfordshires*.
Source: *Herts. Advertiser, 5th June 1915.*

Lord Cavan thanks the 1st Herts. Territorials.

As Brigadier-General Lord Cavan's final special order ran:
28th June - On leaving the Brigade to take command of a Division it would not be seemly to recall the various actions since 18th September in which it has been my privilege and my delight to command you, but I may say this - whether in action, in trenches, or in billets, no unit of the *4th (Guards) Brigade* has ever disappointed me, nor has any Battalion ever fallen short of that great standard set by our predecessors. We welcomed the *1st Herts Territorials* at Ypres, and most worthily have they borne their part with the rest of us. To you all I convey the gratitude of a very full heart, and I wish you Good-bye and God Speed.
Source: *Kipling, Rudyard. The Irish Guards in the Great War: 1st Battalion.*

The effect of gas.

Private A. Mayes, 'B' Company, 1st Bedfordshire Regiment writes to a friend in Welwyn:

I have quite recovered from the gas now, a peculiarity of this gas is that one rarely loses consciousness. I will endeavour to describe to you the sensation. When the wind is right, the Germans fire a shell over us and you see a green cloud of smoke rolling along the ground to you. When it envelopes you all the air disappears and you start gasping for breath, and as you gasp, this stuff fills your lungs until you haven't the strength to gasp at all, or move hand or foot.

All the time one's brain is clear and you know what is going on around you, but you cannot breathe. All your strength seems gone too. If the gas does not blow away, it is all up to you. When it does, some are too far gone and gradually sink. I could not walk ten yards.

Source: *Herts. Advertiser, 5th June 1915.*

Noise of the guns.

Farrier-Corporal Mitchel, 8th City of London Post Office Rifles, in a letter to his home in Abbots Langley:

I have not had my boots off for three weeks now and my poor feet don't half feel sore. On Sunday we had another heavy bombardment. It was amazing and I was dumbfounded, almost speechless, to hear the guns. No kettle-drum could have kept time with them. It drives the enemy mad.

Source: *Herts. Advertiser, 5th June 1915.*

With thoughts of home.

Private Herbert White, 2nd Bedfordshire Regiment writes to his father at 42 Fishpool Street, St. Albans, from hospital:

> While I lie in the trenches and the battle rages hot
> My thoughts are of dear old home, the ivy-covered door;
> And I picture you, dear father, as the days go slowly by
> Waiting, waiting nobly, while the tear-drops dim your eye.

I saw again in dreams, Dad, the place I used to roam,
And wonder if I'll live to see again the dear old home.
Do not fret or pine for me, though sorrow fill your heart,
For your sweet influence lives, and I must do my part.

The harder task by far is your lot to bear,
But cheer up, brighter days shall dawn
                                        and joy shall end despair.
                                                Herbert White.
Source: *Herts. Advertiser, 12th June 1915.*

'On guard duty in the trenches'.

Private Frank Henson, 'B' Company, 1st Hertfordshire Regiment writes to his wife in London Road, St. Albans:
Last night I was on guard in our trench so I did not get much sleep. I could hear the Germans knocking in stakes and fixing up barbed-wire entanglements, but we could not shoot at them because we had a patrol out and we might have shot our own men.

This morning I also went on periscope guard. The Germans started shelling our trenches and one of the shells burst close to me and a piece of shell hit me on the shoulder but did no damage, only stung my arm for a little while, but smashed the periscope I was looking at. One of our fellows had his rifle and bayonet smashed,
Source: *Herts. Advertiser, 3rd July 1915.*

Lord Cavan's Staff Captain is killed.

Lord Cavan writes to Mrs Brabazon, widow of Captain Ernest Brabazon:
Jerry and I spotted a place where we could do good work with a machine gun some 1,000 yards from the enemy, well hidden by high crops. We settled down to shoot with Howitzers and then turn to the machine guns as the Germans bolted. It was timed for 4.30 p.m. and Jerry went to see all was working well in the highest spirits.

After a little while the enemy spotted the place and started to shell it, but there was a dugout handy and he and another bolted into it. One shell pitched close to the dugout but did not explode, but knocked off the roof and the back of the dugout. The *Irish Guards* got Jerry's companion out exhausted except for a broken and twisted foot. It was a little longer before they could reach Jerry. They found that he was dead from suffocation, and possibly stunned by the roof fall.

We simply loved him. I can never tell you what he was to me not only as a Staff Officer, but as a friend. He was priceless, invaluable and never wearying in his work for the Brigade.

Ernest Brabazon was not a Hertfordshire man, but his sister was Violet, was married to Viscount Grimston, son of the 3rd Earl of Verulam. Before the war, Ernest Brabazon had often stayed at Gorhambury, St.Albans as a house guest and taken part in shoots on the Estate.

The Chaplain of the 4th (Guards) Brigade at No.4 Field Ambulance Station of the 2nd Division also wrote to Mrs Brabazon:
18th June - I feel I must add a few lines both because I was, before I came out here, Headmaster of Dover College where he was educated. It was only yesterday I was talking to him, and he seemed, then, as always, so delightfully happy. I do not think I ever met a man who seemed to love life and (the) soldiering life as much as he. You doubtless know how greatly he was loved by the Brigadier and the Headquarters staff, but not only by them, but by all who knew him. The end must have mercifully come very quickly for him. The grave is in a beautiful place near the church at Cambrin.

Revd. F. de Lushington.
Sources: *Gorhambury Collection & Herts. Advertiser, 24th June 1915*.

A narrow escape.
Private Roberts, 1st Hertfordshire Regiment writes to his parents:
25th June - Just behind our lines, a machine gun battery was firing and the Germans started shelling our trench. One burst just behind our parapet so I and the chap with me, moved into the next reverse, about five yards away just as a shell fell right into the trench where I had

been standing, smashing my rifle, water bottle and the book I was reading had a shell go clean through it. My air pillow got eight or ten holes in it!

Source: *Herts. Advertiser, 3rd July 1915.*

'In the Dardanelles and Gallipoli'.

Private Fred Corley, writes to Mr George Wood, Headmaster of Priory Park School.
[Private Corley's parents lived in Sopwell Lane]:
Just a line to let you know I am alive and kicking, in spite of the Turks. Perhaps you have read in the papers of the work the *Lancashire Fusiliers* have done here. I will try and give you a brief outline of our regimental landing. We landed at 6 pm. on 25th April. We were towed by tugs to within 200 yards of the coast and then they let us go, and the sailors then rowed to within fifty yards of the shore.

They were potting at us all the time from the shore, and a few sailors were hit beside our own fellows. The boys jumped in about four feet of water and made haste to get on the land and under cover from the Turks' rifle and machine gun fire. Can you picture us, wet through and shivering from the cold, grasping our rifles and getting into the best place we could out of way of that fire, and eagerly looking for a Turk's head above us to have a pop at. Well, we were like that for ten minutes and then the order came, "Fix bayonets and charge the hill". I wish I could have seen it as a spectator, not because I didn't want to be in it, but because it must have been a sight of a lifetime.

Amid shouts of "Come on, *the Lancs*", and "Are we downhearted?" we charged the hill. We got to the top and drove them out of their trenches into others further back, and we kept them back until other regiments had landed. We have kept the Turks back, in fact we are driving them back. They made a night attack on our trenches. There were thousands of them all shouting *Allah, Allah!* and trying to get through. Needless to say the boys beat them by pumping fifteen rounds per minute into them. Next morning they left all the dead for us to bury.

My opinion of the position they held was it was impregnable. If we

63

had our battalion defending it, a brigade never would have been allowed to land, never mind a battalion. The place we landed at is now called *Lancashire landing*. The Generals say it was the finest thing that they had ever seen in their lives, and that we made history. I can tell you we feel very proud of our doings, what was left of us ... After all said and done we only did what was expected of us by our King and our Generals. We were always reckoned to be a good regiment: we have showed it now anyway.

Source: *Herts. Advertiser, 25th June 1915.*

Humour and horror of the war.

Driver A. Hardie, A.S.C., 153rd Infantry Brigade, lives in Ramsbury Road, St. Albans (and was senior clerk at the Labour Exchange, before enlisting). He writes to Mr. A.E. Harmer, manager of the St. Albans Labour Exchange, now running the Exchange with a temporary staff.

We are attached to the Indian Corps, and the tales you read of them in the daily papers are by no means exaggerated ... . We are fed very well considering the circumstances, and well provided with cigarettes and tobacco, but it will be an absolute feast to get pastry or cake again.

You would laugh at our fellows trying to speak French. They learn one or two phrases, and whenever a Frenchman speaks to them, they use the same phrase whether it applies or not. It is a great scream and generally ends in gesticulating.

As regards sleeping accommodation, it varies a great deal, especially near the firing line, and if we happen on a clean farm we consider ourselves lucky, as some of the places are in a filthy condition, and you wake up to find rats running all over you. I have only slept in a building about four times since I landed. My friend and I invariably put up a bivouac made of waterproof sheets; you do know then that it is clean. If we can't manage to do that we sleep in a waggon.

If is wonderful how the Germans seem to make a point of shelling every church within range, and some are absolutely ruined. One church and churchyard which has been shelled recently has been reduced to a heap of stones, and the shells have exploded with such terrific force that the coffins have been blown into the air and the bones and and shrouds of the persons lie about the place, and in one case a stone tomb has been opened, showing the preserved body.

I don't think the people realise the damage these 'Jack Johnson's do. I never dreamt it was anything like it. Two of the fellows attached to our Brigade have gone quite mad with the noise and strain of the continued bursting of the shells.

Source: *Herts. Advertiser, 12th June 1915.*

Another V.C. Hero.

St. Albans is particularly interested in the following announcement in the *London Gazette* of the King having been graciously pleased to approve the award of the Victoria Cross to Lance-Corporal Leonard James Keyworth, *24th County of London Regiment (Queen's) Territorial Force:*

"for most conspicuous bravery at Givenchy on the night of 25th-26th May, 1915. After the successful assault on the German position by the 24th Battalion, London Regiment, efforts were made by that unit to follow up their success by a bomb attack, during the progress of which 58 men out of a total of 75 became casualties. During this very fierce encounter, Lance-Corporal Keyworth stood full exposed for two hours on the top of the enemy's parapet. and threw about 150 bombs amongst the Germans, who were only a few yards away".

Lance-Corporal Keyworth came from Lincoln where his father is a tailor. It is from a letter to his sister that the family learned something of the deeds which won him the Victoria Cross. For some months at the beginning of the war, he was billeted with Mr and Mrs L.J. Titmus, 63 Heath Road, St. Albans.

"Although I knew that I had been recommended for a distinction of some sort for the incident at Givenchy on the night of 25th-26th May, I did not learn that I had secured the V.C. until mid-day on 5th July. It was in this way. I was up in the trenches and I got a note from the Sergeant-Major in which he said he had a copy of *Lloyds News* announcing that I had been awarded the V.C. Naturally I was very excited, because I never thought that my action would bring me the decoration which all soldiers covert. I thought, perhaps, it might be the D.C.M., and therefore, you can understand how anxious I was to get back from the trenches and read for myself the good news. I may explain that the copy of the paper was brought over by a soldier who left England on the Sunday, and arrived up at the billets next day.

As for the fight at Givenchy, I consider that I was only carrying out the orders given to me by my officer to throw bombs against a certain point in the enemy trenches. I simply did my duty - as I told the Colonel when I was called before him, and he said that my name had been forwarded for a distinction.

The attack in which the bomb-throwing occurred was directed in the evening of 25th May against a section of enemy trenches which wound round a small hill. Our artillery fire was so accurate that when we were ordered to advance we found practically no opposition from the enemy. My company moved against the trenches on the hill top, and we quickly dug ourselves in and made a sand bag parapet there. We were about forty yards from the enemy there, and I was told to throw bombs against a point in their trench to prevent them forming up.

Previously to that, however, I had seen Lieut. Chance of 'A' Company, lying shot through the legs and unable to move. I started over the parapet with the intention of trying to bring him into cover, but as the German fire was so murderous I suppose he saw that it meant certain death for me and so waved me back.

When I began throwing bombs it was about eight o'clock and beginning to get dusk. It is quick work and not a little dangerous to throw bombs. You light the fuse and you have to get rid of the thing in five seconds. One of our men was killed because, being shot in the right arm, he could not get rid of his bomb.

Amongst my impressions of that night are the sizzling of the fuses. In all I flung about two hundred bombs. I remember standing on the parapet of our trenches aiming at the enemy. I remember crawling out over the ground to get nearer Germans, with supplies of bombs, and feigning to be dead - the hill was strewn with bodies, alas! - when they let off their flares to detect any surprise attack. I continued "bombing" the Germans until midnight and a comrade tells me afterwards that I wanted to go back and throw more, but I don't recollect saying that. Two days afterwards the Colonel sent for me. The officers had spoken to him and he asked me what I had done. I was quite surprised, and answered that I hadn't done much - only my duty.

But he sent my name to headquarters, and so I came to be lined up at Buckingham Palace to receive my V.C. The King was in uniform. He shook me by the hand, inquired of my age, and seemed taken aback when I told him I was twenty-two.

Out there, by the way, I have so far borne a charmed life. At Givenchy my chums were shot down all around me, and I got a bullet through my pack and one through my mess tin. And I have a fragment of shrapnel which dropped on my neck, after I had been in the trenches only a short time. So far, however, I have escaped without a scratch.

Yes, I enjoyed throwing those bombs on the Germans, and shall be ready to do it again if the chance comes.
Source: *Herts. Advertiser, 10th, 17th and 24th July 1915.*

A keen alert soldier.

"A through good sportsman, who was bound to make his mark if he got the chance," was the opinion of his commander at the headquarters of the *Queen's County of London Regiment (T.F.)*, in New Street, Kennington, London. Both officers and men are delighted at the news of an act of heroism which adds fresh lustre to a corps which has distinguished itself in a manner second to none at the front.

"I enlisted him myself," said Captain F.B. Galer, the adjutant of the *3rd Battalion,* "and I well remember him as one of the pick of one of the finest Territorial battalions you could wish to see".

"He was a splendid footballer," Lance-Corpl. Butterworth, a friend stated, "and we always liked to get him in our team when we had matches against other companies. He was always the best of sportsmen in every sense of the word and was liked as well as any man in the company. Although he excelled at football, he was good also in other games, including cricket. I've no doubt his experiences in the cricket field helped him considerably in the bomb-throwing".

"They were all splendid and very good fellows" said Mrs.Titmus, of Heath Road, where he was billeted with four others. "He came to us in November, after being billeted in Culver-road Hall. If anybody wanted help in a game of football, he was always ready, and was always playing football on the Heath".
Source: *Herts. Advertiser, ... July 1915.*

Essex Brigade inspected at Gorhambury.

The battalions comprising the *Essex Brigade* were inspected at Gorhambury Park on Wednesday morning. There was an early muster of the troops and the battalions, fully equipped, marched to Gorhambury Park in warm summer weather which, to the lay weather expert, seemed to indicate a glorious summer day. The weather continued all that could be desired until almost the close of movements, when the ominous appearance of heavy clouds was followed by very loud thunder-claps, flashes of intense vividness, and a pelting rainfall, which rendered it extremely unpleasant.

The Brigade, which received the Inspecting Officer with a general salute, was in a position on the magnificent stretch of sward to the right of Gorhambury, the residence of the Earl of Verulam, which is admirably adapted for military movements on a fairly large scale. The Brigade which was put through varied movements, which were carried through with a precision and effectiveness that demonstrated the value of the long course of training it has gone through since the mobilisation. The concluding stages of the review consisted of skirmishing work in extended order, which provided a striking spectacle for the small number of spectators in the Park.
Source: *Herts. Advertiser, 17th July 1915.*

The Sign.

Private Wright, 24th Battalion, London Regiment writes:
In our marches we often come across some very interesting sights; we often pass through a village where the only thing that remains of what was a church is the Crucifix, standing solitary and high out of the runs.

69

It strikes me as a symbol: and in my imagination I have labelled it "the Sign".
Source: *Herts. Advertiser, 17th June 1915.*

Spy up a tree.

Driver A. Hardie, Army Service Corps, with the Gordon Highlanders, formerly employed at St. Albans Labour Exchange, writes to the manager, Mr. A.E.Harmer:

By a piece of luck last evening I met Barber (who was also employed at the Labour Exchange). The poor chap seems to have had a rather rough time, but is quite all right at present. Soon after his battalion came here, they were parading out of their billets for rifle inspection, when a shell burst close to them, killing eight and wounding sixteen of his platoon. He was lucky enough to escape except for a small piece of shell that struck his face.

You are not really safe in many of the places round about here, as spies seem to abound everywhere. I was on night guard a little while back, and about two o'clock in the morning we noticed someone close to our horse lines, and when we challenged him he went off on a cycle. We tried to follow him, but it was pitch dark and we missed him. We found when we came back that he had formed a pile of straw, and I suppose that he was about to light it. Had he done so it would have given away our position, and we should have been shelled, immediately afterwards, but it just shows the work spies are doing out here. One of our interpreters was found in a tree signalling one night last week, and it is unnecessary to say he was shot shortly afterwards.
Source: *Herts. Advertiser, 17th July 1915.*

"I shall never forget the sights of that day".

Corporal F.G. Marshall-Williams, 21st Battalion, London Regiment (1st Surrey Rifles) writes to Mr. George F. Wood, Headmaster, Priory Park Boys' School, St.Albans from hospital in Eastbourne, Sussex:

We were told to take the trenches at Givenchy. We took them, with the result we got chopped up. I got through the charge all right, and stayed in the German trench all night. At about 4.30 in the morning the enemy started to shower shells into us. It got so bad that we were told to evacuate 'the blooming thing', which, by the way, was practically demolished by now.

I got one in the shoulder which knocked me down for the time. There was absolutely no cover, and we were at the mercy of them. When the order was given, we all started to crawl on all fours for the communications trench in order to get out. When we got there the Huns were there, dropping petrol bombs on us. I could not go any farther, and dropped down where I had crawled to, which was between the captured and the original trench. Whilst I was lying out there, waiting to be fetched in (sixteen hours), I got all the rest of my wounds.

I shall never forget the sights of that day. At night, when I and the other unfortunates were taken to the ordinary dressing station, there were 1,400 there waiting to be dressed and sent away. The trenches were full of dead, and the fields where we all charged over were simply covered with them.

Source: *Herts. Advertiser, 17th July 1915.*

At an advanced dressing station.

Private Arthur Hardacres, 6th London Field Ambulance writes:
Our section is now at an advanced dressing station, about two miles from the firing line. Our building is rather a fine one, and the French people have equipped it with beds, etc. French and English soldiers are admitted, and Sisters of Mercy help to nurse and superintend the cooking of the whole hospital.

This part of the line is fairly quiet so we are not over-rushed with wounded. We had an exciting time the other night. About midnight the Germans started to shell this village. News came to hand that a shell had exploded in the billet of the *17th Battalion.* 50 were wounded and four killed outright. We were kept busy for some time, although I am pleased to say the majority of the wounds were slight.

Source: *Herts. Advertiser, 17th July 1915.*

71

'Billy' Grenfell is killed.

War Office, London to Lord Desborough.

3rd August - Deeply regret to inform you that Second Lieutenant G.W.Grenfell was killed in action on the 31st July. Lord KItchener expresses his sympathy.   Official, Secretary of State.

Source: *Hertfordshire Record Office. Panshanger Collection D/ERv C2681/2.*

Lieutenant A.C.Sheepshanks to Lord Desborough.

1st August - Bill died splendidly, leading his men over open ground, up hill in the face of tremendous fire from a machine gun. His Platoon-Sergeant saw him pitch forward with a bullet in the head and thinks he was hit again in the side as he fell. He must have been killed instantly as he was not seen to move afterwards. His platoon all loved him, and he had somewhat inspired them with a fighting spirit.

Source: *Hertfordshire Record Office. Panshanger D/ERv C2347/238.*

N.S.Talbot to Lady Desborough.

16th August - I was able to get out last night and bury Bill's body. [Previous attempts to find it had failed]. During a counter-attack, a Lance Corporal found the body and his identification disc, which was subsequently dropped on its way to Battalion headquarters. We were able to retrieve his wristwatch and flask, but we couldn't find a ring. The grave is 250 yards due south of Hooge, on the Ypres to Menin Road. I am having a wooden cross made up by the *Pioneers, 3rd Battalion.*

Source: *Hertfordshire Record Office. Panshanger Collection D/ERv ...*

After the Great War, his grave was not found. His name is among those inscribed on the Menin Gate, Ypres through which so many young men marched out into battle.

Second Lieutenant G.W. 'Billy' Grenfell was the brother of Captain Julian Grenfell who died from wounds received in action, in May 1915. Lady Desborough, had, in 1913, inherited the Panshanger Estate, near Hertford. It is possible, that the deaths of these two brothers contributed to the decision, made by the family in 1920, to sell part of the estate to those who were to build the Second Garden City in England at Welwyn Garden City, Hertfordshire.

Viscount Grimston writes to a former employee.

Viscount Grimston, Grimston Tyres Ltd, St. Albans writes to Private C. Paynes, 'C' Company, 6th Bedfordshire Regiment who has been wounded and is at No. 6 Convalescent Depot, France:

12th August - I am sorry to hear you had the bad luck to be wounded, but it is something that you have been in *the great push* and come out alive.

As you may have seen from the paper we have been told a good deal more of what is going on in France than we were ever told last year. Possibly that is because what we are doing this year is successful, whilst what we did last year was not. Possibly Sir Douglas Haig believes in as much publicity as can be allowed safely. At any rate it brings the fighting much more home to one.

The following fellows who used to work here have been wounded - E.R.Addington, Beasley, Crouch, Freeman, Gough, H.Lawrence, J.Lowe, L.Page, G.H.Windmill, A.Willmott, Adams, G.Bedford. I do not know if you knew any of them, but in case you did, I give you all their names.

Freeman and Crouch were wounded some time ago and have been discharged. Freeman is back here at work. Crouch has not yet made up his mind whether he will come back or not.

Addington, Beasley, H.Lawrence, J.Lowe, L.Page, A.Willmott (who was badly burnt in the chest) and G.Bedford are all in hospitals, either in England or France. Adams, died of his wounds.

We are fairly busy here, not because we have got such a great deal of work to do, but because we have not got many men to do it, and such men as we have got, are inexperienced in rubber work. Wishing you a speedy recovery.   **Grimston**.

Source: *Gorhambury Collection. Business Correspondence, 4th Earl of Verulam.*

Hay for the Forces.
Useful hints for farmers.
In consequence of the erroneous idea, which prevails in some districts, that the Military Authorities intend to commandeer the stocks of hay in the country at whatever price they deem reasonable, and without regard to the amount required for use on the farm.

The President of the Board of Agriculture and Fisheries desires to make known as widely as possible, the policy of the Military Authorities in respect of the acquisition of hay.

[1] The Military Authorities are ready to buy, at its fair market value, any suitable hay which is offered to their purchasing officers by the grower.

[2] It is not the intention to acquire hay which is proved to be wanted for use of the stock on a farm.

[3] Soft meadow hay and clear clover hay is not required, as a rule, for Army purposes.

[4] In view of the short hay crop this year, the Military Authorities have decided to reduce materially the quantity of hay purchased in this country.

Source: *Herts. Advertiser, 24th July 1915.*

Lord Cavan receives fresh orders.
Whilst in England on leave in July 1915, Lord Cavan was summoned to Windsor Castle to receive the honour of *Commander of the Order of the Bath* [Military Division] from the King. Whilst on leave he was ordered to report to the War Office and there was ordered to form a new *Guards Division*. It had been proposed that one of the Brigades of the new Division should consist of the four Battalions of the Grenadier Guards. Cavan disagreed and argued that it could lead to the loss of more officers and men of one regiment than it might be possible to replace. His arguments won the day and the new Division was made up of a mix of the Grenadier, Coldstream, Irish, Scots and Welsh Guards. There appears to be little hard evidence regarding the

formation of this new Guards Division other than Cavan's own recollections and those of his A.D.C. who was Cuthbert Headlam, his brother-in-law. Cavan returned to France to his existing command as O.C. of the 50th Division. Fifteen days later he was relieved of the command and returned to London where he received fresh orders and the new Guards Division joined the war in the Autumn 1915. The Prince of Wales, joined Cavan's staff and remained with him until September 1918.

Sources: *Cavan's memoirs; Compiler's research.*

National Registration Act, 1915.

The President of the Local Government Board, Whitehall, London SW has written to the Lord Lieutenants of Counties in England. By order of the Vice-Lieutenant of Hertfordshire, the letter was published, in full, in the Herts Advertiser, from which this extract is taken:

20th July - The National Registration Act received the Royal Assent on Thursday last, and under Regulations which have just been issued by my Department, the enumeration of the population between the ages of 15 and 65 will take place in the middle of August.

The Act contemplates that a Register will be formed in each borough and urban or rural district under the direction of the local authority of the area.

It is most important that this work should be conducted as expeditiously as possible, and it is desirable that the local authority should have abundant help for the purpose. ...

Source: *Herts. Advertiser, 31st July 1915.*

Enumeration districts arranged.

The preliminary work of the National Registration is well in hand. The city [of St. Albans] has been divided into 54 districts - 24 in South Ward, 17 in North Ward and 13 in the East Ward. The enumerators, have been selected from voluntary workers who have expressed their willingness to serve. Each person will be responsible for 100 houses and it is estimated that 350 forms will be required by each enumerator.

Work on distribution will begin on Monday, 9th August and collection [of the information] must be completed by Wednesday, 18th August, and the whole of the forms, books etc. delivered in proper order by Saturday, 21st August.

Source: *Herts. Advertiser, 31st July 1915.*

General commends good work.

Private T.W. Barker, 'A' Company, 1st Norfolk Regiment writes:
We have just come out after a long spell in the trenches, for a few days' rest. Things were very uncomfortable during the cold, wet, season. We were at "Hill 60" with the Bedfords - the only regiment I have seen where I have met some St. Albans fellows. I am the only St. Albans fellow in our Regiment. I am in touch with [the city] and used to reside in Bedford road and worked at Sanders' Nurseries. I am kept in touch through the good old "Times "[Herts Advertiser], which is sent to me by my aunt in Bernard street. I was very proud and also sorry to read of the St. Albans V.C. as I knew the brave fellow slightly.

We have just been inspected and highly praised by the General Commanding the Second Army for the good work we have accomplished.

Source: *Herts. Advertiser, 31st July 1915.*

Help for the Belgian refugee fund.

The Directors of the St. Albans Cinema, Chequer Street, whose excellent programme has continued to attract crowded houses, organised a "Belgian Day" on Thursday. The programme included an intensely interesting drama entitled "His Sister's Honour" the topical spirit of which was introduced in realistic scenes of incidents with the contending armies on the Belgian frontier. The entertainment was liberally patronised by the citizens and the Belgians who are resident with us. It is estimated that the show will produce, in round figures, £22 towards the fund for their support.

Source: *Herts. Advertiser, 31st July 1915.*

Putting up barbed-wire entanglements.

Private Percy Mitchell, 1st Army Cycling Corps writes home to Abbots Langley:
Since my arrival in the theatre of war, we have been engaged in very risky work in the putting up of barbed-wire entanglements in front of the firing, and some times only 35 yards from the German firing line. On my first journey to the trenches I had shells screaming overhead and bullets flying by with a 'ping'. Of course, this work must be done at night, but star shells light the place for miles around, and then you must stand still for safety. We have to leave the trenches before daylight and get off the sky line, or we would either get a coal box planted among us or a machine gun would wipe us off the earth. It came down "cats and dogs" on my fifth night engaged in this work, but we had to finish it and the water came up to calve of our legs and we were absolutely drenched to the skin.
Source: *Herts. Advertiser, 7th August 1915.*

Billeting Allowances reduced.

The Army Order issued last Friday fixes the allowances for a soldier billeted in a private house and reduces it to 17s 6d a week and 15s 0d for each additional soldier. This is the same rate as in most towns.
Source: *Herts. Advertiser, 9th September 1915.*

Taking ammunition over the top.

Private E. Wells, 'A' Company, 22nd London Regiment writes to Miss A.E. Groves:
We had held the line at Givenchy for a few days, and were back resting, when we had the order to give in our overcoats and turn out on parade. We were then rushed up to a communication trench behind the firing line to wait until the charge was over. The *24th Battalion* passed us on their way to the firing line. We could hear the chaps shouting as they attacked, and saw the red and green star shells go up, indicating that the attack had started and the trench gained. We were moved up into the reserve trenches, and it was terrible to see the chaps lying seriously wounded or dying, as we had to step over many to get along. The first of the prisoners were brought along - two hulking great square-headed fellows they were - looking as miserable as a

'dying duck in a thunderstorm'. We then got the order to take ammunition over the top to the new trench.

Our trenches were being shelled heavily all the time, and there was a continual stream of wounded going out. It was on this job that Corporal Wood, our section commander was last seen. Another Company of our Battalion was busy digging a communication trench between our firing line and the new one. When the day broke, it still found our chaps busy. The officer came along and told some of our chaps to go and relieve the men in the new line; they managed to get there without any casualties, but it was not a pleasant job, as they had to lay flat in the boiling sun for about nine hours, and to move in this part, meant a bullet through the head, as the Germans were only forty yards away.

We had to sit in the reserve trenches until we were relieved in the evening, and the time has never dragged on so much as that day did. It seemed more like a month, and we were getting shells in galore, and the fellows were being bowled over like ninepins, but they stuck to it, and after we were relieved, and on our way back we were like a lot of schoolboys on a holiday!
Source: *Herts. Advertiser, 14th September 1915.*

Hertfordshire Regiment's farewell to the Guards.

Reuter's' News Agency reports on the Hertfordshire Territorials' farewell to the Guards Brigade:
All the way down the line the men were greeted by the cheers of the comrades they were leaving - cheers given with a vigour and enthusiasm that showed the real feeling behind them. The shouting rippled down the road until it faded away in the distance, only to be succeeded by another great outburst as a fresh battalion came into sight. Every officer at the head of his company; every man's head turned sharply to the right was greeted by the General with a grave salute, which, from its very formality, had the character of a leave-taking, as expressing affectionate esteem and real personal feeling at parting with old friends. That feeling was reflected in the face of every

man there, and is a remembrance that the Guards will ever treasure.

Perhaps the heaviest hearted there were the men of a battalion of *Hertfordshire Territorials*, the only non Guards regiment in the *Guards' Brigade* who were being left behind. From their long association with the *Guards' Brigade*, they have gained the title of the *Herts Guards*, and naturally they could not restrain a wish, clearly expressed on their faces, that they were going with their old comrades.

The last man had passed, the strains of the band had almost died away, and now the Brigade transport was rattling by. The General Commanding the *Guards' Brigade*, who, astride his horse beside the Divisional General, had watched his men filing past, took a last handshake all round, and then, turning his horse, galloped swiftly off in pursuit of his disappearing troops. A last salute to the stretcher-bearers bringing up the rear, a distant roll of drums, and the Guards had gone, followed by the heavy hearts and fervent good wishes of their many friends in the 2nd Division.
Source: *Herts Advertiser, 23rd October 1915.*

A pedlar of all wares.

About 3rd September we left our trenches in order to leave all our valuables and superfluities in a place of safety, returning to the line the following day in fighting order. Dressed in the latter 'rig' a man resembles somewhat a pedlar of all wares, for although the pack is discarded, the haversack is made to contain all sorts of useful and useless articles - iron rations and shaving tackle, dubbin and soap, mess tins and bootlaces. Festooned around the ordinary webbing equipment are sandbags, both ball and battle-bandoliers of small arms and wire cutters, and last but by no means least, smoke helmets and respirators.

Thus arrayed, we returned to the trenches and subjected the Huns to a most gruelling four-days' bombardment.
Source: *Herts. Advertiser, 23rd October 1915.*

A great fight.

Sergeant Allan, 2nd Border Regiment writes to his parents in St.Albans:

We went into the trenches and laid low until 4 a.m. next morning when operations began. It was a splendid sight. First our Engineers and Artillery prepared the position, and after half an hour, my Company were given order to advance. We all climbed over our trench together, and to my astonishment began to walk towards the Germans. When we had got within 100 yards of their trench, they opened into rapid fire, and we had to get whatever cover we could. I myself and a man who was in my section jumped into a shell hole, which provided good cover. We lay there for about ten minutes, which seemed like hours, when I heard the Captain who commands our Company tell us to get ready to charge.

On the word of command we charged, shouting like fury. The Germans, about 200 in number, swarmed over the front of trench and proceeded towards us with their hands up shouting "Mercy, comrades" Our officers took great care in seeing that we did not see some of them off. One German officer shot one of our lads, but he had not a chance to shoot any more, as one of my platoon, on seeing this distardly act, shot him immediately. The prisoners were escorted back by another Company, and we moved forward. Shells were dropping all around us by this time, and we rushed on towards the trench. When we jumped into it, we found another 100 men in the dugouts. We soon had them out, and they were sent back, so that made us 300 prisoners.

By this time our other companies had joined us, and we pushed off again, after we had partially reorganised. We moved off at the trail, in slow time, as the German second line was about 400 yards further on; we remained like this until we got about 50 yards from them. We charged, and to our surprise not a German was in the trench.

We captured four light field guns and two machine guns. All of them were red hot; undoubtedly they had just left them and had retired up the communications trench into a village about 500 yards further on.

We had not been in this trench very long when the Germans gave us our reception, a rapid fire, but we had not many casualties here. Most of them occurred when we first moved forward. I might add that I was the only N.C.O. left in my platoon by then, and out of thirty men, only nine answered their names. I am thankful only a few were killed; the majority were wounded, some severely.

We hung on to this position until nightfall. Then we reorganised and moved further over to the right of the line, to take up a weaker position. About 1 a.m. the next morning the Germans counter-attacked, but by Jove! what a time they must have had. We lay behind our trench as thick as mustard, and every rifle was at work. They soon turned round and fled back, save those that we either killed or wounded, which must have been many. We were relieved that night and went further back. We were by this time tired out, as the weather was not at all in our favour. I am sure the *Border Regiment* did its share, as our Brigadier General has told us since.
Source: *Herts. Advertiser, 23rd October 1915.*

Battle of Loos: a graphic account.

Bombardier G.E. Paines, 18th Battery, 7th London Brigade, who was stationed at Boxmoor in the winter of 1914 writes:
The big battle is still raging, but our boys in the *2nd London Division* have been given their biggest test. My goodness! It was a smash and no mistake. A heavy towering sky greeted us, when, at an early hour, we rose to give our guns their morning toilet on Saturday, 28th September. Rain had fallen heavily during the night, doubtless caused by the heavy firing of the previous night.

The enemy had evidently scented danger and had brought three observation balloons as near our lines as possible. The order "Eyes front" was passed along the battery and our first shot of the battle was fired at 5.30 a.m. We fired a few preliminary shots to register our range and target. Then "battery, fire, ten seconds" rang over the telephone. Methodically we load and fire our guns, a shell screaming over at intervals of ten seconds. From all sides the crack and crash of artillery

81

is heard and this firing continues for 3½ hours. The enemy's fortifications - barbed wire, trenches and lines of communication are all shelled in turn. The enemy returns our fire to what they surmise are our artillery positions and trenches. All guns cease fire at a pre-arranged signal. Will they succeed?

The air is thick with fumes and smoke. We see little as the village obstructs our view. The sound of guns and the crack of rifles is heard on all sides, whilst we stand ready at our guns to fire again if required. The news trickles through that we have broken their line, the line that has remained immovable for ten long months.

The first wounded men appear over the crest of the hill. Two more appear to be walking together. One of them has his left hand shattered to a pulp. He asks me for something to drink. It is the first thing that a wounded man asks for. A wound causes great thirst. I obtain hot tea for them both. The other chap has his right arm badly hurt. Both are attended by a Red Cross officer; they have already been to the advanced first aid post where they have had their wounds roughly bandaged. They had then walked 1½ miles to the advance field hospital. We had met them on their way. They informed us that the enemy's first line of trenches have been taken. Wounded men can be seen swarming over the crest from all sides - Germans as well as our own men.

Then appears a sight to gladden a soldier's heart. A batch of 300 prisoners escorted by our boys with fixed bayonets, are seen along the road to our right. They are halted in the rear of us so we have a good view of them. There are young fellows of 19 to 20 years of age and men of 50 to 60 years among them. Some are defiant, others dejected. Some give us buttons, knives, watches etc. as souvenirs. There are those that can speak English. They are taken over by our cavalry and escorted to a place of incarceration already prepared for them. We continue to support our infantry all day and through the night. I obtain a splendid view from a neighbouring coal stack of an extensive battle towards Hill 70. What a sight!

We fired until our guns were practically red-hot; the heat from the breech could be felt where I sat, on the left-hand seat of the gun. Still it was good; we were getting a bit of our own back.

The Huns admitted afterwards that our artillery was superb. All the artillery that was stationed at Apsley, Boxmoor and Hemel Hempstead were in it. These are the boys who you saw many times strutting along in their clean boots and nicely polished buttons at Boxmoor, but the only polishing they have time to do now is polishing off the detestable Hun and all that he stands for.

Source: *Herts. Advertiser, 6th November 1915.*

A game of football behind the trenches.

Lance-Corporal F. A. Groom, 'C' Company, 1st Bedfordshire Regiment writes:
We have a bit of sport now and again, such as boxing and football. We are the best team in the Company, but we had a very stiff match last Sunday - that is our day of sport, because we get half-a-day.

We played the 2nd East Surrey Regiment last Sunday, and after a fast and good game came out on top. As we were playing the guns were rattling, but we are quite used to them. Our officer is a thorough sportsman; he is a good footballer.

Source: *Herts. Advertiser, 6th November 1915.*

Woman's Volunteer Reserve.

On Friday evening, Mrs Bailey presented to the officers, non-commissioned officers and girls of the Woman's Volunteer Reserve, a stretcher for the use of the Reserve. The W.V.R. was started in London in 1914 to train and equip girls of all ages and ranks so that their services could be offered to the State at any time if necessary, such as signallers, despatch-riders, motorists, camp-cooks etc.

In May 1915, a branch was started in St.Albans with the Countess of Verulam as president. The Reserve meets on Thursdays and Friday evenings in the Deanery Parish Room from 8.15 to 9.00 p.m. for drilling, signalling and physical drill. Stretcher drill is shortly to be added to the classes. Members also have opportunities of learning first aid and home nursing. There is plenty of room for more recruits, and if any girl is wondering how to spend part of her free time in war work let her apply to the Hon. Secretary.

The "khaki-girls" are not "playing at soldiers", but they are being trained in the first duties of soldiers, such as implicit obedience, loyalty and self control.

Source: *Herts. Advertiser, 20th November 1915.*

Trench warfare is monotonous.

Trooper Archie Hickman, Hertfordshire Yeomanry writes from Gallipoli:

9th September - Front Row, Shrapnel Corner, the Trenches, Somewhere. - I've just sent an invitation to the jolly old Turks, who are about 250 yards away, to come and join me in a tin of real spring water, just to celebrate my birthday. All we got back was some more scrap iron, which fortunately, missed my address.

We are having a terribly rough time of it out here, but so far I am not feeling any the worse for wear. It's a case of day and all-night business, as our ranks are so depleted through casualties and illness, that it comes a bit thick on those left standing up and a rest of three hours is looked upon as a great luxury. For eight days I have had neither a wash nor a shave and have lived like a rabbit in the ground.

I am sorry to say that in our great advance, our casualties were very heavy, and included our dear old Colonel, who was liked and admired by all ranks. We had to go up about three miles and the Turks had all their guns trained on us: in fact, it was like a real "Brock's benefit" and to see the shells bursting all round, looked like the lot of us being wiped out entirely. Still, our regiment was really lucky compared with some of the others who lost more than half of their number. This trench warfare is not a bit "sporty". In fact it gets awfully monotonous and I get far more thrills out of a game of "nap". The battleships bombard every day, and as the big shells go over us they rumble just

84

like a train in a tube tunnel, and we are pleased they happen to be non-stop so far as our trenches are concerned. We can gaze upon the sea from our trench and this afternoon. as a birthday favour, I am walking over to have a bathe, the first for over three weeks, although we have been scarcely out of sight of the water.

Four or five of us do the cooking together, but I've come to the conclusion that whichever way we cook it, it's really bully beef all the same; but the unkindest cut of all was when a shell caught our fireplace and moved it on about fifteen yards.

Sunday 12th - Still merry and bright: had a lovely bathe on Thursday, though it meant an eight-mile walk to get to it. At night I was on listening patrol, lying about 150 yards from the Turks' trenches, and on the wet ground it was awfully cold. I've just received the papers up to the 15th August, which are most welcome as we have been without any reading matter at all for a week.

Monday morning. Been trench-digging all night, and now we are having a real English shower. The trenches are terribly muddy, but the old Turks have got it as wet, so we're evens.
Source: *Herts. Advertiser, 30th November 1915.*

A Chaplain's experiences.
From a letter to the Methodist Recorder, the Revd. S.J. Sullings, Wesleyan Chaplain with the 1/5th Battalion, Bedfordshire Regiment who was billeted with Mr. and Mrs Dolling, Victoria Street, St. Albans for several months:
We are having a rough time, but that does not matter. We endure hardness as good soldiers, and we all bear the burden together.

On Saturday I went into the dressing station and stayed all week-end. I conducted two services, while not far away the battle was raging and snipers were busy. At each service I spoke from *Hebrews*, 11th chapter: *He endured as seeing Him who is invisible.* How the men appreciate one's ministry and one's presence. It is worthwhile coming.

One of the lads who was at the morning service, went on 1,000 yards to dig himself in with the others, and a sniper caught him, and by 5 p.m. he was back in the dressing station badly wounded. I had a chat with the Headquarters staff, and a cup of tea, and finished up an exciting day by bringing back to base (three miles) a young officer who was suffering from nervous shock. One day here among the sick and wounded and dying, bucking them up and getting among them cheerfully, is of more value than twelve months service in peace time. Source: *Herts. Advertiser, 2nd December 1915.*

1/5th Bedfordshires in the Dardanelles.

Lieutenant-Colonel Brighten, Commanding Officer of the 1/5th Battalion, Bedford-shire Regiment writes to the Mayor of Luton:
4th September - Dear Mr. Mayor, The first consignment of fly nets has arrived. Will you thank the Mayoress and all who have worked for her in this on my behalf and on behalf of the officers, N.C.O.'s and men of the Battalion, not forgetting, of course, yourself, and those who helped you organise and provided the funds? Will you say that no more acceptable present could have reached us at the moment, although we are not troubled with mosquitoes, which they were really intended to provide against?

We are in some trenches now, where we are simply eaten up with ordinary flies. These trenches were taken over by us in a very dirty condition, and consequently it is absolutely impossible to get rid of the flies, though we have done what we could to mitigate the nuisance. At any rate, with a net over one's head, life becomes more bearable. The men appreciate them very much indeed, and it is very good of you to have responded so readily and promptly to the suggestion put forth by me.

I expect by the time this reaches you, you will have had news of us - not good, as our casualties have been very heavy, and we have lost many that we could ill-afford to lose. But they have done splendidly, and I am prouder than ever of them, and particularly of those who have fallen. All went down like men, with their faces to the enemy.

It is giving no secrets away to say that we were in one of the new landings. We did not take part in the original landing, but we were in one of the great pushes, two or three days after we landed. This country is a particularly wicked one to fight in - very hilly, with deep dongas [dry watercourses] and covered with thick scrub. By reason of this one cannot see the enemy, whereas they are able to pepper attacking troops with shrapnel from positions away on the further hills, and even very often, as in our case, to absolutely enfilade us with fire.

We were told to take a certain hill, and we did it. For the next few days we held it and consolidated our position in the face of some opposition until relieved and drawn out of the firing line for a bit of a rest. But in this country one soon learns that casualties have got to be faced if we are to do anything at all. I have now got only seven officers, including myself, so you can see we are short-handed. As things have turned out, we could have done with a smaller number of fly nets. However, we will take care of those which are not wanted at the moment, and there will be a number of men, who were only slightly wounded, who will come back to duty in the near future, and we shall issue nets to them as they come along.

Since the action we have been moving round into another part of the line, and have been in the first line trenches for the past six days. We are expecting relief (though only into the second line trenches) this afternoon. You will be glad to hear that the men are in good spirits, and full of fight. Their digging, which accounts as much as anything, is extremely good, and they do a tremendous amount of work.

The rations are wonderful. How it is done I don't know, but we had among other things, an issue of eggs the other day, and with the excellent bacon we get we were able to make a splendid breakfast that morning. We do not get much bread at present, but that cannot be helped. We get *Maconochie's* meat and vegetable ration a good deal, and that, as you no doubt know, is wonderfully good either hot or cold. We also get a certain amount of rice, dried potatoes, onions, and such things, so that we do not often have to fall on plain "bully" and biscuit.

Above all we get a small ration of cigarettes or tobacco. I think the men like that the best of all. If they can get their smoke, it makes a wonderful difference to their spirits. Of course, the ration is only a small one, and does not go far, but it is something.
Source: *Herts. Advertiser, 5th December 1915.*

Life in Gallipoli.
Among the bullets, birds and heather.
Mr. E.G. Getcliffe, an assistant master of Harpenden County Council Schools, in 2/2nd London Regiment writes from the Dardanelles to Mr. Watts, the headmaster:
We have been on the Cape Helles side of Gallipoli over three weeks. Our stay in Egypt was a most enjoyable time and all too short. Our band, formed since the beginning of the war, frequently gave concerts at *Shepherds Hotel* and the *Continental*, and also in the beautiful Esbekich Gardens, and was often spoken of as the best military band in Cairo.

We began to think that we should be retained as part of the occupation in Egypt, but one day General Maxwell reviewed us and seemed pleased with everything he saw. A few days later we travelled to Alexandria and embarked. We were in harbour for two days and then hitched up to a larger vessel with Australians.

We travelled to Gallipoli on a very fast turbine steamer packed like proverbial herrings. We tried to appear perfectly comfortable but we were really ill at ease because we knew so little of our destination and the method of landing. We came ashore in the darkness, reaching land dry shod. Then we crept along up a steep incline, hearing reports of guns in the distance. To arrive at a strange house and to be told to find one's sleeping apartment and to get to bed in the dark would be a strange experience certainly, but imagine yourself on strange soil being told to find a dug-out, unpack your kit, and settle down without lights of any kind! I found a dug-out and settled down as best I could.

Since that eventful night we have seen some sights that have stirred us and other sights that have moved us deeply. Our Battalion is attached to the famous Naval Division, which has lost so many splendid men during the six months of the Gallipoli campaign.

Last Wednesday we returned to our rest camp after our second period in the trenches. Our training in Malta and Egypt was certainly not calculated to make us into trench fighters; experience is ever the best school. We have learned to keep our heads down when in the trenches and to get the best possible cover when under shell fire. Several days ago we were returning from the trenches when the Turks opened fire, and several men were hit.

This is a lovely morning; the sun shines brilliantly; the day is cloudless. All around there is heather, marred in this district by digging operations. Gallipoli must have been a beauty-spot a year ago, when its vines flourished and its heaths were unspoiled. Birds sing joyfully and one could be peaceful if it were not for the sights and the sounds that tell of war.

Source: *Herts. Advertiser, 11th December 1915.*

Roll of Honour for Welwyn.

The roll of honour for Welwyn contains the names of 135 soldiers and sailors. Four have been killed in action, two have been wounded and are prisoners of war, and fourteen have been wounded.

For Woolmer Green, there are 35 names on the list, seven of those have been wounded.

Source: *Herts. Advertiser, 11th December 1915.*

The finest Territorial Regiment out there.

Sapper A. Mayes, Royal Engineers, of Welwyn writes:
Coming up by train from Southampton, I was in a compartment with seven Guardsmen. During the journey, Territorials became the subject of conversation. One of the Guardsmen mentioned the *Herts. Regiment.*

Without letting on that I was a Hertfordshire man, I asked what sort of lot they were and it was unanimously agreed by all that the Hertfordshires were the finest Territorial Regiment out there.
Source: *Herts Advertiser, 11th December 1915.*

At the St. Albans Recruitment Station.

Up to Thursday afternoon, about 320 names had been received under the scheme initiated by Lord Derby. This brings the total since mobilisation to 1,665. In addition there have been 230 names for the *Herts Artillery* and constant enlistments for the *Herts Infantry Battalion (T.F.)* and *Herts Yeomanry.*
Source: *Herts Advertiser, 15th December 1915.*

The Fighting Bedfords.

Private S. Burrows, 2nd Bedfordshire Regiment writes:
This European War has proved to every thinking man
The glorious Bedford Regiments are still a fighting clan;
They've fought in strictest honour, have stood their ground like men,
Have faced grim death like heroes, when fighting three to ten.

Outnumbered by the Germans, they've made their courage tell; /hell;
They've made them yell for mercy, they've made made them run like-
When charging for their trenches, they've charged with one idea;
The Bedford boys have got there, and filled their hearts with fear.

They've made the "Squareheads" cut and run,
They've made the rotters dance,
The Bedfords used their bayonets well, and made the beggars prance;
We've took their trenches, caned their hides, and made them all retire,
Because we are the Bedford boys, the men of vim and fire.

Our officers are gentlemen, and heroes every one,
Are handy with the bayonet, and skilful with the gun;
Will lead a charge with coolness, will laugh and joke at death,
Will scream defiant war-cries e'en with their dying breath.

We know at times the Bedford lads are reckless to a fault;
They'll drink and be quite merry, but their prestige does not halt.
When ordered into action, they charge with bulldog pluck,
No other blessed regiment can leave them in the ruck.

All honour to the Bedfords, the men of British birth;
"Hats off" to British officers, the men of sterling worth.
The Union Jack and pride of race will prove to Kaiser Bill
That Englishmen to swallow are a very bitter pill.

Source: *Herts. Advertiser, 15th December 1915.*

St.Albans City Policemen enlist.

The last of the single men of the St. Albans City Police Force have
enlisted. P.c.'s Bennett and Hallett have obtained the necessary
permission and joined his Majesty's forces within the past few days.

In addition to these, sixteen married members of the force have
attested under Lord Derby's scheme. With the two latest enlistments,
there are now with the colours twelve members of the St. Albans City
Force out of a total strength of 35.

The depletion of the ranks has naturally involved much additional
work on the men who remain in the force, and in order to meet, to
some extent, the shortage, the Head Constable is anxious to enrol all
available men who are ineligible for the Army as special constables,
and desire that they should make application at the City Police Office.

Speaking of the work of the special constables already serving, the
Head Constable states: "They have been of the greatest assistance, and
I cannot speak too highly of the work they have done".

Source: *Herts. Advertiser, 18th December 1915.*

St. Albans Chaplain with the troops.

*The Revd. F.H. Wheeler, Pastor of Trinity Congregational Church, St. Albans, talks
of his work and experiences near the firing line. He spoke on Sunday evening and the*

church was crowded to overflowing and his talk was listened to with the closest attention and the most sympathetic interest. Here are some extracts::
"I am now as near to the trenches as it is possible for a chaplain to be. I have always managed to get up somewhere near, but now I have managed to get to within a quarter of a mile, and I suppose that I will have to be satisfied with that. I wish to describe to you, in a word picture, the surroundings of the town or village in which I have my billet. If you travel back with me you would find something like this.

After I had left the coast, I travelled inland for some hours, creeping as only French supply trains can creep along, and ultimately we arrived where I could see afar the flicker of star shells in the sky and hear, the ominous rumbling of the guns. I would now be about fifteen miles from the front. As I went on, I past through the searching scrutiny of countless sentries and guards until I approached to within three miles of the front. Up to this point the French villages seem perfectly normal. Here and there a house may have collapsed as the result of long-range fire, the inhabitants living there much as they had done, the land being cultivated as if no war is going on, and the boys and girls in the streets, with groups of Tommies about them and having the time of their lives.

Getting nearer to the line, the fields become bare, not having been sown last autumn. Further on there are holes in the fields, at the sides of the roads and sometimes in the road itself. By this time I can hear not only the loud rumbling of the big guns, but also the sharp crack and jerky rattle of the machine guns and of rifles as well. Now I have got to where it is not described in newspapers as a health-resort. Here the road goes on ahead for two miles, and at the end of it is a little wood, and in the middle of the wood and grouped around is the village where I have been staying now for three months. On the right are the Germans, not more than six or seven hundred yards from the road. The British trenches are within sight of their positions. I have to travel on horseback and have to make my horse go as hard as it can as the road is swept from end to end and from side to side by such fire as makes it almost impassable. The village is now a mass of ruins, one vast waste of brick, charred wood and broken masonry. The gardens are ploughed up and cut through with trenches and run across with barbed wire. The church is a mere shell, the walls alone remaining with a little bit of the tower standing.

We are all supposed to live in dugouts in the ground and are becoming like some species of mole. In fact we cannot feel safe at night unless we are in these dugouts.

We have been having a very bad spell of weather, with snow, sleet, rain, frost and ice and some of the coldest days that I have ever remembered. I have been told that the men have better conditions this year than in 1914. This year they are better equipped and clothed and fed as no army has before been clothed or fed.

My work among the men has only increased my admiration for them. I have been amazed and delighted at their splendid honesty, their untiring integrity, and their quiet, heroic going-on through conditions that, to the least of it, are appalling. They are burning to get to grips with the enemy. It is "OK, to get over that parapet and that barbed wire. If we could only get there, you would see what would happen".

This is what happened the other day. A deserter came over from the Germans. Poor and miserable he was. He had had enough of it. He came staggering with his hands up, and our men rushed and brought him in. These men have been dying to get at the Germans. What do you think they did? The first thing that happened was that a Tommy took the German into his own dugout and gave him his own breakfast, and went, himself, hungry until dinner-time. Was it not splendid? That is the sort of men they are out there. Talk about the death of chivalry. Surely there is no end to chivalry in the Army. It is an honour to serve them, and I pray to God to help him to serve them better than I do.

My work goes on as usual. Winter conditions make it more difficult to hold services, but we hold them. We meet in dugouts underground. We hold concerts in dugouts underground and we muffle the sound as much as we can, as it is altogether too risky to make much noise in a village which is only four hundred yards from the German lines.

On a previous Sunday, I arranged to hold a service in a nice respectable-looking barn, but on the Sunday found it stocked with beer barrels. I did not see why we should not hold the service and we sat the men down among the barrels and set a brazier in the midst. It was one of the heartiest services I have ever taken at the front. We had a Communion service with a beer barrel as the Communion table. What did it matter if the Lord of the Communion was there. The men were going back to the trenches next day, and before that week was out some of them won an undying name for themselves and some had their last reward.

Within the time I have been out there I have found that some men feel that in the Communion service a kind of passport to Heaven. I always try to take it out of their minds that their is anything magical about their Communion service. It is a a service of solemn memory and consecration.

In a letter to this church's magazine, I mentioned a striking thing that I have witnessed. "In a deserted church in my village, there is only one thing intact, and that is the figure of the crucified Lord, stretched out upon his cross. No-one could scarcely put a finger on any part of that place which had not at some time been rent or torn with shells or bullets, but there was no mark on that crucifix. Untouched, it stood amidst all the desolation. I have seen the same thing happen before. A village I was in three months ago was exactly the same. It is very strange. When the guns have done their work and when the world is rent and torn with desolation, when the slaughter and anger of men had swept like a tide over the earth, there was one thing that remained standing still, lifting it head and shoulders above all the wreck and loss and confusion. It was the Cross of Our Lord and Master Jesus Christ that remains, though all else has gone.

"In the Cross of Christ I glory, Towering o'er the wrecks of time; All the light of sacred story, Gathers round its head sublime".

Mr. Wheeler returned to France on Tuesday.
Source: *Herts. Advertiser, 18th December 1915.*

The Revd. F.H.Wheeler's talk, as reported, was in the third person. and I have written it as a first hand account, in the first person.

A Soldier's suicide after overstaying his leave.

The story of a St. Albans man who, having overstayed his leave, was found dead on the Midland Railway line, was told at an inquest held by the Coroner - Dr. Lionel Drage, at the Town Hall, St. Albans on Wednesday morning.

The deceased was George Herbert Lawrence, *3rd Battalion, Bedfordshire Regiment.* When asked, his father, Walter Lawrence of 38 Warwick Road said that he did not know his son's age, neither was he aware of the regiment to which he belonged.

George Lawrence had come home on a week-end leave on 11 December. He last saw him alive last Sunday (19th December) at dinner time. He was then in good health. He never had anything wrong with his mind. He had never threatened to do away with himself. The deceased should have returned to his regiment a week ago, last Monday but had overstayed his leave. A Witness added: "We kept telling him he ought to go back".

His mother, Emily Lawrence, said that when she was lighting the fire on Monday morning, her son had come downstairs, put on his boots, took his cap and went off out of the back door. He said nothing to her. She noticed he was wearing civilian clothes. When asked if she thought that odd. She replied that he had previously worn his uniform.

.../

Later on that Monday morning, Arthur Hodges, a ganger in the employ of the Midland Railway Company said that about 7.50 a.m., he was informed by a driver on the down slow line that a man was lying midway between Sandpit lane and Dead Woman's hill. He proceeded to the spot and found the deceased and sent to the station and to the police and the body was removed to the mortuary.

The jury found that the cause of death was extensive injuries to the head and neck, the result of an engine having passed over him and that he placed himself on the railway with the intention of self-destruction.

Source: *Herts. Advertiser, 27th December 1915.*

Coping with German snipers.

Both in 1914 and 1915, the British army was prone to be being "picked-off" by the more expert German soldiers who successfully sniped at them. In 1915, a former big-game explorer - Hesketh Hesketh-Prichard began to show those at the front how to counter this activity.

Major Hesketh-Prichard was the husband of Lady Elizabeth 'Lily' Grimston, one of the six daughters of the 3rd Earl and Countess of Verulam.

Writing after the end of the war, Hesketh-Prichard recalled how he taught the British army to deal with German snipers. By chance, between Christmas and the end of 1915, he was asked to demonstrate issues of "sniping and observation" at a range near where the Guards Division, who were part of the First Army were situated. During those few days, every company in the Division was summoned by the Officer Commanding, to send an officer to a class organised by Hesketh-Prichard.

The Guards Division was commanded by Lord Cavan from August 1915 until January 1916.

"There has always been, in certain quarters, a prejudice against very accurate shooting. While sniping is the opportunism of the rifle, musketry is its routine. In September and October 1915, superiority lay with the Germans, and the one problem was to defeat them at a game which they had themselves started. For it was the Germans, and not the British who started sniping.

At the end of 1914 there were already 20,000 telescopic sights in the German Army, and the snipers had been trained to use them. To make any accurate estimate of how many victims the Hun snipers claimed at this period, is naturally impossible, but the blow which they struck for their side was a heavy one, and many of finest soldiers met their deaths at their hands.

Only the man who was a sniper in the trenches in 1915, can know how hard the German was to overcome. For the German Army, the Duke of Ratibor had done good work for the Fatherland when he collected all the thousands of sporting rifles and sent them to the Western front. Armed with these the German snipers were able to make wonderfully fine shooting. Against them, lacking, as we did a proper issue of telescopic-sighted rifles, we had to pit only the blunt open sights of the service rifle, except here and there where the deer stalkers of Scotland (who possessed such weapons) lent their Mannlichers and their Mausers. But for these there was no great supply of ammunition, and many had to be returned to their cases for this reason.

At this time, the skill of the German sniper had become a by-word, and in the early days of trench warfare, brave German riflemen used to lie out between the lines, sending their bullets through the head of any officer or man who dared to look over our parapet. These Germans, who were often Forest Guards, and sometimes Battle Police, did their business with a skill and a gallantry which must be very freely acknowledged. From the ruined house or the field of decaying roots, sometimes resting their rifles on the bodies of the dead, they sent forth a plague of head-wounds into the British lines. Their marks were small, but when they hit they usually killed their man, and the hardiest soldier turned sick when he saw the effect of the pointed German bullet, which was apt to keyhole so that the little hole in the forehead where it entered, often became a huge tear, the size of a man's fist, on the other side of the striking man's head.

The German Army had a system of roving snipers; that is, a sniper was given a certain stretch of trench to patrol, usually about half-a-mile, and it was the duty of sentries along his beat to find and targets for him.

On one occasion I had gone down on duty to a certain stretch of trench and found a puzzled Private with a beautiful new rifle fitted with an Evans telescopic sight.

"That is a nice sight", said I. "Yes sir". I examined the elevating drum, and saw that it was set for a hundred yards. "Look here", I said, "you have got the sight set for a hundred. The Hun trenches are four hundred yards away".

The Private looked puzzled. "Have you ever shot with that rifle?" I asked. "No, sir". "Do you understand it?" "No, sir." "How did you get it?" "It was issued to me as trench stores, sir." "Who by?" "The Quartermaster Sergeant, sir".

[When ever possible] I examined German prisoners. One point cropped up over and over again and this was the ease with which German snipers quite frankly owned that they were able to distinguish between our officers and men in an attack, because, as one said naively: the legs of the officers are thinner than the legs of the men". There are hundreds and hundreds of our officers lying dead in France and Flanders whose death was solely due to the cut of their riding breeches. It is no use wearing a Tommy's tunic and a webbing belt, if the tell-tale riding trousers are not replaced by more commonplace garments.

In 1915 there were very few loopholes in the British trenches, where as the Germans had a magnificent system. In the early days when I used to be told at Brigade Headquarters that there was a German sniper at such and such a map reference, and I was to go and try to put him out of action, I very rarely found a loophole from which I could reconnoitre him, and as every German sniper seemed to be supported on either flank by other German snipers, looking for him with one's head over the top of the parapet was, if a continual practice, simply a form of suicide. I used, therefore, to have a couple of sandbags filled with stones, and it was thus that one got an opportunity of a good look at the German trenches without fear of receiving a bullet from either flank.

Source: *Hesketh-Prichard, Hesketh. Sniping in France. 1922.*

On the outside wall of the *Black Boy*, Bricket Wood is a stone plaque, which commemorates the actions of one man who served in the Great War:

"LEST WE FORGET"

JOHN GEORGE EGGLETON

LEFT THIS HOUSE

JUNE 30th 1916

TO FIGHT FOR HIS KING AND COUNTRY

AND FELL IN ACTION IN FRANCE

APRIL 15 1918, AGED 27 YEARS.

In Letchmore Heath, near Radlett there are at least three similar stone plaques. Two are on the front of houses. One is above a front door. It is possible there are others elsewhere in Hertfordshire.

Contents: 1916

Are St. Albans men forgotten?

Lance-Corporal Rolph, No. 5 Platoon, No. 2 Company, 1st Hertfordshire Regiment writes:

"Will you kindly publish the letter which I enclose, taken from the local paper of a small town in Hertfordshire, known as Hitchin, a town which has not forgotten that there is such a Regiment as the *Hertfordshires*. They need a regular supply of candles and cigarettes every week for their men. I have two men from Hitchin in my section, and they are never forgotten by their townspeople. I think a town like St. Albans could do the same for the men of the Herts. and Beds. Regiments. I am a St. Albans fellow, formerly in the employ of Messrs. Slaters, High-street, and I feel very much that the lads of St. Albans are forgotten".

The following is the matter enclosed in the above letter:

"As is well know, for many weeks past a regular supply of cigarettes and tobacco, together with candles and certain medical comforts, have been sent to local men in the *Hertfordshire Regiment,* at the front, by the *Hitchin and District War Comforts Committee*. In addition to *No.4 Company*, which includes the men of Baldock, Royston, Stevenage, Knebworth and Welwyn, regular supplies have been sent to local men in other companies of the *Hertfordshire Guards*, and this week the Hon.Secretary - Mr. C. Loftus Barham, jun. has received the following letter -

from Private B. Cotton, No. 5 Platoon, 2nd Company, a Hitchin man whose wife is living with her father at the Red Lion, Bucklesbury, Hitchin:

I am writing this letter on behalf of the men from Hitchin and district in No.2 Company, *1st Hertfordshire Regiment* to thank the Hitchin War Comforts Committee for their great kindness in sending us cigarettes and tobacco, which we receive regularly from Sergeant-Major Langford of the No.4 Company.

If the people in the other towns could see the pleasure it gives the men to receive such things from home, and if they knew how it bucks the men up to know that the people of their native towns think of and appreciate the great sacrifice which they have made, I am sure that they would do for the men from other parts of the county what you have done for those from dear old Hitchin and neighbourhood.

There is one town I would like to mention, in particular, and that is St. Albans. The people of that place seem to forget that there is a *County Regiment in Hertfordshire,* and anything they sent out here is sent to the *London Divisions,* the men of which were billeted in St. Albans last winter. The men of this Company feel this very much. Good old North Herts men!
Source: *Herts. Advertiser, 1 January 1916.*

A clasp to the Victoria Cross.
Among the notices of those killed in action, mention is made of those who have been decorated for their work in the field. It included:
For conspicuous conduct and devotion to duty in the field, Captain A. Martin-Leake, V.C., *Royal Army Medical Corps* was received by the King at Windsor Castle on 24th July, when he was handed a clasp to his Victoria Cross.
Source: *Herts. Advertiser, 1st January 1916.*

Blown up on the His Majesty's Ship, Natal.
Able-Seaman Ernest Gray, aged 21 years, of 25 Harley-street, St. Albans had a lucky escape when a fearful explosion on aboard *H.M.S. Natal* blew her to pieces and sacrificed the lives of hundreds of gallant men belonging to the Navy. Young Gray's escape was simply miraculous, and singular enough, apart from the natural shock he has sustained through having lost so many comrades. He does not appear to be much the worse in health after his awful experiences.

When the explosion happened he was on the deck of the *"Natal"* and was blown clean up in the air, and seems to have alighted on the ship's deck again. With many other comrades he got himself up in the rigging, and shortly afterwards found himself in the water. He was seized by the cramp, but managed to get onto the ship again. One of the ship's lifeboats was alongside, and a friend of his who was in it

appealed to Gray to get into it as well. Gray refused to do so, preferring to see if he could render help to those worse off aboard, and says that when the ship went down, the lifeboat went with it and that therefore it must have been held fast to the ship. Gray swam to safety. About one hundred survivors who were fit and well enough to travel were granted leave. He now has to hold himself in readiness for the Court of Inquiry. Able Seaman Gray has been in the Navy for three years.
Source: *Herts. Advertiser, 8th January 1916.*

Christmas Eve - somewhere in France.

A north country man who found himself in London when war broke out and became a County of London Territorial, was trained in St. Albans and is now a Sergeant, somewhere in France. Here he describes Christmas Eve 1915:

Picture a long cellar with an arched roof - a underground place to store barrels of beer. Of the large building which once stood here *"The Brasserie"*, the cellars are all that remain.

The heaped-up debris overhead renders our refuge practically shell-proof which is fortunate for the enemy is particularly active tonight. Each man who returns from billet guard is restored with a drop of hot tea and remarks that the night is a dirty one. Around the fire we sit, my platoon and I; our harness lies at hand, our rifles (clean as new pins and well oiled withal) rest along the wall, and given an alarm, we can be on the move within two minutes - an efficient fire unit ready to meet any demands. Perhaps we shall be called out as a carrying party, to convey by hand either rations or trench stores to our comrades in the line, for we are in reserve, and maintaining supplies is one of our duties.

We cannot lie down to sleep, for we know we must be ready to move and act on the instant. So we sit around our cosy little fire and sing "Old King Wedneslas" and "Noel" followed by old music-hall ballads. And now they play the Christmas Hymn on their mouth-organs.
Source: *Herts. Advertiser, 8th January 1916.*

The tragedy of Serbia.

An appeal from the Bishop of London and others on behalf of the starving and stricken people of Serbia:

When Belgium was invaded and the refugees who fled from terrorism and outrage sought refuge on our shores, the purse of the nation was opened without stint, and it was for us a point of honour to offer these victims an ungrudging hospitality. Another little nation has now been occupied by the same ruthless invader and once again great numbers of civilians have sought refuge from his rule. They have crossed mountains and traversed roads which the *German Military Bulletin* describes as impregnable and impassable. The greatest number have tramped on foot over roads ankle-deep in mud and mountains knee-deep in snow. ... Need of funds is unlimited. Cheques payable to the *Serbian Relief Fund* should be forwarded to the Hon. Treasurer - the Earl of Desart, 5 Cromwell-road, London, S.W.

Source: *Herts. Advertiser, 8th January 1915.*

With the 1st Herts Battery.

A.G.Parsons, 1st Herts Battery, R.F.A., writes to his mother, Mrs Parsons, 36 Alma Road, St. Albans:

I have plenty to do as I am Q.M.S. on duty for the Brigade this week. It's lovely here to-day, quite warm and sunny. As the road is fairly wide here, and it is much better for everyone, as the fields are so wet that you soon get mud up to your knees when the horses have been standing there.

Source: *Herts. Advertiser, 8th January 1915.*

Separation allowances.

Letters from Viscount Grimston, Grimston Tyres Ltd to Sergeant and Mrs Suttle, Catherine-street, St.Albans:

11th January - Mrs Suttle, I am obliged to reconsider the question of allowances. In cases where there is no hardship and where the dependants are in receipt of as much or more with their husbands away than they received when their husbands were at home. I feel there is no longer need for business to help when it can ill afford to do so. In your case, I am informed by the *Soldiers and Sailors Families*

Association that you are receiving separation allowances of 28s 6d and billeting money of 7s 0d, totalling 35s 6d per week. When your husband was here, he earned on average, 34s 8d per week. For the present, therefore, I shall cease paying the weekly allowance of 10s 0d which has been paid during the last 69 weeks. I hope you have been able to save up a good sum of money against difficult times that are ahead.

18th January - Sergeant Suttle, I'm afraid you don't realise the situation. One consequence of the war is an appalling drain of money. It is being poured out like water in order to win, no doubt. But all the same, you cannot eat your cake and have it. In consequence of the drain, there is but very little money left. When this firm arranged to pay 10s 0d a week to certain of its employees' families, the scale of separation allowances was very inadequate. Later on, the country readjusted the scale of allowances. Since then, in the form of taxes, this firm has been contributing its share to the Government separation allowances. Also, during 1915, it has continued to pay the 10s 0d a week to those where it had already begun to do so. The firm paid these allowances, because it found it could afford to do so. It now finds that it can no longer afford anything, and that is why they must stop.

If the War does go on much longer, it will become a question, whether the firm can survive, as everyone gets poorer, prices will increase and trade will decrease. We have no choice in the matter. We have got to cut down. We are only looking to see that the least possible hardship is inflicted.

Coming to the figures, I must say at once that you have gained in actual cash by being away. Your average earnings whilst here would have been 34s 8d and you would have had to keep yourself and your family. Up till now, your family, without you, have had 40s. 10d. Had you remained here there would have been no promotion. I merely mentioned this because I see, you think that you sacrificed something by going. I cannot agree that 30s. 10d without you to provide for, is less than 34s 8d with you to provide for, and now with the 2s 5d extra

Sergeant's allowance per week, making 33s. 4d, Mrs. Suttle ought to be able to manage. I am sorry Mrs. Suttle was worried over the enquiries Mrs. Green made. It was I who asked Mr. Gape to let me know the circumstances of all those to whom I gave allowances. Mr. Gape is responsible for the work of the *Soldiers and Sailors Families' Association*, and it is the business of the *Association* to see that any cases of hardship are relieved. Mr. Gape asked Mrs. Green to call on Mrs. Suttle and enquire.

From the above, you should see that this firm is merely doing what it is obliged to do so. The real reasons are that the war has dragged on into a second year, and that the country is spending £5 million a day. In a lot of different ways these things react on our business. We have no choice. I am only glad that Mrs. Suttle is at least as well off as she would have been had you not joined the army.

Source: *Gorhambury Collection. Business Correspondence, 4th Earl of Verulam.*

Corporal Alfred A. Burt, V.C.
1st Battalion, Hertfordshire Regiment (T.F.)

Mr "Tommy" Burt, 11 Cross-street, Luton was a proud man on Sunday, when it was made known that one of his sons, who had been recommended for the *Distinguished Conduct Medal* for conspicuous bravery at Guinchy, had instead been awarded the *Victoria Cross*.

Corporal Burt had been a member of the *Hertfordshire Regiment* Territorial Force for some time before the outbreak of war, and as a young man who wanted to get on a bit, had just given up his employment in Hertford and taken a job away from home for the first time. He had been in Basingstoke just over a week when he was called to join his Battalion, and although he had been in France for fifteen months he has not been home on leave.

At Guinchy, on the 27th September 1915, his company had lined the front trench preparatory to an attack, when a large *minenwerfer* bomb fell into the trench. Corporal Burt, who knew the destructive power of this kind of bomb, might easily have got under cover behind a

107

traverse, but he immediately went forward, put his foot on the fuse, wrenched it out of the bomb and threw it over the parapet, thus rendering the bomb innocuous. His presence of mind and great pluck, saved the lives of others in the traverse.

His own account of the event says:
We were in the front trench, ready to go over to the attack. The German trenches were about forty yards from us. A patrol had been sent out, and they had got to the German lines, we were to follow them up. But when the patrol had advanced three or four yards, the Germans open fire on them very heavily with machine guns, rifle fire and everything. The noise was deafening. We couldn't hear one another speak for the noise. It was terrible. I was on the left of our platoon (No.6), and I had to keep in touch with the right of the No.5 platoon. We did not go over the parapet, because as soon as the patrol went out, one man was hit, and they came in. Sergeant Neale, platoon commander of No.5 platoon went out and fetched the wounded man in. It was broad daylight at the time and they practically went out to certain death.

When the order came that nobody of my company was to go over the top, I had to pass the word along. I ran round the traverse and just then the bomb fell right in the trench and there was a general scramble. Oh yes, I knew the nature of the bomb - I had seen dozens of them in use before. They are in a kind of sheet-iron case and contain no shrapnel, but sufficient explosive to carry away three or four yards of the parapet and to kill all who happened to be near it.

I knew what would happen if it was allowed to remain there. It would have exploded before we could have got away: so I went at once and put my foot on it and wrenched the fuse out. When I did so, I bent the case, and had to keep my foot on the bomb for a second or so, while I pulled out the fuse. Then I grabbed it and threw it over the top. It was, of course, harmless, after I had pulled the fuse out. A man named Cheshire who stood near to me and saw what happened. There were quite a lot of St. Albans lads in the trenches at the time. I didn't think much of the incident after that. I took it as a matter of course, and never worried until we got out of the trenches, and then I suppose, the boys mentioned it to the officer in charge of my We remained in the trench until dark and then were relieved by one of the other companies and went back in support. We then proceeded to Bethune and were there for a couple of days. Things went on as usual and we never thought any more about it. About a week later I got a paper from Divisional Headquarters saying that I had been recommended by the Brigadier, and the Commanding Officer of our Regiment, stating that reports of our doings had been submitted, and although decorations and promotions could not be given away in every case, they would like me to know how greatly they appreciated my conduct and that I had been recommended.

Then I was laid up with rheumatism and was in hospital for just over three weeks. I then proceeded to the base to wait for a draft to go back to my regiment. After eight weeks, I was sent to join my regiment. My company was in the trenches and I had orders to wait until they came out and then rejoin them. But before I had a chance to rejoin my company I was drafted to a permanent mining fatigue to assist the engineers. I arrived at Bethune on the Sunday and on the Tuesday morning I was ordered out with a party at 0845. At about ten minutes to seven I was up in my billet, when one of the fellows came to me and said that I was wanted down at the Orderly Room. I told him I had my orders. I thought that was what he wanted me for.

We set off to the Orderly Room and on the way he said "Do you know your name and photo[graph] are in the paper for the Victoria Cross?" I thought he was pulling my leg. When I got to the Orderly Room, I could not get away from the fact for there in the English paper was, as he had said, my photo and the announcement that I had been recommended for the V.C. I can assure you that it took me completely by surprise, because I thought I had been forgotten.

I had seen the name of five other men who had been "mentioned in despatches" and could not find my name there, and I thought the thing had fallen through. Among those recommended were Sergeant Neal, son of the stationmaster at Wheathamstead, Corporal Spinks, Private Hagger and two other patrol men. About half an hour later a despatch rider was sent down with a message from the Colonel, congratulating me on gaining such a great honour for the Regiment and myself. A message was sent to the officer in charge of the fatigue party to release me, so that I might go and rejoin my Regiment. When

I got there my company was in the trenches and when they met me they nearly pulled me to pieces in their excitement.

We remained in the trenches for three days and on the day after coming out, the battalion was paraded and the Brigadier came and complimented the battalion on their excellent work, and those who had the honours or were mentioned in dispatches were called out, and complimented by the Brigadier and the Colonel. When I left for home, the boys gave me a rousing send-off.

News of Corporal Burt's arrival was telephoned to the *Hertfordshire Mercury's* office and a member of staff went at once to see the Mayor and Corporation, who were assembled for their quarterly meeting. He informed them that Corporal Burt would be arriving in ten minutes time.

Discussion had already discussed that there should be an official welcome, but time was too short to attempt anything of the kind. Instead the Mayor sent the Sergeant of Mace to meet the hero at the station and to bring him, in a cab, to the Shire Hall.

Corporal Burt who was in full equipment with mud on him as he had just come out of the trenches, was taken by surprise when he was ushered into the Council Chamber and greeted with a hearty round of applause. The Mayor asked Corporal Burt to convey, from himself and the members of the Corporation, their congratulations to his parents and added that this was only an informal greeting. His Worship grasped the gallant soldier by the hand, and Corporal Burt replied with a modest *thank you, Sir,* and left the Council Chambers. He then went by the cab to his home. It is five years since he had enlisted and he was entitled to his discharge. He has, however, been re-engaged for the duration of the war, attached to the *4th Battalion* at Hertford.
Source: *Herts. Advertiser, 25th January 1916 and other issues.*

Medals for the "Herts Guards".

Company Sergeant-Major A.P.Langford, 1st Hertfordshire Regiment writes to a friend in Hitchin:

What do you think of our new V.C. - Corporal Burt of Hertford? Isn't it splendid?

We now have one Victoria Cross, one C.M.G (Commander of the Order of St. Michael and St. George), three M.C.'s (Military Crosses), ten D.C.M.'s (Distinguished Conduct Medals) and two Russian Medals. No a bad record for a Territorial Regiment and we hope to get more yet.
Source: *Herts. Advertiser* ...

Women to work on the land.

It is proposed by the *Hertfordshire County War Agricultural Committee* that a canvas of women and girls aged between 14 and 60 should be made in each parish to ascertain the number who would be willing to offer their services in view of the shortage of agricultural labour. A register of women will be prepared and be accessible to farmers.
Source: *Herts. Advertiser,* ... *January 1916.*

"Our dead mates heard us go".

A carbon copy of a poem, which may have been the work of Ivan Heald, although it is typed on notepaper of Grimston Tyres Ltd, St. Albans. It is dated 24th January 1916:

So quietly we left our trench
That night, yet this I know,
As we stole down to Seddul Bahr
Our dead mates heard us go.

As I came down the Boyau Nord
A dead hand touched my sleeve,
A dead hand from the parapet
Reach out and plucked my sleeve.

Oh "little I thought" a voice did say
"That ever a lady of Tyne"
Would leave me alone in the cold trench side
"And him a mate of mine".

111

The dawn was springing on the hills
'Twas time to put to sea,
But all along the Boyau Nord
A dead voice followed me.

Oh! what is toward you, mate o'mine
That you pass with muffled tread
And there comes the guard for the firing trench
The trench won by your Dead?

We sailed away from Seddul Bahr,
We're sailing home on leave,
But this I know through all the years
Dead hands will pluck my sleeve.
Source: *Gorhambury Collection. Business Correspondence, 4th Earl of Verulam.*

Captain Charles Vickers, VC.

Captain Vickers, 7th Robin Hood Battalion was billeted in Harpenden in 1914:
He was awarded his Victoria Cross for conspicuous bravery on the
14th October, 1915 in the *Hohenzollen Redoubt*. When nearly all his men
had been killed or wounded and with only two men available to hand
him bombs, Captain Vickers held a barrier for some hours against
heavy German bomb attacks from front and flank. Regardless of the
fact that his own retreat would be cut off, he had to order a second
barrier to be built behind him to ensure the safety of the trench. Finally
he was severely wounded, but not before his magnificent courage and
determination had enabled the second barrier to be completed. A
critical situation was thus saved.
Source: *Herts Advertiser ...*

A prisoner of the Austrians.

News of Nurse Clara Morris, a cousin of Mrs J. Potton, "The Limes", Worley Road,
St. Albans, and a prisoner in the hands of the Austrians has become available:
Miss Morris, a native of St. Albans, has for some years been living in
Australia. About five years ago she came over to England with a view
to taking various diplomas in sanitation and medical science.

When war broke out she joined the *Red Cross Society* as a trained nurse for active service. She was sent to Serbia on Sir Thomas Lipton's yacht *Erin*, and letters were received from her at pretty frequent intervals. Since October last, however, no news has been received, beyond the Red Cross Society's intimation that she was undoubtedly a prisoner in the hands of the Austrians.

The long silence has now been broken. Mrs. Potton has received a letter from Nurse Morris. Writing on 16th January from Serbia, she says: "I am well and happy, and the Austrian army have treated us well. We expect to get our marching orders at any time now. he weather has been perfectly beautiful for this time of the year.
Source: *Herts Advertiser, 5th February 1916.*

From the Parish magazine.

The February issue of St. Saviour's Parish Magazine contains news from members and friends who are serving in the war:

Corporal Sidney Dance, who is serving with an ammunition column writes:
On Christmas Day we were unfortunate in respect of all religious observations, as we were on the march. We thought that we were going into the midst of plenty of excitement, but we found it very monotonous with scarcely a break. One would scarcely credit the state of the roads and camps out here just now; it is quite easy to stick fast in the mud.

Private S. Percy Ives writes:
I saw a battery passing through the town and knowing that Frank and Charlie Christmas and Coker's lot were in this neighbourhood, I looked for the name of the battery. Well it wasn't one that I knew anything about, and just as I was passing on, some little body perched on a great horse, shouted "Hallo Perce". I looked and saw Cecil Calvert just as small and quiet as usual, only a bit war stained! He was as delighted to see me as I was to see him. He has been a driver out here for three months and has seen some action. The funny part of it is that only a few days before I had made up my mind to write to his old

school to find out what regiment he had joined. He is in the *1/10th London Battery*.

Bombardier Charles Christmas writes:
Although I feel quite used to the life out here: a few shells come over now and again, but not to do any damage so to speak. The *1st Herts* have been here before us, for when I went into a shell wrecked house I saw *1st Herts* scratched on a wall.

Sapper Wilfred H. Morley writes:
This is a small village which seems to be made up chiefly of cafes and they sell horribly tasting wine and fairly passable beer. The sale of spirits to troops is forbidden, and for any offence of this kind the cafe is promptly put out of bounds.

The countryside is very flat, and would, in normal times be ideal for cycling; most of the roads are bordered by trees. The demeanour of the people is very grave, almost sad and far from frivolous. They are friendly enough with us and supply us with vegetables, apples and such like things. It is very seldom that we understand each other, but the language difficulty is overcome by mutual laughter.

Company Sergeant-Major Ralph Dunham writes:
Life out here is not so bad as some people imagine. Our food is good and wholesome, and every little thing that can be dome to make us comfortable is done. We have a theatre and plenty of recreation rooms where men are made very welcome.
Source: *Herts. Advertiser, 5th February 1916.*

Second old boy of Hatfield Road School gets V.C.
Second Lieutenant Alfred Victor Smith,
5th Battalion, East Lancashire Regiment, Territorial Force.

The *London Gazette* last Friday night contained the announcement that His Majesty the King had graciously pleased to award the Victoria Cross to Second Lieutenant Alfred Victor Smith :

114

"For most conspicuous bravery. He was in the act of throwing a grenade when it slipped from his hand and fell to the bottom of the trench, close to several of our officers and men. He immediately shouted out a warning, and himself jumped clear and into safety; but seeing that the officers and men were unable to get into cover, and knowing well that the grenade was due to explode, he returned without any hesitation and flung himself down on it. He was instantly killed by the explosion. His magnificent act of self-sacrifice undoubtedly saved many lives".

He was 24 years of age when he died and been a chorister and boy soloist at St. Albans Cathedral. For some years he had been a scholar at *Hatfield Road Boys' School,* whose headmaster was and is Mr. J. Roe. When the *Herts. Advertiser* representative called at the school, Mr. Roe checked the school records:

"Young Smith was born on 22nd July 1891 and was admitted into the school on 28th October 1901 - or early in his eleventh year. The removal of Chief Constable Smith to Burnley led to young Smith severing his connection with Hatfield Road School on 23rd June, 1905, so that he had been at the school for four years, and was fourteen years of age when he left".

Mr. Roe remembered the boy well: "He was a very bright, keen, intelligent lad, of good address, and of much promise. He was a remarkedly good boy. He had a very good voice, and this is why he became a member of the Cathedral Choir for a period. He and Mr. Roe's own son were chums in those schooldays and Smith was consequently a frequent visitor to the Headmaster's house.

At the outbreak of war, Smith immediately applied for a commission with the *Burnley Territorials* and he became a Second Lieutenant in October 1914. From Burnley he went to Southport, where with four other officers and a draft detachment he volunteered to be sent to Egypt, where he arrived on 11th April 1915. On 13th May he landed in the Dardanelles. He saw action with the *Royal Munster Fusiliers* and the *King's Own Scottish Borderers,* but in July, fell ill with dysentery, and was invalided back to Alexandria. On return to general duties, he went

115

through a course of bombing and was appointed Brigade bombing officer in October. Since then he has been complimented and mentioned in *Orders of the Day* for his handling of bombs, grenades and trench catapults. In one of his letters home he stated that he liked the work and in one night had used over 700 bombs to knock down fire screens and "bird cages". A feature of all his letters was the praise he gave to the men. He was killed three days before Christmas Day 1915.

Colonel W.E. Sharples, 5th East Lancashire Regiment of Accrington wrote to his parents:
Please accept my sincere and heartfelt condolences on the sad and irreparable loss you and your wife have sustained by the death of so promising a young gentleman, whose future career seemed so bright, but was so suddenly cut short. He was so universally loved by all.

This is the second hero to have attended Hatfield Road Boys' School for Private Warner, *Bedfordshire Regiment (see page 45-48)* had been at the school between 13th January 1890 to 14th April 1893; and from 1st May 1894 to 11th December 1896. The Roll of Honour of the Hatfield Road School will be a very long and proud one when it is complete. It is already known that over three hundred old boys are serving with the Colours.
Source: *Herts. Advertiser, 11th March 1916.*

"The terrible trek".
Mrs Green of the Scottish Women's Hospitals for Foreign Service, who was in the historic retreat from Serbia gives a vivid description of the terrible two hundred mile trek and the great privations suffered by those brave British women who went to assist Serbia in the hour of her direst need.

The meeting was held at the Deanery at the invitation of Mrs. Blenkin, wife of the Dean of St. Albans, in connection with the St. Albans Branch of the National Union of Women's Suffrage Societies.

116

Harrowed by the reports of reports of the terrible sufferings of the Serbians, she volunteered for service in Serbia and was sent to Meladenovatz, about eighteen miles from Belgrade as home sister, and found a very full and satisfactory life awaiting her. Incidentally, Mrs. Green stated that the camp kitchen was presided over by an Austrian prisoner "Charlie", who had been for some years in the kitchen at the Trocadero, London and for eleven years in the L & N.W. Hotel, Liverpool. They had a very busy life in the camp, their day beginning at five and and often ending at eleven or twelve at night. Things went on quietly until 17th September when they heard heavy firing all day, and on the night of the 19th September the very tents vibrated with the firing of those terrible siege guns across the Danube. Mrs. Green went on to describe, in some detail, the events of the days which followed and the assistance which they were able to render to the wounded and refugees who were brought from Belgrade.

On 12th October their Austrian orderlies were taken away and they were ordered to evacuate. They started packing all the equipment and by five o'clock they arrived at the station, with all their belongings including the floors of their tents. Instead of taking a few hours to get to Kragnjevatz, they spent two whole days in the train and shared their food with many wounded soldiers. They were being continually sidetracked to allow military trains to pass. At Kragejevatz they were given a large empty building, which in a few hours, the doctors and nurses converted it into a hospital with six hundred beds. Within a few days 1,045 patients were admitted. Then they received orders to evacuate, and had to go to Kraljevo, where they were given one of the wards in a military hospital where a French and a Russian unit were working, and within a few days it was arranged that they should take over the hospital as a dressing station as the wounded were coming in with terrible wounds, which had not been attended to for several days. Very soon they had orders again to evacuate, and got out barely three hours before the Germans arrived.

Before leaving Kraljevo, Sir Ralph Paget, the commissioner for all the

British hospitals in Serbia, spoke very seriously to them, and urged them to try and escape, though he said that they would have a very hard struggle to get across the mountains, as the winter snow and frost had already set in, and the roads were very difficult and dangerous. The only alternative was to remain where they were and be taken prisoner by the Germans. By doing so, they would be hampering the poor Serbians, who had to share their food with them, and were most anxious to see them safely out of the country, as they felt that they owed the nursing units a deep debt of gratitude for their splendid work during the typhus plague in the spring. So finally after signing an official document to say that they were travelling over the mountains at their own risk, the party started from Kraljevo having first distributed their hospital equipment and blankets among the Serbs so as to leave as little for the enemy.

They retreated with the Army. She went on to describe the great difficulties on the "trek" regarding food. Everyone was hungry and so much food got lost or stolen that for many days their supplies were pretty meagre. A Serbian doctor had managed to get, for a half-pound tin of cocoa, motor-transport and sufficient petrol to take their party on a three days' journey. Poor Austrian prisoners sold their overcoats, shoes and shirts for a slice of bread, and consequently many of them died on the mountains from cold and exposure.

Mrs Green said that they found walnuts and chestnuts very sustaining. Onions also helped them, eaten raw with bread, and one night they had quite a banquet with fried onions and wild sage which they found growing at the roadside. To her, the greatest hardship was the want of water for toilet purposes. Many days they had to be content with rubbing their hands and faces with snow. The Serbs all carried small water bottles, and never began to eat a meal, however scanty, without first pouring water over their hands.

The mountain roads through Montenegro were terrible, and so were the monotonous plains in Albania, but she would always look back with the greatest horror upon the road from Kraljevo to Rashka. It had thus been described to perfection: "The whole road was a living snake, with human heads for scales. It coiled across the plains, zig-zagged up the mountains and writhed down again into the valley. It was a strange sight, that valley with the slow muddy river flowing and the human stream hurrying on".

Motor-cars lurching frantically in the deep mud ploughed through the human flood. There were bullock carts too, but they were slow, then a bustling throng of soldiers and peasants with army waggons and bullock carts intermingled, streaming along the winding, restricted roadway with on one side the steep mountain walls rising abruptly, and on the other side a precipitous descent to the river below. For two whole days the road never varied, and it was impossible to find a spot to rest for the night. "All we could do" said Mrs. Green "was to stop our carriages on the brink of the precipice, and sit there until morning, hoping that our guards could ward off all the passing vehicles, as it seemed to us that the slightest touch would send us over the brink". All through the terrible retreat at frequent intervals there were furious blizzards of sleet and blinding snowstorms broke over them, adding cruelly to their sufferings. Now and again vehicles broke down, blocking the road and jamming streams of fugitives for miles back.

"The night before we arrived at Rashka," said Mrs. Green, "we found a fairly open space, and camped for the night. We had supper around the most wonderful camp fire I have ever seen, and it was a curious sight to see us seated round the fire, all sharing our supper with friends and enemies alike. Serbian officers, Austrians, English, and Scottish doctors and nurses. After supper, the Serbians, who are a very musical people, gave us quite a grand concert, with solos, duets and part-songs, a French woman and one of the Austrian doctors sang beautifully and several of our Sisters sang. The Serbs were deploring the fact that none of them could sing an English song in our honour, when to the amazement of everyone, a young Austrian student lustily sang a verse of 'My heart's in the Highlands' ".

The speaker went on to tell of the arrival of the party at Rashka and of

119

the increasing difficulties and privations connected with their journey to the coast attending to dressings for the wounded, and feeding starving fugitives where opportunity occurred. She told of an accident that befell a motor transport wagon containing some of their nurses, which, owing to the to the dangerous state of the roads, went over a steep precipice. One of the nurses was killed and they had to bury her in a little cemetery by the roadside. Going from Mehavitza, where they procured stores for the mountain journey, they arrived at Leipsan, where forty women were all packed into one small room, and the men of the party slept in the narrow passage outside. The difficulty in procuring salt and the unpalatable nature of the black bread that they had to eat were commented upon, and the speaker spoke of a banquet of potatoes boiled in bovril that they partook in a stable, and afterwards felt so festive that they started singing "Tipperary" and were going to wind up with "God Save the King" when the French people who were sharing the stable joined in lustily, and a girl sang several songs most exquisitely. Then they all joined in, and the rafters of the stable fairly creaked when they responded by singing the "Marseillaise".

After spending a night at Sueareka in a tiny room where forty-three of the party had to sleep in their wet bedraggled garments, they were glad to get up at dawn and get into the fresh air.

The snow was very deep and the road terrible with dead animals, bullocks, horses, ponies and goats. Half-way to Prizren they found a poor Albanian lying dead in the snow. Many times when they felt inclined to sit down in despair, the picture of that poor dead man spurred them on and kept them going to the end of the day's march. Afterwards it was no uncommon sight to see poor, tired out human beings lying dead on the roadside. ....
Source: *Herts. Advertiser, 25th March 1916.*

"Soldiers" Home Circle.

The "Soldiers Home Circle" at Spicer-street, St. Albans, continues to be as popular as ever among the soldiers and the letters and postcards posted from the box at the writing materials' counter total several hundred a week, apart from those which are written there and posted at a future time.

The billiard table and bagatelle tables are in constant use; they have, in fact, had to have new covers.

On Wednesday, a company of the *Staffords[hires]* were entertained at a smoking concert, by the kindness of Captain Clay. The hall was crowded and the various items were vociferously applauded and encored, especially those contributed by Privates Welsh and Magee, the latter's mandolin solos being very fine. Cigarettes and tobacco, and beer for those that liked it were provided by the officers, and lest the abstainers should feel they were left out of the reckoning, the Committee of the *Soldiers' Home Circle* decided to supply all temperance drinks free on that evening.
Source: *Herts. Advertiser, 1st April 1916.*

The youngest Brigadier in the British Army.

Henry Page Croft leaves the command of the 1st Hertfordshire Regiment and takes command of the 68th Infantry Brigade:
Leaving this gallant company [*Hertfordshire Regiment*] for new surroundings was a depressing moment in a day when all this changed and I lived in a different atmosphere amongst total strangers. I was appointed to command the *68th Infantry Brigade, 23rd Division* which comprised the *10th and 11th Northumberland Fusiliers,* and the *12th and 13th Durham Light Infantry.* On reporting for duty, my senior staggered me by informing me that he thought it only right to say that he strongly disapproved of a Territorial officer being appointed a brigadier! He was a gallant old gentleman with many excellent qualities, but what a start.

Nothing however could have been more delightful, than the relations with my own command. My battalion commanders were all regular officers of long standing and with previous war experience, and two of them were old enough to be my father. I was thirty-four and at that

121

time, the youngest brigadier in the Army; and yet these fine old soldiers gave me total and devoted service and'went out of their way to make my task easy, responding with the greatest readiness to my smallest request.
Source: *Croft, Henry Page. My Life of Strife.*

Talbot House, Poperinghe.

I expect some of you will ask what TOC means. Well, not a lot! But it has nothing to do with the Grandfather Clock which goes tick-tock! It is a signaller's way of pronouncing the letter 'T'. Why call 'T' Toc? Just run your mind over our alphabet and you will see that several letters end with the sound 'E'. So to make a signal clear to the receiver, signallers called 'B' Beer, 'D' Don, 'P' Pip, 'T' Toc and 'V' Vic. Other words end with the sound 'A', so 'A' Ack. 'M' was called Emma.

So Toc is 'T' and 'T' is the initial letter of the name Talbot. He was a young officer killed in the First World War. His brother, well known to me, was one of the Senior Chaplains. H stands for House, so we have got 'Talbot House'. That was an old oast-house in Poperinghe, Belgium, which the Army took over [in 1915]. They turned it into a sort of rest house for soldiers waiting for the troop-train to take them on leave to 'Blighty' (England); or for those who had returned from leave and were waiting for transport to take them back to their units.

On my first visit to 'Toc H' it was crowded with men getting some refreshment, joking and laughing. The person in charge of the house was the Revd. Philip B. Clayton, known as "Tubby". No need for me to tell you why! a splendid man who had the knack of keeping order and everybody happy.
Source: *The Revd. Canon Lovell writing. Junior Choice, in. Hertford Hundred West Parish Magazine, September and October, 1991.*

'Tubby' Clayton was an original character: he made everyone welcome. It would be hard to imagine any one less military-looking that "Tubby". He was short and round. "Clothing" wrote a contemporary, was always a trial. Buttons would persist in coming off, breeches would gape at the knees, shirt-cuffs would wear out ... "

Officialdom thought that the club might be called *Church House*, but the Revd. Neville Talbot, the Senior Chaplain had other ideas. He insisted that the house be called Talbot House after his own, younger brother, who had been killed in July 1915. As 'T' in signaller's language is 'Toc' so Talbot became 'Toc' and House became 'H' and thus Talbot House became known as *Toc H*. And so more than eighty-five years later it is still known as Toc H, and after the war, Toc H became an alive organisation, and remains so at the beginning of the 21st century. century.

All were welcome at this house: it wasn't a club for officers, nor was it a club for the men. It was for everyone.

Canon Lovell recalls the accommodation:
On the first floor there was a quiet room (no talking) fitted out with comfortable arm-chairs where one could sit and perhaps have a doze, or read the London-newspapers, or write a letter home. The top floor was turned into a Chapel, where one could go and say prayers, and a great many did so. A carpenter's bench was found in the garden or back-yard. It was used, in the Chapel as an altar, most appropriately as Jesus was a carpenter, and worked with Joseph, his father, at a bench. Hanging on the wall by the chaplain's room was a written Toc H rule, which read: *All rank, abandon ye who enter here.* From General to Private 'Tommy' all were equal. Nobody was allowed to 'presume' by his rank. Here was a thriving place where soldiers serving on and around the Ypres Salient wanted to go. They were welcome and were welcomed.
In 1918 the house did close when Poperinghe was overrun by the enemy. At the end of the war, the house, which had belonged to a Belgian banker and stockbroker, was handed back to him. Eleven years later, in 1929, Lord Wakefield, who created the lubricating oil - *Castrol*, bought the house and donated it to *Toc H* organisation.

I visited the house in the summer of 1998 and was welcomed by the curator, and shown round by a couple, who themselves had lived at some time in Potters Bar. Year by year, students from British schools and elsewhere visit this living shrine on visits to the "battlefields of the Great War". Many pilgrims to the Ypres Salient visit the house, which provides self-catering accommodation for groups.

Toc H Headquarters is at - 1 Forest Close,Wendover, Aylesbury, Buckinghamshire HP22 6BT.

Lord Cavan visits Talbot House.

In 1916, Lord Cavan assumed command of the XIVth Corps, and at a time when the war was not going well, he became burdened with the 'misery and horror of the war around him'.

"I came away from the trenches after having spent the whole of a grim day witnessing the destruction upon my men. As I left the line - the torrential rain, the bitter cold and as the evening approached 'Hate began to break my spirit'. As I pondered the tragic happenings of the previous year, my car came to the outskirts of Poperinghe. I left the car and buttoning my trench coat around me, I walked directly to the doors of Talbot House and entered. I was greeted by Clayton's batman who asked me if I wanted to see his master. "No" I replied, I have come to say my prayers".

Without much ado, I climbed first the stairs, and then the ladder that led to the 'Upper Room'. Here I saw one officer and three men kneeling at the benches. I knelt down and prayed as I had never prayed before that 'Almighty God would give me comfort, self-reliance, courage and would take away despair! I never knew how long it was before the answer came; but come it did, and I found myself being upheld. At first came quiet - a sense of peace and my confidence revived. I felt as if an overwhelming burden had been lifted from me and that I was free and strong once more. I rose from my prayers - refreshed and renewed, knelt again to render parting thanks and descended the stairs and went out into the darkness and walked alone, back to my Corps Headquarters".

Source: *Lever, Tresham. Clayton of Toc H.*

124

All rank, abandon ye who enter here. From General to Private all were equal at Talbot House, Poperinghe, which remains, today, at the heart of the Toc H movement.

The address for Toc H is given on *page 124.*

The Chapel, known as the Upper Room, where many went to say their prayers, or make their holy communion.

UNDERWOOD T.
VINE W.
WALKER C.
WALLINGER H.
WARD H.A.
V.C.WARNER E.
WARNER R.J.
WARRINGTON J.
WATSON B.C.
WATTS F.W.

The Menin Gate memorial which records the names of soldiers and men who fell in the Ypres Salient, but who have no known grave.The Memorial Registers, kept within the Menin Gate record the names of those listed. They include Private Warner, Lieutenant 'Billy Grenfell', and 100 officers and men of the Hertfordshire Regiment, who died on 31st July 1917.

City Police attached to Hertfordshire police.

Mr. E.P. Debenham, Town Clerk of St. Albans received on Wednesday, an Order from the Home Secretary intimating that on and after 1st June (the following day), the *City of St. Albans Police Force* "shall for the purposes of control and discipline be treated during the continuance of the present war, as part of the police force of the County of Hertford". Source: *Herts. Advertiser, 3rd June 1916.*

Mayor of St. Albans' Shilling Fund.

to raise 100,000 shillings from St.Albans and the neighbourhood for the British Red Cross Society and the Order of St. John of Jerusalem. Previous total published - 11,301 shillings. New total - 11,721 shillings. Source: *Herts Advertiser, 16th June 1916.*

Local men at the Battle of Jutland.

On Wednesday of last week the greatest naval battle recorded in the history of the world commenced in the North Sea, and continued throughout the night. The news did not reach the public until Friday. On Saturday, the Comander-in-Chief, Grand Fleet, stated that our total losses amounted to eight destroyer boats. A closer estimate of the losses and damage sustained by the enemy fleet showed that one Dreadnought battleship of the Kaiser class had been blown up and another had been sunk by gunfire. Of three German battle-cruisers, one was blown-up, another was seen to be disabled and stopping, and the third was observed to be seriously damaged. One German light cruiser and six German destroyers were sunk and at least two German light cruisers were seen to be disabled. Further repeated hits were observed on three other German battleships that were engaged. Finally a German submarine was rammed and sunk. Germany announced to the world that she had beaten the British fleet, but when Admiral Jellicoe cruised off the German coast on the following day and challenged the Germans to finish the fight there was no response.

Among the local men who had seen action were Ships Steward's

Assistant, Frederick Archibald Brown, son of Mr. H.E. Brown, newsagent, Holywell-hill, St. Albans who had joined his ship only a fortnight when he had the thrilling experience of going into action. Leading Stoker Frederick Palmer, elder son of Mr. and Mrs. F. Palmer, of Romeland-hill was also privileged to take part in the great battle. Mr Alfred E. Smith, Hill Street has a son, W. Smith, who has been in the Navy for about seven years. He has had a message from his son "We have been in action, and came off all right". Among the wounded in Sub-Lieutenant Alan Cory Wright. Two local victims are named as Petty Office John Rothven, of Little Berkhamstead and Assistant Paymaster Lewis Tippen, of Beresford House, Watford. A former resident of Harpenden, Dr. George Shorland, is on the official list of casualties among officers serving in the ships which took part in the great naval battle. Surgeon George Shorland was of H.M.S.Invincible which was one our ships that was sunk.

Source: *Herts. Advertiser, 10th June 1916.*

continued on page 127

Bricket House, Red Cross Hospital.

A meeting of the committee of the Voluntary Aid Detachment (Herts 38) was held at Bricket House. Mr. Walter Reynolds, High Sheriff of the County presided. Also present were the Countess of Verulam (vice-president), Lady Thomson (vice-president), Mrs. Hall, Mrs. A.N.Boycott (Commandant) and Dr. Lipscomb.

The Commandant's report showed that the hospital has been in full occupation since its opening on the 9th December 1914, and that the average daily number of beds occupied during 1915 was 34. In the spring of 1915 many hundreds of outpatients had also been treated. The Royal Army Medical Corps have attended to the medical and surgical work of the hospital. The nursing staff consists of three trained nurses, two by day and one for night duty. Under them has been the staff of V.A.D. Nurses. of whom an average of 12 have attended daily, and one for night duty. The Quartermaster, among her other duties, has now organised the sewing room, where many willing helpers regularly give their services in mending hospital linen and attending to soldiers' kit, a member of the detachment having this under her care. The kitchen department is carried on entirely by voluntary help. The head cook or her deputy attends daily, with usually two members of the detachment, and at least four other helpers for washing up and scullery work. A recreation room has been erected in the grounds by the Mr. A. Holland-Hibbert, County Director of the British Red Cross Society, being paid for from funds placed at his disposal.

The accounts showed that an appeal in August 1914 had raised £214 15s 0d. Of this £24 5s 10d had been expended by 31st December 1914. Receipts for 1915 came to £1,950 1s 11d of which £1,744 was received from the Government for the maintenance of patients. The Herts Branch of the Red Cross Society granted £58 16s for the salary of one of the trained nurses. Most of the remaining £147 5s 11d was composed of donations from friends, collections and entertainments organised for the benefit of the hospital. The committee expressed their thanks to the V.A.D. members, helpers and friends ...

Source: *Herts. Advertiser, 10th June 1916.*

127

St.Albans City Tribunal
Attested men seek exemption from military service.

Three cases heard before the Tribunal. It has met on five days out of the last eight - The case of Edwin Eddy, for whom Mr. A. Ernest Gibbs (Messrs Gibbs & Bamforth) proprietor of the *Herts Advertiser*, applied, had been adjourned for a week to enable Mr. Eddy, who is the head of the commercial department of the firm, to produce a medical certificate from Mill Hill. The certificate stated "Fit for service (but not general service) in garrison or provisional units." The Town Clerk said that it would probably be some time before Mr. Eddy would be called up. The Military Representative agreed. It was decided not to grant any exemption.

Seth William Green, New Grange-street, hairdresser and tobacconist, said he was unable to get an assistant. He had had the business for ten years; had advertised to sell it, and had advertised for a manger, but had received no replies, and if he went to the Army, the shop would absolutely have to close. It was a lock-up shop, and he had two rents to meet. - Six months' conditional exemption.

Thomas Joseph Ballard, aged 35, married, No.75 St.Peter's-street and Hackney-road, Bethnal Green, had had his application remitted to St. Albans by the Bethnal Green Tribunal. Applicant stated that he carried on business as a wholesale fruiterer, having a business at No.25, George-street, St. Albans and would have to close the shop up if he enlisted. In reply to the Mayor, applicant said he had a monthly agreement respecting the tenancy of the shop with Mr. Alcock. He had no lease; there was no name on the shop. Applicant said he had taken business from his brother-in-law, who prior to that arrangement, had employed him as manager. Goods were sent to St. Albans in the name of Osborne, and the applicant still traded in the name of Osborne. Mr. Osborne had a good many shops. Applicant said he had a stall in the market which was run on the Saturday by paid labour. The Tribunal decided not to grant any exemption. Applicant: No time at all to settle my business? The Chairman: No time at all.
Source: *Herts. Advertiser, 17th June 1916.*

128

NOTICE PAPER to be sent to men who belong to the Army Reserve under the provisions of the Military Service Act, 1916.

[In accordance with the provisions of Section 24 (2) of the Reserve Forces Act, 1882, "evidence of the delivery at the last registered place of abode of a man belonging to the Army Reserve of a notice, or of a letter addressed to such man, and containing a notice, shall be evidence that such notice was brought to the knowledge of such man."]

Surname _Swain_

Christian Name _Thomas_

Number in Military Register (Army Book 414) } _250_

Address _Colney Heath_   Class Number _5_
Nr. St Albans

You are hereby warned that you will be required to join for service with the Colours on the ___ 8 MAR 1916 ___ 191 .

You should therefore present yourself at _62, QUEENS ROAD, WATFORD_

on the above date, not later than _9.30 A.M._ o'clock, bringing this paper with you.

*This will be struck out if the man resides within 5 miles of the place at which he is required to present himself.

A Railway Warrant is enclosed herewith.*

___ _R. J. Saunders_ ___ Signature.

2 3 FEB 1916 Date.   _Capt_ Rank.

62, QUEENS ROAD, WATFORD Place.   _R. O._ WATFORD Appointment.

N.B.—Particular attention is called to Section 15 of the Reserve Forces Act, 1882, which provides that where a man belonging to the Army Reserve is called out on Permanent service, and such man, without leave lawfully granted or such sickness or other reasonable excuse as may be allowed in the prescribed manner, fails to appear at any time and place at which he is required on such calling out to attend, he shall be guilty, according to the circumstances, of deserting, within the meaning of Section 12, or of absenting himself without leave within the meaning of Section 15 of the Army Act, 1881.

(5724.) W. 16793/5846. 300,000. 2/16 C. P., Ltd. Forms/W. 3236/1

RAILWAY WARRANT for Journeys in Great Britain.   Army Book 408.

This Warrant must be presented to the Booking Clerk at the Station where the holder is authorised to commence the journey, when a railway ticket will be issued in exchange.

The Directors of the _L nw Rly._
Railway Company are hereby requested to provide conveyance as shown hereon.

Date **8 MAR 1916**

Station from _St albans Lnw Rly_

Station to WATFORD. Junc

Single or Return _Single_

No. of Warrant	This Warrant is NOT† chargeable against the Public.	Duty, (If not under route, state below whether for a RECRUIT, for a man on DISCHARGE, or for what other service.)
2	Initials of Issuing Officer } _After_	
№ 969153	† If the cost is chargeable to the Public, strike out "NOT" and initial.	_mob._

The particulars on the back of this Warrant should be fully completed.

(Signature) _R L Fletcher_

(Rank, &c.) _Capt R O WATFORD._

	Number to be conveyed. To be filled in by the Issuer.	To be filled in by Railway Company.	
		Ordinary fare.	Amount payable at Military Rate.
Officers, 1st Class			
Soldiers, 3rd Class	_one_		
Women & Children 12 years of age and upwards at fares for adults			
Children between 3 and 12 years of age, half fares for adults			

	No.	§Weight, including Contents.			Mileage.	Rate.
		Tons	Cwts.	Qrs.		
Guns and Limbers						
4-Wheeled Vehicles						
2-Wheeled Vehicles						
Total Weight of Guns, &c...						
Horses or {In horse boxes						
Mules {In cattle trucks						
Bicycles						

Total £

To be filled in by Booking Clerk.	No. of ticket issued_____ Date_____
	Route via_____
	(Signature)_____ Station_____

Counter-Signature of Official representing Railway Company_____

Any alteration in the Warrant which may be absolutely necessary must be verified by the signature of the person who makes the alteration.

§ The weight of baggage and stores not packed in Army Vehicles must be excluded separate forms to be used for traffic not so packed.

Railway Warrant issued to Thomas Swain, 8 March 1916

Operation Order No.76

27th June 1916.

The 2nd Battalion, Bedfordshire Regiment will be in support and on the night of X/Y will be disposed as in Appendix Z.

2 Vickers Guns will be attached to this Battalion and one will move with 'A' Company and one with 'D' Company. Lewis Guns will work with their companies.

Each man will carry on his person, 170 rounds Small Arms Ammunition [S.A.A.] and 2 hand grenades. Each bomber will carry 10 bombs.

Water is scarce and the utmost care will be exercised.

Each man will carry: Waterproof sheet, Pack (without Greatcoat); Rifle and Bayonet; 170 rounds S.A.A., 2 Mills Bombs, 1 Iron Ration; also unexpended portion of 'Z' days ration.

Bombers, Gunners and Stretcher Bearers will carry: Rifle and Bayonet (except No. 1 and 2 Lewis Gun Teams), 50 rounds S.A.A. (except Bombers); Lewis Gunners will carry 170 rounds; Rations as above.

All men will carry a filled oil bottle, pullthrough and flannelette. Picks and shovels will be carried by all men in proportion of 1 pick and 3 shovels. Each man carrying wire cutters will wear a white patch on the shoulder strap.

National Hospital for wounded soldiers, Napsbury.
1916-1919.

Inmates at the Middlesex County Asylum, Napsbury, south-east of St.Albans, along the southern boundary with London Colney, were removed in May 1916, so that a National Hospital for Wounded Soldiers could be established there.

Although erected and equipped on the most approved, modern methods, for the housing and treatment of those suffering from diseases of the mind, its adaption as a general hospital for wounded soldiers has resulted in extensive alterations and additions. When completed it will afford accommodation for 1,500 patients and in times of stress that number can be increased to 1,800. The number of nurses will be in the region of 300 and detached accommodation is being adapted in the ground to provide a nurses' home.

151 men, who came straight from the firing line were the first convoy of wounded to arrive at the hospital in June. A detachment [25] of the Royal Army Medical Corps have been specially drilled as an ambulance unit. So well was the work organised and carried through, that within an hour of the arrival of the convoy at Napsbury railway station (on the London Midland Railway), every patient making up the convoy was comfortably lying in his bed at the hospital.

The Officer Commanding the Hospital speaks in terms of unqualified praise of their performance: "They all did their work remarkedly well", he declared. The only criticism I heard was offered by an orderly on the train, who observed: "I see this is your first convoy: you have dealt with it so quickly!" "personally, I consider the performance was very creditable. At other places, they have boasted at getting a convoy dealt with in two hours: we did it in half that time, and did it entirely in our own way".

The men who come here for treatment are fortunate indeed. Spacious, sunny wards are brightened by beautiful flowers. A staff of Army nurses with their quiet, grey uniforms, edged with scarlet and flowing white line head-dress, move busily about the wards, and under them, the ordinary hospital staff are are serving as probationers. What a haven of rest after the stress of the battlefield!

Under the regime of the War Office, the latest scientific apparatus is being introduced. An efficient X-ray installation has been provided and is in much demand for the location of bullets and other foreign bodies and for the speedy diagnosis of fractures and such like. A man has been wounded in the thigh. The stretcher-bearers lift him tenderly from his bed and he is carried on a wheeled stretcher to the X-ray theatre and the radiographer, having located the seat of the trouble, proceeds to take a photograph of the injury, and thus places in the hands of the surgeon, information, which is invaluable in the treatment of the case. Near by is the operating theatre, admirably lighted and fitted with the most approved appliances. The theatre is of great importance, for there are obvious many cases in which operations are necessary, chiefly for the removal of embedded bullets and such like.

Soldiers reaching the stage of convalescence may stroll or sit in long comfortably furnished galleries, recalling with comrades the stirring times they have passed through. They are provided with plenty of reading matter and there are games and pastimes available. Life passes happily even for those who are obliged to remain in bed. The hospital barber goes on his rounds attending to a convalescent here or a bed patient there. One of the wounded boys brought with him to the hospital, a concertina which had been sent out to him as a birthday present, but did not reach him until he was wounded and in hospital. He is now convalescent, happily, and fills a sphere of usefulness by going round the wards playing *Come to the cookhouse door, boys,* when dinner is ready.

The spiritual ministrations at the hospital are in efficient hands. Sectarian differences are banished; the welfare of the men is the all important consideration. In one ward a veteran pastor seeks to bring consolation to a sick soldier; on the lawn outside the Roman Priest is holding the attention of a group of convalescents, and in another part

131

of the building, the Church of England chaplain is busy.

When the scheme is in full working order, Napsbury will be the centre of a network of hospitals throughout the county, for there are twenty-five auxiliary hospitals with about six hundred more beds to be utilised.

Source: *Herts. Advertiser, ... 1916.*

Note: Between 1916 and 1919 more than 37,000 patients were accommodated at Napsbury Military Hospital. The records survive at the Public Record Office, Kew but were closed until 1995. I have "sampled" the records and found that the majority of patients were returned to their units or sent on leave within a month of their admission. It would appear that very few died, from wounds received in battle.

Battle of the Somme, 1916.

1st July - The British attack on a long front, north of the River Somme. Our orders were to be ready to move at short notice. We were expecting orders to move to trenches near the village of Wailly, three miles south-west of Arras, as it had already been arranged that we should attack from these trenches on 2nd July. Officers and N.C.O.s had reconnoitred this area, but then order for the attack were cancelled.

2nd July - At midday we got orders and the Battalion left Arras and marched to Givencey-le-Noble where it was billeted in a large chateau, its spacious grounds offering good facilities for training. Barely had the men settled down when a despatch rider arrived with orders that the Battalion must be ready to move at the shortest possible notice. All equipment had to be put together, stores packed, horses harnessed and everything made ready to move. Men had to sleep fully dressed with rifles ready. The next day these orders were modified and we actually remained at Givercey-le-Noble until 13th July.

13th July - The Battalion left Givercey-le-Noble at 6 p.m. The march was a long one - a distance of fifteen miles and by the time we arrived everyone had had enough. The billeting party had got billets allotted

St. Albans Cemetery
Cross of Sacrifice
Erected in 1920.

The cross is
found only in
larger cemeteries.

Soldiers' Corner, St. Albans Cemetery.
Private Winter and Private Gillin were buried in August 1916.
Burials continued until 1920.

IN LOVING MEMORY OF
THOMAS KENT for 46 years Churchwarden of this Abbey
who died 23rd April 1917 also of his wife
EMILY SELINA who died 25th April 1914
Also of two of their sons
HAROLD 2nd Lieutenant South Wales Borderers
who was Killed near Ypres 4th Aug 1917 and
LIONEL VICTOR Lieutenant South Wales Borderers
who was Killed at Oostaveine 31st July 1917

IN MEMORY OF THE OFFICERS AND
MEN OF THE HERTS YEOMANRY WHO
GAVE THEIR LIVES FOR KING & COUNTRY
IN THE GREAT WAR 1914-1919.

LIEUT-COL. S. GURNEY SHEPPARD D.S.O.

ABBOTT TPR. D.G.	CLARK L.CPL. J.W.	GRIFFITHS TPR. A.F.	MASSON TPR. J.
ALEY TPR. F.	CLAYTON L.CPL. G.E.	HALL TPR. S.	MATTHEWS TPR. A.E.
ARCHER TPR. G.	COLLINS TPR. A.	HALLUM TPR. E.E.	MATTHEWS TPR. L.
ARNOLD L.SGT. A.W.	COOKE L.CPL. H.	HARRADINE TPR. R.G.	MILLAR TPR. H.P.
ATKINS L.SGT. P.A.	CULVERHOUSE TPR. H.H.	HARROWELL TPR. F.	MILLER TPR. H.
BARNARD TPR. W.J.	DAVIES TPR. A.	HICKMAN SGT. F.H.	PADDON TPR. H.L.
BARRATT TPR. C.J.	DELL S.S.CPL. W.G.	HOLGATE TPR. A.H.E.	RUDD TPR. W.J.
BEST TPR. E.	DEARDS TPR. E.	HOWARD TPR. W.H.	SMITH TPR. S.A.
BRAND TPR. J.	DWYER TPR. C.	HUMPHREYS TPR. W.S.	SMITH TPR. W.A.
BRIDLE TPR. A.	EAST SQM.SGT. A.G.	JOLLY LIEUT. F.	STEVENS L.CPL. S.
BROWN TPR. S.H.	ELLACOTT L.SGT. S.A.	JONES TPR. A.S.	WALDER SGT. P.J.W.
BUCKEL L.CPL. S.E.	EVERETT TPR. H.J.	KEMPSTER TPR. J.	WALL TPR. H.W.
CARLILE MAJOR E.H.H.	FARR TPR. P.	KNOWLTON SGT. J.H.	WARD TPR. C.W.
CARROLL L.SGT. E.S.	GINGELL TPR. J.S.	LOVESAY TPR. B.	WHITING L.CPL. E.J.
CLARKE TPR. F.	GOUGH TPR. J.R.	MASON TPR. H.D.	WILSHAW TPR. D.G.

WOODMAN TPR. T.F. COOPER S.SGT-M.W. WOODS TPR. A.R.

ERECTED BY THEIR COMRADES OF THE REGIMENT.

Two memorials in the War Memorial Chapel, St. Albans Abbey.
1. The Kent family, whose two sons died within four days
of each other in the Third Battle of Ypres, 1917; and
2. The Herts. Yeomanry Memorial which lists those
who died during the Great War. The Yeomanry
served at Gallipoli, Egypt, Mesopotamia and Palestine.

Boulogne Eastern Cemetery, France where Julian Grenfell of Panshanger, near Hertford is buried. Best known for his poem *Into Battle*. Graves here are laid flat, for fear of subsidence.

A war cemetery at Loos, France in which there are graves of Hertfordshire men.

Queen Eleanor's body rested at St. Albans on its final journey
from Lincoln to London in 1290. Frank O. Salisbury painted
this large canvas in 1908, and it hung in his studio at Harpenden
until 1918, when Alderman Faulkner, Mayor of St. Albans,
bought it in recognition that the allied armies had captured Jerusalem.
He presented it to St. Albans Abbey, where it hung until October 1973.
The painting was cut from its frame and stolen. It has never been found!

and guides at the entrance to the village, showed Platoons to their billets. Everyone was dead tired and soon fell asleep.
Source: *Bedfordshire Record Office. Bedfordshire Regiment, War Diary.*

First stage of the "Big Push".

Lance-Corporal Maurice E. Webb, King's Own Yorkshire Light Infantry writes, from hospital to his parents, Mr and Mrs. G.G. Webb, Redbourn of the fighting on Saturday, 1st July 1916:

Four days before 1st July we filed into the trenches with orders that we were going over the top the next morning but one, and then at the last moment that was cancelled. Well, our battalion being the first to go over in our division, had to remain in the trenches until the time re-fixed for the attack. I was due to go over with Mr. Nott, our new officer in Headquarters' line - that was the 6th line.

The first line was to get out of the sap at 7.25, which was five minutes to Zero - Zero being 7.30 a.m., the time set. The sap we were in was between ours and Fritz's front lines. The attack was to be preceded by an intensely heavy artillery bombardment lasting an hour, so precisely at half-past six such a roar broke forth, and I shall never forget it. I know I was laughing and shivering at the same time. Fritz was retaliating on our front line, so we were between both, and it was most unpleasantly close. During the continual roar some very heavy crashes were heard, and the sap shook and pieces of shell were continually falling in on us. These heavy crashes made me doubtful, and I asked Mr. Nott if they were Fritz's trench mortars, and he said "No, it's our twelve-inch shells falling on their front line". They do make a splash-eh, Webb" This eased me considerable.

Well at last our officer said "first line, get ready" which they did. They were to crawl as close to Fritz's trench as our artillery would allow them. Then came our turn, and we got out on top and felt relieved a bit, although the bombardment was still going on, but it had lifted a bit farther back. Dozens of Machine Guns were going, and Mr. Nott had to shout to me to tell me it was better to walk than to crawl, for my right and left chums had each received a bullet in the chest and lay still. He said that we should only get hit low, barring shells. Our front line should have been well over Fritz's front line by the time we got out, but nearly all the lads had been fetched down, and my first impression was that our attack had failed.

Mr. Nott was shouting 'push-on, push-on!' and he was going for all he was worth. Just as I reached the front line something seemed to shoot up my leg, and I must have shouted, for Mr. Nott shouted, "Never mind, Webb; I shall see you later". Then I fell in Fritz's trench, and he went straight on. I have heard that he was wounded and returned safely. I'm glad, too, for he was a nice fellow. The first I saw of Fritz's trench was a German making for me and I said Good-bye', for I had dropped my rifle as I fell and hurt my wrist. Anyhow, he didn't' reach me. Someone must have seen him, for he was hit in the mouth with a bomb that somebody threw, and then a fellow jumped into the trench and finished him with a bayonet. I didn't see who the fellow was, for he pushed on for more. I then reached for my rifle, and I had the satisfaction of dropping a few, as they came out of dugouts, some with their hands up.

Then someone dropped behind me and gave me a start. He was one of the *Somersets*, and was also wounded, but in the thigh, and he started crawling to a wounded German officer and started to bandage him up when the officer shot at him with his revolver, the bullet going through the lad's tunic, so the lad gave him a round and had a souvenir in the revolver. I looked at my foot, and my boot was off, for the bullet was explosive, and had made a gash at the bottom, whence it came out. It must have hit the bone too, for I could hardly move, and I noticed this morning the doctor here has marked 'Fracture' on my paper over the wound.

Anyway, *Somerset* and I started to crawl back; and it was a crawl, too, what with our wounds and old Fritz still shelling. Our Engineers were walking across the top whistling and singing with large bundles of material on their backs, and carrying all kinds of tools, so we knew that the attack was going right.

I got as far and had to stop on a piece of a ledge in the trench, feeling pretty queer. While I was there there, an officer came and sat beside me and he was covered on the face, neck, and body with shrapnel wounds, his tunic being in shreds, and he could not speak. When I looked at him again he was dead.

Then an artillery fellow saw me and carried me to the dressing station on the field. Since that dressing, I have been through several dressing stations, including one on a railway station whilst travelling to Rouen. I, with a few others, was fetched out of the train and re-dressed, as my foot was bleeding again. At one place a German prisoner, wounded, was speaking English, and one fellow remarked how bad and thin the Germans looked, and he replied: "No wonder, your artillery cut up all our transports the last few days that were trying to reach us". He said: "You have the finest artillery in the world". At another dressing station, a German doctor was doing good work, and one of our doctors said he was very clever.

"Anyway, I am feeling much better now I'm settled in bed, but it will be some time before I turn out."
Source: *Herts. Advertiser, ... 1916.*

Munition workers' outing.

There were a number of munition works' outings on Saturday and several parties travelled through St. Albans on Saturday morning and evening in brakes. There were some stoppages for refreshments. The thing that took notice was the number of young men employed at these factories and the remark was expressed that it was about time a regular clearing out took place.
Source: *Herts. Advertiser, 16th July 1916.*

Harpenden children entertain wounded soldiers.

Twenty wounded soldiers from Napsbury Hospital were entertained by the girls and boys of the County Council School, Harpenden. The soldiers were conveyed there by brake and the ride proved most enjoyable. Throughout the afternoon songs by the children and solos by the teachers interspersed with games and competitions kept the soldiers entertained. Refreshments were provided and when the "Tommies" returned, each went away with the overflow of good things. Lusty cheering from the youngster marked the soldiers' departure.

Source: *Herts. Advertiser, 16th July 1916.*

More wounded arrive at Napsbury.

Two days after having taken part in the "Great Push", 180 wounded soldiers were receiving attention at *Napsbury Military Hospital*, near St. Albans. There are now 800 wounded at the hospital. The services of the *Ambulance Section, St. Albans Company, Hertfordshire Volunteer Regiment* are invaluable in removing the wounded from the train to the Hospital.

Source: *Herts. Advertiser, 16th July 1916.*

Private Houses lent as hospitals for wounded.

A list of private houses in Hertfordshire that are being lent as hospital

Blackmore End - 168 beds   (Malay States Hospital)
Boxmoor House - 20 beds   (Mrs. Bouwens)
Underfield, Boreham Wood - 8 beds   (Mrs Jarvin Dickson)
Codicote, near Welwyn - 24 beds   (Mrs J. Pierpoint Morgan)
The Institute, Croxley Green - 35 beds   (J. Dickinson and Co.)
Ken Cottage, Hadley - 10 beds   (Mr. R.F. Sandon)
Goldings, Hertford - 16 beds   (Mrs. Reginald Abel-Smith)
Wallfields, Hertford - 20 beds   (Convent of the Sacred Heart)
Ewen Hall, High Barnet - 40 beds   (Congregational Church Deacons)
King's Walden Bury, Hitchin - 40 beds   (Mr. T. Fenwick Harrison)
Rosehill, Hoddesdon - 33 beds   (Mr. R. Barclay)
Bragbury, Knebworth - 15 beds   (Mrs S. Leger)
Little Heath, near Potter's Bar - 18 beds (Mrs. Nathan)
The Studio, Rickmansworh - 16 beds   (Mr. E. Beckett)
St. Augustine's Hall, Rickmansworth - 20 beds   (Father Julien)

Source: *Herts. Advertiser, ... July 1916.*

Marjorie writes to 'Daddy'.

Two letters written to 'Dear Daddy' from 29 Glenferrie Road, St. Albans were handed in to the Museum of St. Albans when they were setting-up an Exhibition to remember the 50th anniversary of the ending of World War II, 1945. One letter is included:

12th July - Dear Daddy, I hope you are very well. I did like it at Grannies [sic]. We had a shower of rain before I wrote to you. After dinner, Mamma, Granny and me went out and got caught in a shower and had to shelter in a fancy shop for about ten minutes.

On Tuesday we went to Harpenden and had a look at the shops and then went on the Common and sat a little. I did not sit as long as Mamma, but threw stones in the pond and then we went out to tea at 'Bobbies'. After tea we had a look at the shops we had not looked at and then we went on the Common again, but much farther - mainly to the top and then turned back again to look at Mr. Howard's shop, when we saw Miss Woril, and again we went up to the Common and back again and sat down for about five minutes. We were just in time for the train.

It turned out nice on Wednesday morning and Mamma said we could go by the river and ask Mrs Groves if you could come, but it went so dull that Mamma sent me to Mrs. Groves, to ask if she would come for a walk if it kept fine. She said that she could but it turned out wet so we could not go. Mrs. Grove came in he afternoon with her winter coat on and brought a lovely bunch of rambler roses.

Kisses and Love from dear Marjorie Tonge, to dear Daddy.
Source: *Museum of St. Albans.*

Call for nurses.

Both *Red Cross* and *St. John's Ambulance* are calling for more nurses. Demands made upon nurses by the military authorities are very heavy and cannot be met out of existing supplies. There must be many women who are not giving their whole of their time and service to the war, and who have no ties which prevents them from doing so. We earnestly call on these women to come forward and help us in this emergency, and thus enable us to answer the call of the sick and wounded men.

Source: *Herts. Advertiser, 3rd August 1916.*

With the Trench Mortar Bomb Section.

Private Eernest Kingham, 7th Bedfordshire Regiment writes from hospital of his section's involvement in the Great Advance. He was 19 years old when the war started and has been in France since June 1915:

We went in at ...., and a pretty stiff job it was. Our Battalion did lose some men at that time. I was with the Trench Mortar Bomb Battery, so therefore I had to go over with them, and if you remember 1st July, it was a very hot day and all the Battery except the men with the gun had to take eight shells with them, so that you can guess what it was like. At seven o'clock in the morning we each had a tot of rum. At half past [seven] the first men went over; a quarter of an hour after that the second wave went; we went after that, and then they went over in platoons, and I can give you my word it was a sight to see the poor fellows being pipped off, and a better sight to catch the prisoners. Well, I was lucky to get through that lot all right, and after that, several days in the trenches. Then this other advance came off. I managed to get through the work of the bombardment all right, and we were just thinking about going up to reinforce the others, when over came a big-un and exploded. It was then I managed to stop a piece, and am glad to say that it was only a flesh wound. It went in one side of the left leg above the knee at the back, and came out of the other side, making a nice-sized hole.

Source: *Herts. Advertiser, 3rd August 1916.*

Belgian refugees take offence.

The President and Secretary-Treasurer of the Belgian Sporting Club, Letchworth write to the Revd. John H. Bailey, Vicar of Norton, Letchworth on 9th August.

Sir, It is only today that we are able to answer your letter of 20th July, and we must say that its contents very much surprised the members of our Committee.

We cannot in any way accept your protest on our playing matches on Sundays. Our men are working eleven hours per day for a fortnight each month on daywork; the other fortnight when on night duty, they work 10¾ hours a night. They have not the same privilege of the British workers of having a half-day off on Saturdays and a great deal of our men are even working on Sundays until 12, 1 or sometimes till 5 and 7 o'clock.

Do you think these men need no fresh air, no recreation at all. Most of these men are discharged soldiers or soldiers on leave. Some of them were in the field since Liege, or Louvain ... . Do you think that these fellows, at least, after helping the Allies, with all the remainder of of their power, may do some sport during the 4 or 5 hours they do not work in a week. You will very very easily find out at the Ministry of Munitions that the output per head, has not been equalled up to now by any other factory in the United Kingdom!

Furthermore, we beg to point out that in no way are we your visitors. The Belgians are citizens because they pay the same taxes, but higher rents as you do.

At every match or meeting we make a collection of money, 50% of which is distributed for charity.

Please bear in mind that since their childhood, our people are accustomed to do sports on the Continent as a rule they have no leave in the week and work 10, 11 and 12 hours a day.

Yours faithfully,
for the Belgian Sporting Club.

The Revd John H. Bailey noted on 29th April 1931. I agree to this. I should probably not have written this protest today.

Source: *Hertfordshire Record Office. D/P75/3/3 - Revd. John H. Bailey collection of letters.*

War Graves in Hertfordshire.

116 graveyards and cemeteries contain 869 war graves of men who died in the Great War, 1914-1918. Of these, 68 were in the Bedfordshire Regiment, 30 in the Hertfordshire Regiment and 7 in the Hertfordshire Yeomanry. Of these - 632 were soldiers of United Kingdom units; 81 were German interned civilians; 50 were in the Royal Flying Corps or Royal Air Force (1918 onwards); 36 were in the Royal Navy; 21 were in the Australian Imperial Force; 18 were in the overseas Military Forces of Canada; 16 were Austrian interned civilians; 12 were members of the German army; 7 were in the Belgian army; 6 were Royal Marines; 3 were members of the South African Overseas Expeditionary Force; 2 were members of the Women's Royal Air Force; 1 was in the Royal Australian Navy; 1 was in New Zealand's Expeditionary Force; 1 was in the Queen Mary's Army Auxiliary Corps; 1 was an Australian munitions worker and 1 was a Voluntary Aid Detachment member of the British Red Cross.

Source: *Commonwealth (formerly Imperial) War Graves Commission Memorial Registers: Great Britain and Ireland. Vol. IV - Cemeteries and Churchyards in the County of Hertford, 1-116. 1930.*

Of these, the greatest concentration of graves is in the St. Albans Cemetery, Hatfield Road, St. Albans (entrance opposite to St. Paul's Church). The St. Albans City Council agreed, in July 1916, to set aside part of the cemetery as a soldiers' burial ground. The site is to the right of the main avenue, where there was erected in the inter-war years, a Cross of Sacrifice, as may be found where there are substantial numbers of war graves in the United Kingdom and abroad.

When established, the Superintendent was instructed that the ground may be used for general unpurchased and purchased graves. A separate enclosure by the western boundary of the cemetery contains the graves relating to the Second World War, 1939 to 1945.

In total there are 177 war graves in the cemetery, of which 111 are in the two "Soldier's Corner" sites. In addition there are other burials around the cemetery, the earliest being for 1915. At one time there were 4 American graves, but these have been removed and re-buried in the Midlands. 5 German graves remain in unmarked graves. Surely over 80 years after the end of that war, it is time for steps to be taken to record these graves, as has been done elsewhere in parts of France and Belgium.

Like war graves elsewhere, the headstones are maintained by the *Commonwealth War Graves Commission* [CWGC]. Other than the five Germans, names are recorded in the Cemetery Register which can be consulted at the Cemetery Office. In November 2001, the CWGC appealed for schools and young people to become involved in caring for these "shrines" as happens abroad.

Whilst the main Remembrance Day ceremony takes place at the Civic War Memorial in St. Peter's Street, St. Albans on or near to the 11th November each year, a service is takes place on the Sunday nearest to "*Anzac Day*" in April when those who died and are buried here are remembered by members of local churches, veterans organisation and the community living in Fleetville, St. Albans.

Among the burials in the cemetery is Private Dennis Adams, *2nd Bedfordshire Regiment,* who died on the 29th July 1916 at Winchester of wounds received on 1st July 1916 on the first day of the Battle of the Somme. Private Adams, who joined up on 12th August 1914 was married and left a widow and child, and before the war had been employed at Grimston Tyres. He was the eldest son of Mr. and Mrs. C. Adams, Offa-road, St. Albans.

He became entangled in the barbed-wire barricade. Owing to the dense smoke and shell fire, he was separated from his battalion, and found himself in a German trench. The German soldiers were very civil to him and took him below and handed him a cigar. In the meantime the British troops raided the trench, and Pte. Adams was shot in the back by a German, the bullet penetrating his lung. He laid in the trench with a dead German for seven or eight hours and though wounded severely, was quite conscious. Pte. Adams, while lying in hospital,

141

spoke very highly of the R.A.M.C. having to go through fire and shells to reach him.

Source: *Herts. Advertiser, 15th August 1916.*

First interments in Soldiers' Corner.

The first interments in the special plot of ground in St. Albans cemetery set apart by the City Council for the burial of soldiers took place on Monday, when an Australian was accorded military honours, and on Thursday, Private Winter, who was buried in another portion of the cemetery in the ordinary course some few weeks ago was re-interred in "Soldiers' Corner, under an order from the Home Secretary.

Separated by nearly half the earth from his kith and kin, Private William Marken Gillin of the *Australian forces* died at *Napsbury War Hospital* during the week-end from wounds received in action. The burial took place on Monday afternoon, the *Army Veterinary Corps* [A.V.C.] making the arrangements. A gun carriage was procured from the Artillery Depot at Luton and on it the coffin was conveyed from the Hospital to the cemetery, accompanied by an A.V.C. firing party and two trumpeters and a following party of about 50 men of the *Royal Flying Corps*. The graveside ceremony was conducted by Revd. Dr. John Power (Roman Catholic Priest). After the service, the firing party fired three volleys over the grave and the trumpeters blew "Last Post". Messrs. Goodchild and Son were the Undertakers.

Source: *Herts Advertiser, 2nd September 1916.*

Zeppelin brought down in Cuffley.

One of Germany's latest monster raiders was brought down in Cuffley on Sunday, 3d September 1916. Thirteen Zeppelins were spotted to be involved in this raid on south-east England, but only three machines approached London. Around the area a number of bombs were dropped but fell mainly on open fields doing little damage beyond tearing holes in the ground and the killing of farm stock. On the triangular green in front of the church, a signpost was felled by a bomb scattering fragments in all directions, tearing up the fence and a tree in

.A privately owned grave.
Lieutenant John Greathard
Royal Flying Corps.
in St. Albans cemetery.

Private W.M. Gillin
buried August 1916
(see page 142)

His remains were
exhumed in 1918 &
buried here.

Source: Cemetery
Burials' book
1914-1918

Among the Soldiers' Corner
graves are 50 that have
headstones arranged in pairs

2nd Private W. Evans *(left)*
Private W. Winter *(right)*

Needlework undertaken by men at Napsbury Military Hospital.
It was purchased by St. Albans City Council (*see page 238*), but
I have been unable to trace whether it has survived, and where?

Ward at Napsbury Military Hospital, which nursed over 37,000 soldiers
from 1916 until 1919. Contrary to popular belief, the majority, who arrived
by railway, left for home or their regiment within a month of arrival!

an adjoining garden and leaving a large hole. There was some damage to property in Cuffley village: two houses, lived in by elderly widows, had walls torn out, but apart from being shocked, were themselves unhurt. The south-eastern corner of the church was damaged with masonry flung all over the churchyard. The vestry and the organ were also damaged.

A young woman, aged 26 years was killed outright by a bomb, which fell within two or three yards of where she was standing behind her home, and her young sister aged 11 years had her right leg shattered. The Commander of the airship and his crew of sixteen were all killed. Their bodies were removed from the tangled wreckage and at the inquest, which opened the following day, it was reported that they had no identity discs. Later they were buried at Potters Bar cemetery.
Source: *Herts. Advertiser, 9th September 1916.*

Eye-witness reports.
In Ware.
A postcard of London Road, Ware, postmarked 9.15 p.m., 4th September 1916 and addressed to Miss Figgest c/o Mrs Johnson, The Crossways, St. Flora Road, Littlehampton, Sussex:
Dear Annie, - Just to let you know am at Ware. All well, going home Tuesday. Dear Annie, you will see the X on the same sides as the houses. Well Annie, I must tell you there was a dreadful raid early Sunday morning. Had just got off to sleep when we was woke up with the noise of a Zeppelin coming over. Well we got up and clung to one another on the side of the bed, and it passed right over our place and dropped where you see the X. We went to see the ruins last night about half-a-mile of Ware. Will tell you more in a letter. Love, Mother.
Source: *Private collection.*

The Elderly Lodgekeeper at Cuffley.
I had been awake at about one o'clock, but must have gone off to sleep again. It was about two o'clock, when I was next awakened by a terrific bang. My missus said to me "There's a bomb", so I jumped out of bed and went through the kitchen and opening the back door, I could see

a bit of light over the cricket field. We were nearly 'frit' to death, in the pitch black and all. I went back to the bedroom and tried to get my clothes on, and as I was doing so there were more bombs - one, two, three. My missus has been laid up for three months with a bad foot, and she was trying to get something on her foot when the ceiling came in. I lugged hold of her and got her out somehow, and took her to the house of the schoolmaster opposite. God knows how I did it; I don't. Accommodation has now been found for us at the bothy in the park.

Holiday excitement.

Miss Willy, who is living for a six-weeks' country holiday at "East Ridgeway" a charming little villa, situated no more than a hundred yards from the spot where the airship fell and directly in its path recalls:

We were roused about three o'clock in the morning by the guns going off, but the first thing we saw on waking was a brilliant light which made the house and all around it as bright as day. It was a most uncanny light, very white and fearsome. When we looked to discover the source of of this, we saw the Zeppelin falling straight down from the sky, nose first, and it seemed impossible that it could miss us. Its passage through the air was accompanied by a tremendous noise, like the roar of an express train, as if the engines were going, and it seemed as if it were broken in two. I was very frightened. In a few seconds the blazing mass had reached the ground, but I heard no noise from the impact, probably because the ground was so soft and wet. As it touched earth, however, the great light which had died down for a few seconds, flared up again, with great intensity, and once more died down, although the great thing continued to blaze furiously for some time afterwards.

Source: *Herts. Advertiser, 9th September 1916.*

Farmer's vivid story.

Mr. E. Littlechild, Castle Farm, Cuffley describes what the monster looked like:

I got my clothes on and came downstairs and went out of the front door. Looking up towards Enfield I could then see the Zepp. in full flare. It seemed to be travelling very unsteadily, as if they had no control over it, towards Northaw. When it got over Northaw, which is

144

on the opposite side of the valley, it made straight for this house. We didn't know what to do - whether to remain in the house or to come out. Having been outside, we had just got inside when my daughter, Kathleen, said she would like to have another look at it, and when we got outside the door, the airship was exactly over the house, and it was a mass of flames, but I believe the engines were still going. It was sailing horizontally. It was so low that I thought it was going to fall into the pond close by the house, but it passed over the lane into the Church Field and there fell to the earth nose downwards. I went at once to the field and saw there the Zeppelin, a burning, blazing heap. Several people came out and assisted the police to throw water upon it. We were afraid to go too near at first, because there was a constant popping of bullets from the machine gun.

I helped to release one of the Germans from the wreckage. The lower part of his body was burnt, but his chest and face were not much disfigured as far as I could see in the semidarkness. He had his hand on a lever, and his head was bent forward. I lifted up his head and found he was dead. We then pulled him out and laid him with the others beside the hedge.
Source: *Herts. Advertiser, 9th September 1916.*

Inquest and funeral of the crew.
On the day following, Monday 4th September, Dr. Lovell Drage, the Coroner held an inquest on the bodies of the sixteen members of the Zeppelin crew at The Plough Inn, Cuffley. It became clear that a British airman - Lieutenant William Robinson had been responsible for bringing down the airship, under difficult and dangerous circumstances. The King has graciously awarded him the Victoria Cross for his conspicuous bravery.

The War Office states that the dead men were to be given a military funeral. The following day, the bodies of the crew, having lain in Cuffley Church were brought out and placed on the back of a lorry and a trailer behind. The coffin of the Commander was placed on a separate motor wagon. The procession journeyed to Potter's Bar

Cemetery where a brief service was held by the Revd. G.R.P. Preston, Vicar of Potter's Bar. Arrangements for the funeral were made by members of the *Royal Flying Corps*.
Source: *Herts. Advertiser, 9th September 1916.*

Doctors joining up.

Sir Charles Longmore, Clerk to the Herts. Insurance Committee reports on the arrangements made by doctors who are joining up:
Doctors A. Binning (Hatfield), H.R. Grellet (Hitchin), C.E. O'Keeffe (Tring) and H.C. Wimble (Oxhey) are joining the *Royal Army Medical Corps*, and they had made arrangements to secure medical attendance and treatment for the insured people on their lists, by other doctors.
Source: *Herts. Advertiser, 9th September 1916.*

Painting a historic episode.

It is interesting to note that the Admiralty have decided that the name and deed of Jack Cornwell, the sixteen year-old boy who, although mortally wounded, stuck to his post in H.M.S.Chester in the Battle of Jutland, shall be honoured in every possible way as an incentive to the boys of the future, and that the commission of this heroic lad has been given to Mr. Frank O. Salisbury, so well known in Hertfordshire. Mr. Salisbury has ascertained from Cornwell's mother that another son, a few months younger, is very much like the boy who has laid down his life, this he will be considerably helped in his difficult posthumous portrait. "Dr. Macnamara," said Mr. Salisbury, "has promised that every possible advantage and convenience shall be accorded me. I expect that I shall do a large amount of the detail actually in the ship itself, and I am hoping that the captain will be able to reconstruct the scene for me to a great extent". Mr. Salisbury will begin his work soon, and it is hoped that the picture will be ready for the [Royal] Academy in the Spring.
Source: *Herts. Advertiser, 23rd September 1916.*

Utter desolation on the battlefields.

The Revd. F.H. Wheeler, writes to the members of Trinity Congregational Church, St. Albans:

Villages, the names of which are in your newspapers day by day, are as familiar to me as those near your own city. But no words of mine can convey an adequate sense of the utter desolation of these hard-fought fields. Villages have been so completely wiped out that only a few charred tree stumps remain to indicate where once children played and the labourer returned at evening to his cottage home. There are hillsides so ploughed up by shells that scarcely a square inch of grass remains - in which Trinity Church could be comfortably placed, the tombs of perhaps a hundred fighting men.

I have walked in these captured villages, and explored these German trenches, with their maze of subterranean passages and dugouts, three storeys down, replete with every comfort. I have tasted the effects of "gas" and crouched in shell holes and trenches from the too pressing attention of enemy shells. I have carried the wounded down these scarred hillside, and buried the dead by moonlight on fields of battle where they fell. I have worked with our splendid doctors, and succoured those - British and German - who could thank me only with their eyes. I have met our men in all the conditions of their life, and shared their perils, hopes and fears.

Source: *Herts. Advertiser, 28th September 1916.*

Film of the Battle of the Somme.

Viscountess Grimston writes to her husband who is away on business:

Arthur [her brother] has come back from Egypt, where he has been guarding Turkish prisoners on two months sick leave, after having had pleurisy. He looks very well, better than I've seen him looking.

As soon as May goes I'll get him to come down here. I went up to see him at Aunty's yesterday and we sent to see the Battle of the Somme [film] at the Scala. There were crowds being turned away there, so we went to the Marble Arch cinema, where we eventually got in. The pictures are wonderfully taken, and give one a vivid idea of what it is

147

like out there. One sees the actual advance out of the trenches, and a good way across no man's land until the few mén who haven't, by that time fallen, disappear into the smoke which hangs over the enemy trenches.

Mrs. Glossop got the news of the death of her son, Bertram, on the Somme. This only leaves her Billy, who had to rejoin his ship yesterday. Poor little woman. Bertram had been twice wounded.

There was a nice thing at Bricket House yesterday. The man who usually helps to clean *Ward D* was reading his newspaper, and thought I wouldn't disturb him, so began cleaning round the ward alone. The only other occupant was a Scottie, who wasn't fit to help me. I was quite unconscious that he had noticed the other man's omission until I heard "Will ye no help the lassie"?
Source: *Gorhambury Collection.*

Prisoners of War Help Committee.

Mr. W. Duoro Hoare, Honorary Secretary, writes to the Mayor of St.Albans:
25th September. Dear Mr. Mayor, You will remember that your predecessor in July 1915 signed an appeal for funds for the above which was sent out to all the Hertfordshire papers: I was appointed Honorary Secretary to it.

The Fund has progressed satisfactorily ever since and is still providing for every known prisoner in the *Bedfordshire Regiment* who comes from Hertfordshire, the *Herts. Territorials* and any Herts men who are not provided for by their Regimental fund. We send our men a 5s 0d parcel every week, 4lbs. of bread from Berne, weekly, and occasional gifts of tobacco and cigarettes. We also try to provide them, as far as possible, with any little extra for which they ask.

Under the Act of Parliament which has recently been passed the Accounts have to be audited every three months and a Committee has to be formed and the Charity registered. This I have taken steps to do and I enclose a copy of the signed Balance Sheet up to the 15th

September this year. The Lord Lieutenant and the Vice Lieutenant [Lord Hampden and Lord Essex] will serve on the committee and I shall be most grateful if you will allow me to add your name to it.
Source: *Hertfordshire Record Office. St. Albans City Archives.*

The audited statement of receipts and expenditure from 6th July 1915 to the 15th September 1916. recorded receipts of £1,796 4s 10d, with £920 5s 5d in hand.

Wounded arrive at Napsbury Railway Station.
Work of the 3rd Battalion,
Hertfordshire Volunteer Regiment: St. Albans Ambulance Section.

In spite of the fact that the train was due to reach Napsbury at the inconvenient time of 1.15 in the afternoon, thirty members of the Section paraded in Marlborough-road at 12.45 and were conveyed to the hospital station in the fine new ambulance waggons presented for use of the section by Messrs. Freshwater and Messrs. Lee.

The men were punctually on the spot, but the Red Cross train did not arrive arrive until nearly two o'clock. Meanwhile the ambulance men got all their stretches in readiness, with blankets, pillows, rugs etc. in position. The two new waggons were joined by five others belonging to the British Red Cross Society and the St. John Ambulance Detachment bringing more stretchers and other necessities. Eventually the long hospital train, bearing its weight of patiently borne agony, drew slowly up to the station, and backed to the little siding platform, which became again a very hive of activity.

First out, were the seventy "sitting" cases, who were able to walk to the motors and ambulance cars waiting to convey them to the hospital.

As each case left the train the word "surgical" or "medical" as the case may be, was announced, and the carriers were directed by Dr. Wells to this or that waggon, and the driver again, was directed to the east or the west hospital. Every patient wore a ticket, explaining who he was, and the nature of his trouble.

There was no jarring, no undue hurry, and yet, with all the great care exercised, the removal was quickly effected. It was easy to see that the wounded themselves appreciated the little acts of kindness accorded them. In some cases a pillow was raised for an uncomfortable patient; in others, a blanket or rug was re-arranged; tired, or perhaps sleepless eyes were thoughtfully shielded from the sun during a momentary wait.

One poor fellow had to handled with especial care; he had several ribs fractured, and was in a severe condition; in one or two other cases, limbs had already been amputated; while many legs and arms were fixed in bandages. In one case a young fellow's face was marked and marred with shot; in another the whole head and nearly all the face was swathed in bandages. It was astonishing, however, how many were cheerful, and were calmly smoking cigarettes - surely our soldiers' greatest solaces under all conditions! - and it was somewhat amusing to see how nearly all "hung-on" to the little printed cotton bag, containing one knows not what valuable articles.

As each two or the long coaches were cleared, the train was drawn up a little further to bring two more opposite the platform. The seven ambulance waggons passed unceasingly to and fro, Dr. Wells directed the whole of the removals, and by three o'clock the work was completed, and the last batch were on their way to the hospital.

Then the stretchers were closed, the blankets, rugs and pillows were gathered together, and placed in the waggons, members of the Section taking their places with them, and in twenty minutes the peacefulness of the pastoral scene, temporarily disturbed, re-asserted itself, for train, wounded, motor waggons, ambulance men, and even the Stationmaster had vanished - gone to other necessary duties.
Source: *Herts. Advertiser, 28th September 1916.*

150

Royston Emergency Committee.
Precautions to be taken against Air Raids.

Immediately it is known that a hostile aircraft is in the neighbourhood, the Public are requested to put their Houses, Shops and other buildings in darkness either by the aid of very dark blinds or putting the lights out altogether so that no visible light may be seen from the outside.

All Special Constables have been ordered to turn out on duty at once, on hearing officially of such aircraft, and see that all lights in the neighbourhood where they reside, including all street lamps are, at once, put out, and not re-lighted until the Police say all danger is past.

Source: *Hertfordshire Record Office. D/P/13/29/18.*

Zeppelin crashes at Oakmere Farm, Potter's Bar.
Sunday, 1st October 1916.

Mr. R.E. Groves, principal, St. Albans School of Art and Crafts, a member of the 3rd Battalion, Herts. Volunteer Regiment had an excellent view of the death struggles of the ill-fated Zeppelin from his residence in Blenheim Road, St. Albans:
It was about a quarter to eleven on Sunday night when we received the alarm and at once we went into Sandpit-lane, where we distinctly saw a Zeppelin. It was picked out by searchlights and from that time they did not let it go, except momentarily. It manoeuvred about a great deal and seemed to be using its utmost endeavours to escape from the range of the searchlights, darting first this way, then that, and then shooting upwards. It reminded me more than anything else of a fish in a small pond of water trying to escape.

We distinctly saw through field-glasses, shells bursting above the Zeppelin. Then a lull came in the firing, and after a second or two, a small glow appeared at the nose of the Zeppelin, which at that time, looked like a long silver pencil, owing to its great height.

The tiny glow rapidly swelled out into a big round ball of light, and the huge thing turned on its end and nose-dived towards the earth.
Source: *Herts. Advertiser, 7th October 1916.*

The farmer upon whose land at Oakmere Farm, the Zeppelin fell, gave this account of his experience to a "Daily Chronicle" representative:
We were awakened by the sound of the guns and we got up. I went into the garden and from where I stood the Zeppelin seemed to be right overhead. Thinking she might be preparing to drop bombs, I brought my wife and two children into the garden away from the house.

We had not been watching it many moments when the airship burst into flame. It was then, apparently, right over my house, and looked as though it would fall right across the roof. It was burning furiously, and blazing masses were flying away from it during its descent. As it got lower and lower - it did not seem to fall very quickly - I saw it would fall into the fields behind my farm buildings. I ran through the stable yard and down a by-lane leading to some grass fields. In the corner of one of these were some large haystacks, and I was afraid that these might be set on fire. When I reached the spot I found they were all right: but about 200 yards away the remains of the Zeppelin lay blazing furiously.

I dare not go very near to it as the heat was very great and because ammunition was exploding at intervals. I afterwards discovered that this was machine-gun ammunition and it seemed that a large quantity was carried as some was found in boxes unexploded, afterwards. The Zeppelin had broken into two pieces.
Source: *Herts. Advertiser, 7th October 1916.*

Captain H. G. Bushby, Manor House, Wormley, on forty-eight hours leave from Banbury recounts:
At about 11.55 p.m. I woke hearing loud bangs of either bombs or guns

We went to the windows and to the south saw a Zeppelin marked out by two searchlights. It looked like aluminium, softly lit up. It shifted its position to the west and after a minute or two seemed to become stationery at a point I thought was over Chipping Barnet. The guns fired incessantly, and one saw big fat sparks round the Zeppelin. Four times I heard the "whew" of shells - apparently very near. The Zeppelin tried to escape - turning round - rising - and at once moving quickly to the west. The searchlights still held it. Then all the firing ceased and there seemed an endless pause with nothing happening, but there was a continuous rumbling sound overhead from (to me) invisible aeroplanes.

Then there was one loud bang and then another pause. Then I saw a red disc which grew to about the size of the sun, then a red flame which spread until half the Zeppelin was burning. By then I was cheering (in the morning and for two or three days after, I could scarcely speak).

The Zeppelin now began to dive nose down and the flame became a large ragged flare in the sky, breaking up here and there into lesser flames and the whole gradually descending. When it was nearly burnt out it descended to below the tree tops. In the sky a green light: the sign that all landing stages are to be lit up for the aeroplanes to descend. Soon after, I went to bed at 12.10 a.m. on 2nd October.

After breakfast I went to the village and found that boys had bicycled to Potter's Bar and came back with lots of aluminium. I bought two bits of strutts from Reggie Shaw for 5s 0d!
Source: *Hertfordshire Record Office. Captain Busby's Diary, part.2.*

An inquest was held at the Potter's Bar Cottage Hospital on Wednesday. Two facts were disclosed: the Commander had been Captain Mathy and that the airship had been the L31. The funeral of the commander and the crew of the wrecked Zeppelin took place at Potter's Bar cemetery on Thursday. Great secrecy was observed and in consequence few people witnessed it. The arrangements were similar

to those made, in September, for those killed in the airship that was brought down at Cuffley. An Army Chaplain officiated assisted by the Vicar of Potter's Bar. The Commander's coffin was carried by officers of the *Royal Flying Corps* as were the crew. At the conclusion the "Last Post" was sounded.
Source: *Herts Advertiser, 7th October 1916.*

Another military funeral.

A full military funeral was accorded Private John Bonney Eyles, who recently died at Napsbury Hospital [on 3rd October 1916], aged 39 years, from the effect of wounds. The interment was in the "Soldiers' Corner, St. Albans cemetery on Monday. The Revd. Dr. Chadwick officiated, The Royal West Kents supplied the firing party and buglers to play the "Last Post"

Application for exemption.

Application was made on behalf of Frank Leonard Whiteman, aged 40 years, married, of No.28, Abbey Mill-lane, who is sexton at the Cathedral. The Churchwardens, in their application to the St. Albans Tribunal stated that Mr. Whiteman is the only available man who knows his way around the passages of the Abbey in case of fire and that he understands the fire appliances of the Cathedral. He winds the Abbey clock, chimes the bells for services and attends to the chimes, which ring every quarter of an hour. He was also the grave digger. It was necessary for any person who had the care of the safety of the Abbey to be thoroughly well acquainted with all these things and the access to and unlocking of the doors of the approaches to these passages. It was a most complicated system of passages, and in case of any outbreak of fire, the Dean would be absolutely helpless without this man's assistance. It would take years to train someone else! The St. Albans Tribunal refused the application. Asked if the St. Albans Fire Brigade were cognisant of these passages. The answer given was that they were not, not without the assistance of the Applicant who will not to be called up until 1st November. The Abbey authorities were told to introduce an understudy as soon as possible.
Source: *Herts. Advertiser, 7th October 1916.*

Hostile Aircraft.
Letter to all Section Leaders, Special Constabulary, from Hertfordshire County Police Reserve, Hatfield.

In the event of any hostile aircraft being brought to earth in the County, all Special Constables in the neighbourhood should proceed to the spot without delay, and place themselves at the disposal of the senior police officer present. Should the special constables arrive on the scene before a sufficient number of troops can be collected to guard the wreck, they should do all in their power to prevent the remains of the hostile aircraft from being disturbed by the public. Particular care should be taken to prevent any dead bodies from being searched or anything taken from them until the arrival of a specially accredited military officer who will supervise the proceedings, and any fragments of paper or documents or maps that may have fallen from the airship should be carefully preserved until the officer's arrival.

When released from these duties by the military, the special constables will do their utmost to prevent members of the public from carrying off any part of the wreck or its contents or any detached portions that may have fallen at a distance. It is of the utmost importance to the naval and military authorities that all fragments shall be secured, however insignificant that they may appear at first sight. Any person suspected of removing any wreckage or other articles from a place where hostile aircraft, or the wreck thereof descended, is guilty of an offence under the *Defence of the Realm (Consolidated) Regulations*, and may if necessary be arrested and searched.

(Signed) Major S. St.Leger, Chief Staff Officer, Special Constabulary.
Source: *Hertfordshire Record Office.*

Hertfordshire Regiment.

A lieutenant of the Dorset Regiment writes to his parents, on the Wednesday following the "Big Advance":

The *Herts Regiment* did magnificently. They took four machine guns, several officers and 800 prisoners.

Source: *Herts. Advertiser, 11th November 1916.*

155

Fighting on the Somme.

Signaller T.W. Goddard, formerly of Bricket Wood, now of Abbots Langley, serving with London Regiment writes:

A few remarks might be of interest of the fighting now taking place on the Somme. It is quite different from what we experienced at Loos. Instead of the well-dug trenches, we get these hurriedly made, with just sufficient cover to walk along. One is surprised to find that, even as far back as we have driven the Hun, he has been able to build "funk holes" sometimes to the depth of 20 feet. Possibly some French or British prisoner has been forced into some work. These are simply shafts with wooden stays as supports. Out last H.Q. was in one of these, the most uncomfortable we have struck . My little office was composed of earth taken out of the side of a trench with a door and a small quantity of earth on top. It was not exactly shell-proof but it was dry, and with a little doubling up of oneself, it was a fairly comfortable "kip". We had six days here.

At first you imagine that at last we have the Germans "out of the blue". Very little barbed wire is seen: the ground near the trenches is a mess of shell holes. The absence of houses is very noticeable; some of the villages have become notorious are passed through without knowing it. The country is open; few villages and woods. It is the latter where the Huns love to place their machine guns to mow down our men. The woods are badly battered about by shells, but in a few cases there is a fair amount of undergrowth. Before the war the land was purely agricultural, but since the German occupation it has not been touched, so it reminds one of our moors. It is quite a common sight to come across large quantities of German shells of all sizes; now and again a howitzer with the top of its muzzle blown away, so as to be of no value to the wretched British.

The great question, is whether, with the advance made, it is worth the terrible cost. The cost of one small five minute bombardment is tremendous. To the German it is comparatively cheap, as he is checking us mostly by the machine gun, whilst we, to make any progress at all, must use heavy artillery. Before I went down to the

156

Somme I was inclined to think that our offensive was a failure, because on paper we had little to show for the number of lives lost and shells expended. But now I would strongly advise us to continue the struggle so long as the weather permits. Out losses are heavy, but so are the Germans. This must be so, as he is not allowed time to build deep dugouts to counteract our shell fire. Our artillery fire is almost continuous. The trenches occupied before 1st July were so constructed that the large shell sent over would only knock the trench about, and as soon as we started Fritz would adjourn to his dugouts and, with his eye to the periscope, sit in perfect safety.

Source: *Herts Advertiser, 11th November 1916.*

A splendid achievement.

A Lance-Corporal in the Herts Regiment writes from Norfolk War Hospital where he is lying, wounded:

16th November, - I have been admitted into hospital with a shrapnel wounds to the left ankle, received in the advance of Monday morning. Out Battalion moved to Schwaben Redoubt on Sunday morning and took up their 'jumping off' or attacking position on the north-east face of the redoubt in the early morning, on the right of our Brigade. Then followed a tiring time for us - a wait of some three or four hours in shell holes until the appointed time for the attack. All the while our 'heavies' were pounding the Hun trenches into shambles It was very misty when at 5.45 we started forward at the same time that our guns opened a violent barrage on our first objective. I have seen a few barrages, but never one to touch the one we followed that morning. It seemed like a dense cloud of flame moving slowly along in front of us. It was heavy going, the ground churned up and each shell hole half full of water. Men began to fall - two fellows one on either side of me were hit. As I was bandaging them I felt my left ankle go a bit numb. I felt it but could feel any hole or blood so I went on again (this was about 6 o'clock). This time I lost direction in the mist and found myself with the Battalion on our left. I struck off to the right and came across parties of Huns coming back to our lines yelling "Kamerad, Mercy" hands aloft, and looking as frightened as I have seen anyone look.

Source: *Herts. Advertiser, 25th November 1916.*

157

Ministry of Food.
London and Home Counties Local Rationing Scheme.
Table of equivalent weights of meat.

- In the case of uncooked Butcher's meat the following value (including pork) or offal 5p worth.

- In the case of other uncooked meat the following weights:

- **1. Poultry, Game, etc.**

- (a) a bird delivered without feathers, but with offal 12½oz.

- the same without offal 9oz.

- (b) rabbit or hare, without skin, with offal 10oz.

- the same without offal 7½oz.

- (c) Venison or horsemeat with the bone 6oz.

- the same without bone 5oz.

- **2. Bacon and Ham**

- uncooked with the bone as usually delivered 4oz.

- the same, without bone 3oz.

- **3. Sausages**

- (a) first quality (not less than 67% of butcher's meat) 6oz.

- (b) second quality (not less than 50% butcher's meat 8oz.

Source: *Hertfordshire Record Office. D/EHcZ3 (edited)*

158

In a German trench.

Corporal P.M.Hampton, Canadian Expeditionary Force writes to his father, Mr. C.Hampton, School House, Wheathamstead:

On Sunday morning just before daybreak we charged. Out company was in the first wave. My first experience was getting blown into a shell hole on top of our Sergeant-Major who was wounded in the arm. I did my best to fix his first field dressing, and had just got it ready when the stretcher-bearer came. I went forward only to get caught on some barbed wire. I got my pants torn and lost two sand bags. Anyway I got free and got into Fritz's trench. I saw two of them on their knees begging for mercy from a lad my own size. The trench was a shambles. We had three German machine guns that had never had the chance to open fire as our artillery had slaughtered the crews; and what Germans were alive were the most miserable specimens of human beings. They begged and prayed to be sent back to our lines, and were willing to give us everything in the shape of money and watches. They were all searched and escorted back. Then we put the trench into shape for repelling a counter attack. They made three attacks and finally got us out at about 4.30 in the afternoon. We had held their trench since five o'clock that morning.

Source: *Herts Advertiser, 2nd December 1916.*

Rescue from the sea.

First Air-Mechanic Arthur H.Coburn writes to his wife of an rescue in Scotland:

This afternoon we heard the guns of some ship in distress. We all had to turn out and tried to throw a life-line to the wreck which was three or four hundred yrds from the beach. The sea was continually breaking over the ship and there were seven men hanging on to the ropes. From the beach we could see those from the barracks coming along with the lifeboat and we all had to shove the boat out into the sea. Talk about a drenching! We were right up to our waists, and every now and then the waves went right over us. Several of the men were knocked over, but none of us was hurt. In a few minutes the seven men were taken on board. Then we had another soaking, pulling the lifeboat in.

Source: *Herts Advertiser, 2nd December 1916.*

The Long Trench.

Lord Cavan writes of nature studies for Wheathamstead Parish Magazine:

One hot August day I approached the mouth of the Long Trench and was glad to arrive safely with my companion in its towering walls. The first thing that struck me was the number of holes about a foot or eighteen inches below the surface. I expect a good naturalist could have picked out at once the mole-runs from the rat-runs and the countless mouse-runs, but the first captive I saw was a weasel. He fled along the hard trodden bottom of the trench until he came to a softer spot, where there was a trench-board; under this he dived. But neither he nor I had noticed a hanging thistle and a tiny ledge where the pick had not cut clean, and we saw the glorious jump for freedom - on to the thistle, on to the ledge, up again under the hanging wild convolvulus and so to the surface.

A little further on I counted six kestrels, who must have been happy to a degree long denied to their parents. Two years of *"chase defendure"*, no keepers, and in all the vast strip just behind and between the lines, not even a farmer's boy. Fields of perfect corn, thistles, self-sown rye grass, and all the riot of wild flowers that grow in the chalk. Truly the vermin are enjoying the war.

Our Long Trench had been dug for the great battle, and there had been no time so far for revetment, but it will have to be done. Having noticed this we proceeded and came to a 'Seven Dials' luckily all labelled. No one is supposed to take trench maps of our own lines into our trenches, and rightly so, but I defy any officer to find his way when he first comes to a new area without one. In his case I had broken the rules, for I was learning my line, and had a skeleton map, and so took the right street for the spot I was making.

To one coming out of Flanders, where all is flat, to a country where hills do roll, is a true joy. Anyone who has the rudiments of the stalking science can lie hidden, yet observing, and can see not only the enemy's line, but miles and miles behind it.

Source: *Herts. Advertiser, 2nd December 1916.*

160

Tea at Talbot House, Poperinghe.

22nd December. - Each week I have little festivities for various units in the neighbourhood, e.g. nine boys from St. Albans and Wheathamstead way came to tea, and a Sergeant-Major of Police in to supper on Wednesday. So the world wags. .

Source: *Clayton, Revd. Philip "Tubby". Letters from Flanders: some war-time letters to his mother.*

More war shrines dedicated.

On Monday, the Bishop of St. Albans dedicated the tenth war shrine and roll of honour placed in the Abbey Parish, this being placed on the Clock Tower, High street, St. Albans.

A large and reverent gathering assembled in the vicinity of the Clock Tower, among them were several bereaved parents. A procession left the Abbey and went by way of Holywell hill and High street which included the boys of the Abbey choir, Lieutenant A. Williams, carrying the processional banner, Abbey clergy including the Dean, the Very Revd. G.W. Blenkin and the Bishop of St. Albans.

The Bishop, in dedicating the shrine, said: "*To the Glory of God and in memory of the men from these streets who have fallen in the war and in honour of the men who are serving, I dedicate this shrine and roll of honour*". His lordship then led the Lord's Prayer after which he said: "*Oh God, bless our King and country, help our leaders, our soldiers and sailors, relieve the wounded, comfort the prisoners and missing, grant rest and peace to the fallen, make brave the hearts of those who are at home, and grant us victory over our enemies, and to all mankind bring the blessings of peace*".

The Revd. E.H. Evans then read out the 45 names on the list, including four who have fallen in action:- Bertram Glossop, *19th Devons*; Edwin Glossop, *Somerset Light Infantry*; Thomas Powell, *Herts Regiment*; and Arthur Holmes, *Norfolk Regiment*. The Bishop then followed with a few words of encouragement to the bereaved and then pronounced the blessing.

The shrine, like the others placed in different parts of the Abbey Parish, has been made by the boys at *St. Albans Technical School* under the supervision of Mr. R.R. Bunn and his assistant instructors. The rolls themselves have been prepared by lady workers. Above the framework are the seven flags of the Allies, and on each side is a receptacle holding flowers. The result is a bright and very attractive memorial to those who have made and are making so great a sacrifice on behalf of their country.
Source: *Herts. Advertiser, 9th December 1916.*

Flying Fatality.

Lieutenant Crawford Thomas Miller was killed on Friday, 8th December 1916 by the collapse of an aeroplane in which he was taking a flight alone. He was 21 years of age and is home was in Ontario, Canada. He belonged to a Canadian Regiment but was attached to the *Royal Flying Corps*. The Coroner's Inquest held at Napsbury Military Hospital found that the deceased who has been taking his first solo flight in an aircraft of this type, and the jury decided that he met his death by misadventure, and that the accident was due to an error of judgement by the pilot whilst about to land.

There were many people in Fleetville and at St. Albans Cemetery when Lieutenant Miller's remains were buried on Friday, 15th December. The service was conducted by the Revd. H.W. Taylor, nonconformist chaplain at Napsbury. Six officers and six sergeants of the *Royal Flying Corps* acted as bearers. Three volleys were fired over the open grave and twelve buglers clarioned forth the sounds of "The Last Post".
Source: *Herts. Advertiser, 16th. December 1916.*

Recreation Rooms opened.

The Committee of the old Abbey Institute have generously placed the the Institute at the disposal of the Senior Chaplain to the Forces, for the purposes of a soldiers' recreation centre.
Source: *Herts. Advertiser, 16th December 1916.*

Contents: 1917

Somme Battle Honours.

It was officially announced in July, that the King had been pleased to appoint Major-General the Earl of Cavan to be a Knight of the Order of St. Patrick [K.P.].

In the Battle of the Somme honours announced at the end of 1916, Major-General, the Earl of Cavan, K.P., C.B., M.V.O., was raised to the rank of Lieutenant-General.

Source: *Herts. Advertiser, 6th January 1917.*

Military Honours, 1916.

Many military honours have been awarded to officers and men from the county during the year, including the following:

Victoria Cross

Corporal Alfred Burt [Hertford], *1st Hertfordshire Regiment;*
Lieutenant Albert Smith [Burnley and formerly of St.Albans], *5th East Lancashire Regiment, Territorial Force;*
Captain Charles Vickers [billeted in Harpenden, 1914], *7th Robin Hood Battalion;*

Mrs Warner, Cannon Street, St.Albans mother of Pte. Edward Warner, *Bedfordshire Regiment,* attended Buckingham Palace by invitation on 16th November and received from the hands of King George the honour that had been given to her dead son;

Military Cross

Second Lieutenant Paul Dangerfield [St.Albans], *1st East Kent Regiment;*
Captain J.N.Donaldson [St. Albans], *K.R.R.*
Captain Leonard F.Beal [St. Albans], *Bedfordshire Regiment;*
Captain G.F.Bailey [St. Albans], *Yorks and Lancs. Regiment;*
Lieutenant Malcolm Hancock [St. Albans], *Northampton Regiment;*
Second Lieut. H.B.Secretan [Leverstock Green], *West Surrey Regiment;*
Second Lieut. J.A.Bessant [Leverstock Green], *Royal Engineers;*

Military Medal
Sergeant J. Allen [Roestock, nr. Hatfield], *Bedfordshire Regiment.*
Corporal G. Callow [St. Albans], *Hertfordshire Regiment.*
Gunner William Clough [Fleetville, St.Albans], *R.H.A..*
Private R. Folks [St. Albans], *Middlesex Regiment.*
Corporal G. Callow [St. Albans], *Hertfordshire Regiment.*
Private Tom Gray [St. Albans], *Royal Army Medical Corps.*
Private W. Groom [Hatfield], *Hertfordshire Regiment.*
Private J.E.Humbles [Colney Street], *Bedfordshire Regiment.*
Corporal Philip Kingham [St.Albans], *Hertfordshire Regiment.*
Corporal Gerald Massey [St.Albans], *R.G.A.*
Private Alfred Pratt [Redbourn], *Bedfordshire Regiment.*
Sergeant G. Sansom [Redbourn],Worcestershire Regiment.
Corporal J.C.Stuart-Richardson [St. Albans], *Royal Engineers.*
Sergeant S.C.Sweet [Radlett], *Army Service Corps, Motor Transport.*
Lance-Corporal A.Tibbett [St. Albans], *Bedfordshire Regiment.*
Sergeant F. Whitlock [London Colney], *Yorkshire Regiment.*
Private M. Winch [Codicote], *Bedfordshire Regiment.*

Distinguished Service Order
Major L.A. Fanshawe [St.Albans], *Royal Artillery.*

Distinguished Conduct Medal
Corporal H. Brazier, *Bedfordshire Regiment.*
Lance-Corporal Ernest De'Ath [Boreham Wood].
Private Gitto Goldhawk [Kimpton], *Bedfordshire Regiment.*
Corporal J. Ivory [Markyate], *Bedfordshire Regiment.*
Sergeant Frank Neal [Wheathamstead], *Bedfordshire Regiment.*
Private N. Riddell [Watford], *Bedfordshire Regiment.*
Sergeant Oliver Summers [London Colney] (killed in action, 1st July).
Source: *Herts. Advertiser, 6th January 1917.*

Work of the Military Tribunals
The increasing demand upon our military strength, inevitably led to
the two Military Service Acts, which automatically enrolled all men
between the ages of 19 and 40 in the Army, and thus brought the

European turmoil closer to every home. The advent of conscription greatly increased the work which devolved upon the local and county tribunals, formed in November 1915. At the present time the St. Albans City Tribunal have considered approximately a thousand applications, while the county body have decided about double that number of appeals.

Source: *Herts. Advertiser, 6th January 1917.*

Conscientious objectors.

Four sons of Mr. A.R. Dunn, The Aubreys, Redbourn applied for exemption from military service on conscientious grounds. The County Appeal Tribunal ordered that they take up work of a national interest on a farm. At a later date, another son applied for exemption on similar grounds and was also directed to undertake work on a farm.

Source: *Herts. Advertiser, 6th January 1917.*

From St. Saviour's Parish Magazine.

Local men tell of their experiences whilst on active service:

"I always wanted to see other parts of the world, and although the conditions on a transport are not what one would naturally desire, we can certainly get some fun out of it. When in France, I did not have a turn in the trenches, and only got within a mile or so of the front line; my time was mostly spent in travelling with a full pack. I now have arrived at my destination [in the region of Salonica]. At present I am under canvas - rather a crowd with thirteen in a bell tent. The weather is not cold, except at nights, only very cloudy. It is interesting studying the ways and the doings of the people of the land. They look very picturesque in their coloured clothes, and I have seen some ploughing done in the good old fashioned way, with oxen and a wooden plough, after the style of two thousand years ago".

Private Archie Lawrence writes:

"We are living with some Belgian refugees who have told us something of the terrible hardships which they endured when retreating before the German army. There is one tall, bearded old gentleman, who hobbles along with a stoop. When fleeing as fast as he could from the Germans, he found on the roadside an exhausted little child of three years of age. With great difficulty, and in spite of many obstacles in the way, he carried the poor youngster, and now he tends and keeps him as if he was his very own [child]. How few people in England can yet realise what war really is"!

Sapper William C. Potton writes:
I have had to undergo an operation in France. This has been successful and I have made a good recovery. I thoroughly enjoy the services at the military church at the Base, where I am now stationed.

Private Haddow writes:
I have had a long [spell] in two hospitals and am now recovering from my wounds, and am having a short time at home.

Robert Folkes has been promoted to Corporal and is to have, shortly, a well-earned run home.

Driver Cyril Calvert is still in France, and says that they have been through some very trying times, and extremely bad weather. Since his recovery from an accident, he has been serving with the Divisional Ambulance Column.

Lance-Corporal John Watson says that they are still under canvas and found it difficult to keep dry. This is an interesting town, and if it were summer, instead of winter time, it would be a pleasant place to stay in; but under present conditions of short days and bad weather, it is impossible to enjoy the beauties of the surroundings.
Source: *Herts. Advertiser, 13th January 1917.*

In France en-route for Salonica.
Sergeant E.G.C. Ward, with a Signalling Section, now in Salonica, writes to his parents, Mr. & Mrs Ward, 137 Fishpool Street
We had a lovely trip across France - 51 hours in a train! The scenery was very tame and monotonous at first but became quite great as we

progressed. There are large plantations of olive trees and oranges grown in back gardens. For miles we ran alongside a river edged with rows of straight trees all painfully alike. The mountains lay a little bit back from us and the sides of many hills were ploughed - up a slope as steep as Holywell hill, or rather down, as a plough could never have got up when in the ground. The towns look wonderfully clean, but very drowsy. The roads are white and straight. In the north the roads are usually lined with black poplar but down south the chief tree that strikes one is the Cyprus.

Source: *Herts Advertiser, 13th January 1917.*

The Middlesex Roll Call.

A poem, written by Lance-Corporal A.J.Baldwin but sent to the Herts Advertiser by Private F.J. Payne, Middlesex Regiment, of 19 London Road, St. Albans:

'Thiepval'.

The charge it was over, the battle was won,
Some girl lost her sweetheart, some mother her son,
Sadly we heard of a comrade who fell
For the honour of Britain at that fight - "Thiepval".

Their honour they won in that glorious fight,
Those lads who had died for the cause of the right.
There's a price to be paid - the the Germans know well -
For the cold-blooded murder done at "Thiepval".

We fell in for roll-call at the close of the fight,
And some of us there made a piteous sight,
Some never answered - one that we knew well -
For he fell like a hero at that fight - "Thiepval".

Some home will be lonely; some mother's heart sad,
Some lass will be weeping for her soldier lad
Who died in the battle; for the country he fell,
Defending his home at the fight "Thiepval".

Source: *Herts. Advertiser, 13th January 1917.*

169

Maintaining the roads and railways in France.

Mr. H.F. Mence, surveyor to *St. Albans Rural District Council* and a Lieutenant in the St. Albans Company, *Hertfordshire Volunteer Regiment* has been commissioned by the Director-General of *Military Railways and Roads* in France to raise a company of 250 Royal Engineers to go out to France to assist in the maintenance and institution of roads, tracks and railways for the use of transport and troops.

He wants men who have been used to pick and shovel work, or men who are skilled wheelwrights, carpenters and engine drivers, or who have been associated with the varied routine of navvying.

Volunteers are invited from men of and above military age. Rates of pay will be as follows: - Roadmen - 3s a day; N.C.O.'s 4s. to 7s. per day (if over military age); 1s 8d per day; N.C.O.'s 2s 6d to 5s 3d per day if of military age. In all cases the usual separation and other allowances will be paid, and rations, uniform and kit will be provided. All men will go to Borden Camp for a month's training before proceeding to France.

Source: *Herts. Advertiser, 13th February 1917.*

Hertfordshire Regiment.
Report of a raid on the night of 12th/13th February 1917.

The raiders left the canal bank and moved via La Brique and St. Jean to the front the British line and then the assembly position in No Man's Land according to programme. The whole of this movement was carried out without a hitch and without being observed by the enemy.

At Zero minus 2, the raiders advanced to their objectives. The patrol to Argyle Farm found it unoccupied. The two parties detailed to deal with No.3 and No.4 saps (deep and narrow trenches) found these obliterated and also unoccupied. Most of the remainder of the raiding party entered the German trenches and worked over the area prearranged. The found the German wire well-cut and lying about in tangled masses. It consisted principally of rusty barbed concertina wire and knife rests. The trenches themselves were badly knocked about by our shell fire. There is no doubt that the raid was a surprise to the enemy and the few men in the area were at once overpowered. Three Germans were found and one was bludgeoned and the other two captured. A number of dead Germans were seen partly buried in the damaged trench.

The raiders worked beyond their allotted area and it appears that this part of the German line was very lightly held. One N.C.O. reported that he saw a number of Germans in their support line and thinks that they were preparing to counter-attack.

Blue Rockets were fired as a a signal for the raiders to withdraw and they waited in No Man's Land to allow the enemy fire to die down. They then returned to the Canal Bank with the exception of a few who reported, in accordance with orders to Advanced Battalion Headquarters. All raiders were accounted for by 2.00 a.m. The two prisoners both belonged to the 1st Battalion, 161st Regiment. They were brought to Headquarters by 11.54 p.m. and after being searched, were sent under escort to the Officer-Commanding the 1st Battalion Cambridgeshire Regiment. The three officers who led the raid - 2nd Lieutenant F.M. Drury, 2nd Lieutenant R.L. Hardy and 2nd Lieutenant W. Thompson, all returned before Midnight. There were only four casualties, all slight.

Our artillery barrage was exceptionally good. The enemy reply was feeble and fell chiefly on or near our front line, some being sprinkled in No Man's Land. The hostile gun fire consisted of 77mm. shells and 2 or 3 'Minnies'. Small pieces of the enemy's trenches which remained intact were found to be revetted with brushwood and had plank floors. They were dry. There was no trace of gas cylinders, nor were there any arms or equipment lying about.

The raiders carried out the programme exactly as rehearsed.
Source: *Public Record Office. Herts Regiment War Diary [WO95/2590]*

National Service Committee for Hertfordshire.

The first meeting of the Committee was held on Friday at the Holborn Borough Council Offices, High Holborn, W.C. when the attendance included the vice-chairman of the County Council who was voted to the chair; Major Hamilton M.P. representing Mr Neville Chamberlain (whose inability to attend was explained as he had to attend a meeting of the War Cabinet; Mr. Walter Reynolds, High Sheriff and other representative gentlemen.

The Chairman of the meeting (Mr E.B. Barnard) explained that the Government had decided on a certain policy and considered that local authorities were the proper people to give effect to that policy.

Under the previous recruiting campaign and the two Military Service Acts, any man or his employers, considered he should not be in the Army but employed elsewhere, had the right to appeal to his fellow countrymen - people on the Tribunals, who were more or less like himself.

Major Hamilton, MP explained that Mr. Chamberlain intended to make special appeals to women, and at an early date would ask for 100,000 women to assist in agriculture. In the new scheme, the Government wanted men of military age - from 18 to 61 years to volunteer for National Service thus putting themselves at the disposal of the Government for the period of the war. It did not mean that the military age had been increased to 61, nor did it mean that men of military age will not thereby become exempt from Military Service.
Source: *Herts. Advertiser, 20th February 1917.*

Use of pigeons.

Mr. W. Beech Thomas, Place Farm, Wheathamstead talks to a gathering in the Church Schools, Wheathamstead of his experiences as a war correspondent with the Daily Mail:
During the German retreat from the Marne to the Aisne he and a colleague reached a little village, the little clock in the church tower of which it was rumoured to have been used by the Germans for

signalling, the clock hands having been used for semaphore. His friend decided to ascend to the tower to see if he could find any evidence of the occupation. After a hazardous climb he reached the clock room and was surprised to find it littered with egg shells. Evidently the Germans who had stayed there had robbed neighbouring hen roosts for their larder.

In that district, too, they saw the French people carefully tending the graves of fallen British soldiers.

When our troops had arrived in Flanders in the attempt to outflank the German armies, there were no trenches there then, but now there were trenches all the way from the North Sea to the Somme. In the front trenches the men seemed to live normal natural lives, although in many cases they were within forty yards of the enemy.

Dealing with the happenings since the "Big Push" on 1st July, Mr. Thomas told how useful pigeons are for carrying messages. There is a an Officer Commanding Pigeons which is an important branch of our Army. On one occasion when the air was thick and heavy, rendering aerial observation impossible, the telephone wires were down, and the headquarters of a corps could get no information of what was going on at the front. The Commanding Officer gave orders that any pigeon seen must be taken, even if it had to be shot. Some time later in the day a pigeon hove in sight and was captured. To its leg was attached a message which was secured and handed to the General. All crowded round with bated breath while he opened the flimsy piece of paper - and read: "I got tired of carrying this beastly bird!" It is a common thing, said Mr. Thomas, when our men made an attack, to see a man walking along with them, serenely carrying a pigeon basket.

German prisoners are very fond of writing home and receiving letters and they are inveterate grumblers: indeed they might make our our soldiers envious in this respect. If there is one thing a German likes better than being taken a prisoner it is the opportunity of getting clean. After being taken prisoners, they may be seen in their "cages" busily cleaning themselves. The men are very good-tempered, but the officers are very bad-tempered. Mr Beech Thomas said that he had often heard people in England say what they would do with German prisoners, but one did not feel that way when one saw them. He had seen an English soldier and a prisoner walking along arm-in-arm, and another helping a wounded German and giving his enemy frequent "pulls" at his cigarette.

Of the attack at Thiepval, he saw the battle from an observation post situated only 800 yards from the line from which the attack commenced. Until our artillery suddenly started a powerful barrage of fire, the scene was very peaceful. The change was wonderful - and trying. At first he could see every shell going over, but they soon became so thick to observe and made a terrible noise. He saw no men running. They climbed out of their trenches and went off leisurely, apparently. After a while, however, he did see men running, and at first had the fear that our men were retreating. Then he saw that the runners wore green uniforms and knew that they were Germans running to be taken prisoners.

The Battle of the Somme was the biggest the world has ever seen. The daily output of shells had run into millions. The result of all this artillery fire was that the land was torn up in every direction and looked to be permanently ruined.
Source: *Herts Advertiser, 27th February 1917.*

London Colney landing ground.

Situated two miles from Radlett railway station, London Colney landing ground opened in the spring of 1916. Operational squadrons of the *Royal Flying Corps* were based there until May 1917 and thereafter it was a base used for training until December 1919, initially for the R.F.C. and from 1918 onwards for the R.A.F. In the 1920s the nearby Radlett Aerodrome opened and during the Second World War a site at Salisbury Hall (north of this site) was used for the design of a de Havilland war plane.
Source: *Information supplied by Derrick Blunt/Hertfordshire Flying Club.*

Women in cowsheds.

From the cases heard by the St. Albans Rural District tribunal:
Alfred Welch, aged 32 years who was pronounced A1, of The Tin House, Beaumonts, St. Albans, ploughman with Mr. W.H. Moores, of Oaklands Farm, claimed conditional exemption because of the shortage of labour and the necessity of maintaining the food production of the country. Asked if he wanted a trained girl to do work with the cows, Mr. Moore said he knew the work and would not like to see a woman in the cowshed. He was given three months exemption from military service.
Source: *Herts. Advertiser, 10th March 1917.*

Attitudes to girls by farmers.

Mrs. Secretan protested to the St. Albans Rural District Tribunal against the rather discouraging manner in which the effort to place women workers on the land was received by many of the farmers who came before them and by some members of the Tribunal. Mr. Protheroe was shortly going to issue an appeal for hundreds of women workers, and she believed that women would respond the same as they had done to the other appeals in the past, but when they had farmers going before them for help and she offered to find girl labour, she was met with some sort of objection, such as "Girls could not sit up all night with cows calving". She did not see why suitable women could not be trained to look after cows when they were calving.

A short time ago the Committee of the *Stapleford Training Hostel* for Girls inserted an advertisement in eight local newspapers asking farmers who wanted girls to apply for them. Two replies were received. One wanted a farmworker to act as a governess to two or three children as well, and the other withdrew the application for a girl. Mrs. Secretan read a list of sixteen girls who had done most excellently in looking after dairy work under ordinary cowmen and farm labourers. Of course they could not do all the hard work, but it was the dilution of work that helped
Source: *Herts. Advertiser, 10th March 1917.*

175

War shrines dedicated.

Five new war shrines were unveiled and dedicated in the streets of St. Saviour's Parish, St. Albans on Sunday by the Vicar, the Revd. L.S. Westall. A procession was formed and paraded the streets to the different shrines. The names of 321 serving from the parish of 2,270 people at the last census. The shrines are distributed in Walton street (for Sandpit lane, Walton street and Battlefield road - 49 names; Boundary road (for Boundary road and Warwick road) - 74 names; Upper Heath road (for Heath road and Upper Heath road) - 51 names; At the Parish Hall, Culver road (for Culver road and Upper Culver road) - 95 names; and in Sandridge road - 52 names.

On Sunday evening, just before Evensong, the Dean (the Very Revd. G.W. Blenkin) dedicated four more Abbey Parish war shrines erected at the corner of Abbey Mill lane and Orchard street, Fishpool street, Temperance street and Spicer street.
Source: *Herts. Advertiser, 10th March 1917.*

On board the transport "Tyndareus".

The fact that no lives were lost in the boats was due to the behaviour of the *Middlesex Regiment* when disaster struck the transport *Tyndareus* off South Africa.

Private Alfred Arthur Bridges, of 105 Verulam road wrote to his parents: "We had a day off Cape-Town which we left at six o'clock in the morning, and twelve hours later the awful accident occurred. The courage of all was simply magnificent, and the crew worked to their best to rescue all, and I am glad that all were rescued. The ship was in a sorry plight.
Source: *Herts. Advertiser, 24th March 1917.*

Double fatality whilst flying.

The distressing aerial fatality which happened near Radlett about noon on Thursday resulted in the deaths of Flight Lieutenant E.R. Mackay (29) and Second Lieutenant G.S. Raine (24), both of the *Royal Flying*

Corps, whose machine came into collision with another machine piloted by Lieutenant William Jameson Pott, R.F.C. who lies in hospital suffering from injuries received in the collision.

At the inquest held by the Coroner, a labourer - Arthur Andrews, Hope cottages, Radlett, said whilst at work he saw seven or eight machines in the air. Two were close together - one circling and the other taking a straight course, and the latter aeroplane struck the back part of the first machine and it dropped to the ground "like a stone". Lieutenant Mackay was an extremely experienced pilot who had recently returned from the front and Lieutenant Raine was a pupil taken up for instruction. The jury returned a verdict of "Death from misadventure" in each case.

Source: ... Herts. Advertiser, March 1917.

Life at the Ruhleben Prison Camp.

Having spent nineteen months in internment in the German civilian prisoners' camp at Ruhleben, Mr. Israel Cohen, correspondent of the Globe and Glasgow Herald recounts some of his experiences:

He was arrested at the beginning of the war and was subsequently interned at the Ruhleben racecourse, where six men were placed in each of the horse boxes and 150-200 men in the hayloft. The camp was under the direction of the military authorities whose function was to prevent them from escaping, to punish them for committing any offence and to provide them with the necessities of life. They spent eightpence per man per day on rations: Breakfast consisted of coffee made with acorns without milk and sugar. For dinner they had vegetable soup with occasionally a thin shred of meat and perhaps also a bone. Sometimes the soup contained creatures, including worms and beetles! For supper they had the remains of the mid-day soup or some watery cocoa or a herring and a potato in a jacket. In addition they had ten ounces of black war bread made with flour, bran and sawdust. There were frequent outbreaks of diarrhoea. They livened their drab existence with dramatic and musical societies, sports and other athletic exercises. Many men went out of their minds!

Source: Herts. Advertiser, 30th March 1917.

Aerial Fighting.

Cecil Lewis recalls being posted to London Colney landing ground:

I was posted to London Colney to join No. 56 Squadron, which was forming to go overseas. The squadron was to be equipped with the SE 5, the last word in fighting-scouts, turned out by the Royal Aircraft Factory. It was fitted with a 140 h.p. Hispano Suiza engine and two guns: one Vickers and one Lewis. It would do 120 [miles an hour] on the level and climb 10,000 feet in 12 minutes.

When I arrived only one SE 5 had been delivered; but every day during the next fortnight before we left for France experienced pilots were rushed over to Farnborough to bring others, till, on the 5th April, the establishment of twelve was complete.

At last everyone was ready. The machines had been tuned up, the men entrained for overseas, the kits packed and sent off, and only the pilots were left with a pair of pyjamas, a toothbrush, and a towel to cram into the pockets of their flying coats when they left for France on the morrow.

Rooms had been taken in the little hotel at Radlett near by. That evening we all sat down to a cheery dinner and went early to bed, strictly sober!

Eleven o'clock next morning, the 7th April 1917 saw us all in our cockpits, warming up our engines. Because of my many trips across the Channel and my knowledge of French aerodromes we were going to, the honour of leading the squadron fell to me. Waving to our friends below as we soared above them, we climbed into formation and headed for St. Omer, via Chingford, Romford, Gravesend, Maidstone, Folkestone and Calais. The weather conditions were good, the pilots were nursing their engines and keeping fine formation. We made St. Omer in an hour and forty minutes and by four o'clock we had landed safely at Vertgaland.

Source: *Lewis, Cecil. Sagittarius Rising.*

HERTFORDSHIRE
WOMENS WAR AGRICULTURAL COMMITTEE
28 Castle Street
Hertford
April 1917

Dear Sir,

At the last meeting of the committee, the following resolutions were passed:-

(1) That the minimum wage of 18/- for National Service Volunteers should only be accepted as a starting wage for inexperienced workers, where the rate for board, lodging and washing does not exceed 13/-, thus leaving the worker a clear 3/- a week. Where the rate is higher than 13/- the commencing wage should be proportionally higher. It is hoped that in no case will it be necessary for the worker to pay more than 15/- a week for board, lodging and washing. The farmers will naturally realise that as the girls gain in experience, they will expect a higher wage.

(2) That conference is to discuss the question of local billeting and wages rates, and will be summoned in each parliamentary Division consisting of the chairman & secretary of the Divisional Selection Committee, the District Representatives of the Division, any farmers likely to be helpful, and others interested.

The conference for Mid-Herts has been fixed for May 3 1917 at [the] Town Hall, St. Albans at 3 p.m.

As the question is one of great importance, I trust that you will see your way to be present.

Yours faithfully,
LOUISA PULLER.
Organising Secretary.

Source: *Hertfordshire Record Office. St. Albans City Archives.*

179

Hertfordshire Yeomanry enter Baghdad.

Information is to hand that "our" cavalry were amongst the first to enter Baghdad, and that our 'Yeomanry literally rendered yeoman service alongside the British regular cavalry and their Indian native comrades. For obvious reasons we are unable to write specifically, but it is gratifying to learn that our Yeomanry earned unstinted praise from Sir John Maxwell [Commander in Chief, Northern Command].
Source: Herts. Advertiser, 6th April 1917.

Football in Egypt.

Trooper W.J. Symons, 'A' Squadron, Herts. Yeomanry writes:

Being a St. Albans man and a constant reader of your paper, I am sending you an account of a football final in which the Herts. Yeomanry took part, also a snapshot of the team. Can you find space to publish it, as I know what a wide circulation your paper has in Hertfordshire, and I am sure your readers would like to know how the Herts men are faring in different parts of the world during the great war. Wishing you every success for your paper.

The following is the account of the match against 'B' Squadron, Berks. Yeomanry:-
"The match took place on Christmas Day resulting in a win for the Herts Yeomanry by 3-0, whose side included Joe Lane, Blackpool's centre-forward, S.R.Judge, the Watford Orient centre-half, and several well-known Hatfield and St. Albans men. Losing the toss, Herts had to kick against a strong wind, and although Berks. pressed for a time, they could not beat Farmer, who was playing in good style. Herts then took a hand, and Judge cleverly tricking one of the backs, got clean through and scored with a well-placed shot. Half-time came with the score as above. On recommencing with the wind in their favour, Herts completely monopolised the game. Lane, who was playing centre-half, received the ball. Lane, who was playing centre-half, received the ball, cleverly beat three men, and put it in the corner of the goal with an unstoppable shot. Five minutes later Judge received a pass from Palmer and promptly added a third. From now onwards there was simply a bombardment of the Berks goal. Lane scored from a penalty kick, which was disallowed owing to an infringement. At the second

180

attempt he hit the goalkeeper, who cleared. Soon afterwards Smith headed one in which was disallowed owing to spectators crossing the touchline. The game end with the result [3 Herts to 0 Berks].

All the Herts men played well, the outstanding players being Farmer, who saved some very hot shots during the first quarter of an hour, Lane and Judge. The Herts team was: Farmer; Foster and Rolph; Palmer, Lane and Smith; Byrne, Symons, Judge, Sears and Kirby. The average for the four matches played was 26 goals for and 1 against. The winners each received an illuminated wrist watch.
Source: *Herts. Advertiser, 6th April 1917.*

Lost in Salonica.

Gunner B.Massey, R.G.A., son of Mrs. Massey, Ramsbury road, St. Albans writes:
I arrived at Salonica on 26th August 1916. After being at the Base for about two weeks, we moved off to the firing line. I had to act as convoy rider on a motor cycle. For some reason I was delayed, and when I eventually started I took a wrong road and was lost for five days. The fellows in the Battery had all given up hope off seeing me again, but at last I found them, walked into the camp covered with dust, un-shaved and having had no wash for five days. I was altogether worn out.

The same night we got into a position for action, fording the river and our heavy guns wanted some pulling along too. Being then a signaller, I had to lay out a wire, a job one does not run after. The next day we start an bombardment, and we had plenty of 'returns', two being severely wounded, and several slightly wounded, including myself - a piece of shell passing through my shirt and tearing my shoulder; quite enough to be unpleasant. After that I had a bad touch of dysentery.

I was taken off the guns, then to act as a despatch rider, motor cyclist, and the conditions for motoring out here are not at all nice. Roads are practically impassible, and quite twelve inches deep in sand in the summer time. I had a despatch to take to a certain village out here, which was being heavily shelled, and I could not see as we are not allowed to light our lamps in some parts of the country, and I rode my machine into a shell hole and pretty severely injured my leg, which turned to septic poisoning. An idea may be gained of the size of the hole when I say that we measured one and it was 16 feet across and 10 feet 7 inches deep.

I was only in the town of Salonica once, and that was quite enough too, it being a very dirty place. We get a local paper our here now and that is called "*The Balkan News*".

There are plenty of fields with tobacco growing, cotton, and melons galore during the summer months.
Source: *Herts. Advertiser, 6th April 1917.*

A St. Albans bandsman aboard the Tyndareus.

Bandsman Arthur Thomas Kerrison, eldest son of Mr. and Mrs. A. Kerrison, New Kent Road, St. Albans give another account of what happened aboard this transport:
The Admiralty transport *Tyndareus* struck a mine at 8 p.m. on 19th February off Cape Aguilhas, with a battalion of the *Middlesex Regiment* aboard. The mishap took place not far from the spot where the *Birkenhead* was lost, and never was a tradition more worthily upheld than on this occasion. The *Middlesex Regiment* to a man stood to parade, and thanks to the devotion and peseverance of the captain, ship's officers and engine room staff, the ship was saved. A strong south-easterly gale was blowing, and immediately after the explosion the ship began to settle by the head with her propeller well out of the water. The *assembly* was at once sounded, and the men put on their lifebelts and paraded in perfect order. Roll was called, and upon the order *stand easy* being given, the whole battalion began to sing *The Long Trail* and afterwards *Tipperary*.
Source: *Herts. Advertiser, 6th April 1917.*

Four fighting sons.

Throughout the war, the Hertfordshire Advertiser and St. Albans Times provided news of the men of whole families who were serving in the services. Increasingly as the war progressed these accounts, which included photographs, relayed information

182

of those who were wounded or killed in action. Here are details of one such family (as an example) who appear to have survived the war:-
The four sons of Mr. and Mrs. J.C. Blundell of 42 Culver Road, St. Albans. All the sons attended the Abbey School and the the three elder sons were choristers at St. Saviour's Church, Sandpit Lane, St. Albans.

Cpl. Joseph Horace Blundell (29) *Bedfordshire Regiment,* who went to France in the autumn of 1914 and was wounded at Mons. On his recovery he returned to his regiment and was promoted corporal, and later he took part in the "big push" of July 1916.

Driver Harry Blundell, *Herts R.F.A.* joined the Army at the outbreak of war and has been at the front in France for the past seven months.

Private George Blundell, *A.S.C.* and has now been six months at the front.

Private John Sidney Blundell, *London Regiment,* has been abroad for nine months. For six months he was in France and now is in Salonica.
Source: *Herts. Advertiser, 6th April 1917.*

Death of Baroness Kathleen Eckardstein.
granddaughter of the late Sir John Blundell Maple, of Childwickbury, St. Albans.
The death occurred of the Baroness, who was the daughter of the marriage between Miss Grace Maple with Baron von Eckardstein of the German Embassy, who, whilst on a visit to her grandmother, underwent an operation for the removal of her tonsils, but passed away under the anaesthetic.

She was a very strong and athletic girl and had been engaged in war service since the beginning of the war, one of their houses being used as a military hospital. The Baroness was just finishing a course of instruction to qualify as a transport motor driver, and had been through a special course in the repair shop in order that she might take up either Army or hospital work. In order to ensure that she

should be able to stand all weathers, she was advised to have her tonsils and adenoids removed. It is this operation which resulted in her death from heart failure. The interment took place in the family vault at the chapel on Childwick Green.
Source: *Herts Advertiser, 14th April 1917.*

"For an ideal".

Captain Freddie Webster, of Harpenden has been appointed adjutant of the *King's Liverpool Regiment* having previously been adjutant of the *13th Lincolnshire Regiment.*

Since 1914 he has published several works of military interest, which include "Britain in Arms", "Recruit to the Firing Line", "Britain's Territorials", the "Volunteer Training Corps Handbook"; and "Duties".

His latest work is a collection of poems "For an Ideal" which includes one dedicated to Lieutenant Richard Harvey Boys, *2nd Bedfordshire Regiment.*

Captain Webster who interested himself in the revival in England of the Olympic Games, was the author of two books on the 'Games. An old boy of St. Albans Grammar School, he maintained the family tradition for his father, grandfather and great grandfather all received their education at the same school and three generations had practised, as doctors in St. Albans.
Source: *Herts. Advertiser, 14th April 1917.*

Mesopotamia day.

A detachment of 160 men which includes a score of men from St. Albans, under the command of Major Clayton, a former member of the London Stock Exchange, were the first British force to enter Baghdad.

The news, given in a speech at the Stock Exchange, has created quite a thrill of excitement in the county.
Source: *Herts. Advertiser, 21st April 1917.*

From Vimy Ridge to Napsbury.

Its a long way from the Vimy Ridge to Napsbury, and the wounded heroes who arrived at Napsbury were glad indeed to get settled down in comfortable quarters. Two convoys have arrived this week - the first train, which arrived on Monday bringing 160 and the second on Tuesday bringing 120 - all "cot" cases. The work of transferring the men was expeditiously carried out by local sections of the Volunteer Ambulance.

Source: *Herts Advertiser, 5th May 1917.*

Fight in the air.

Lieutenant Rupert Neves, of Maidenhead and a cousin of Mr. D.B. Skillman, Harpenden and Mr S.W. Skillman, Redbourn writes, from a casualty clearing station, of his involvement in a battle in the air:

I am wounded in the side, but it is a chest wound and the bullet, after smashing a rib, came out near the stomach. It was a fight - ten Huns to eight of ours. I was *strafing* a Hun when my gun jammed. He simply rained bullets into me, and I thought it was all over. Then my engine stopped, I just doubled up as I was hit, then a bullet hit my forehead, but by God's good grace, glanced off my leather cap. As the Hun knew I was done for, he went.

I was six miles over the lines, but my emergency tank worked ten minutes, and took me over the lines at 400 feet, the Germans firing like mad. With half my control shot away, I landed 150 yards farther on, hardly able to breathe, and finished upside down. The machine caught fire. I scrambled out, my fur coat and gloves burning hard. Three 'Tommies' "put me out" and carried me into a dug out and I was taken to a field ambulance, and had my wound dressed and brought on here by car - very painful. But I am going to get well. The doctor says it is a wonderful escape and I am very strong!

Source: *Herts. Advertiser, 12th May 1917.*

A hard time in Mesopotamia.

Sergeant A.E. Cartmel writes to his parents, Mr. & Mrs. A Cartmel, Fishpool street:

We are now above Baghdad. My troop was doing advance guard and

185

as my officer was badly wounded a fortnight ago, I led the troop all through the great advance to the infantry, so the *Yeomanry* were engaged in every fight. We were very, very lucky, few men were wounded, and none killed, although six horses were killed, and several wounded. We have had a very hard time doing 30 miles a day and often 16 hours out of the twenty-four on the go, or holding a position until the Infantry relieved us. We are now camped in a palm grove and it is rather pleasant as an occasional shower keeps down the dust.
Source: *Herts. Advertiser, 12th April 1917.*

King's Langley lad receives the V.C.

Private Christopher A. Cox, *Bedfordshire Regiment,* of King's Langley has been recommended for the Victoria Cross for his gallant conduct and devotion to duty in the field on 15th, 16th and 17th March 1917 during operations at *Achiel le Grand.* It is understood that at a time when stretcher-bearers were forbidden to bring in the wounded owing to the heavy fighting, Private Cox brought in several wounded men, carrying them on his shoulder, and was slightly wounded whilst doing so.
Source: *Herts. Advertiser, 12th May 1917.*

Military funeral at St. Albans.

On Friday afternoon, a full military funeral was accorded the late Sergeant Robert J. Amott of the *MotorTransport, Army Service Corps,* who died from injuries received by being crushed between a motor lorry and the gatepost at the depot in London road, St. Albans on 30th March. The cortege started from Napsbury Hospital and proceeded to St. Albans cemetery. The principal mourners were Mr. and Mrs. Amott (father and mother), Mr. F. Amott and Miss Amott (brother and sister) and Private E. Amott, A.S.C. Former colleagues from the Bedford depot followed the coffin which was placed on a motor ambulance, driven by Staff Sergeant Gray together with the drum and fife band and a firing party.
Source: *Herts. Advertiser, 2nd June 1917.*

Wall Hall Hospital.

Mr. Pierpoint Morgan's kindness and generosity resulted in the *Wall Hall V.A.D. Hospital* being handed over to the military medical authorities in the spring of 1915. The premises, formerly a motor garage have been equipped to provide three wards and contain 50 beds. There is a card and billiard room and a large recreation room with a library, games, gramophone, piano etc. Concerts and whist drives are frequently arranged.

Source: *Herts. Advertiser, 23rd June 1917.*

"Behold you unbelieving Turks, 'go and eat and be thankful' ".

Sergeant Fitter Boteler, Herts R.F.A., stationed in Egypt writes to his wife at 11 Portland street, St. Albans of an amusing incident involving a nearby Turkish prisoner-of-war camp.

Not far from here is a prisoner's camp and the prisoners refused to eat their rations and were in a state of open mutiny. An interpreter was sent for, and this is what passed: On enquiring into it an officer found the tins of bully beef were unopened and lying about. He called the chief or head prisoner out, who explained that they were all Muslims, and that therefore they could not eat the flesh of an unclean beast (pig).

"Pig in a bully beef tin? Absurd!" the officer at once exclaimed. So then the prisoner picked up one of the tins, and there on the label was the picture of a pig. It was the firm's trade mark, but the Turks, had come to the conclusion that the tin contained pig, and nothing but pig. The matter touched their religion, and they would have nothing at all to do with the meat. The office tried to explain to them, but they would not touch it, at any price. Then the officer, being a clever sort of chap, thought it over, and an idea struck him. He gathered the prisoners around him, and showed them a box of *Bryant and May* matches, with the *Noah's Ark* trade-mark, and also the ship on the label. Then he opened the match box and said, it being made to the Turks by the interpreter, "Behold, you unbelieving Turks! Within are not ships but matches, even so is it with the tins of bully beef. Go and eat and be thankful." They soon made short work of their rations, and not only

187

ate it all up, but asked for more. I reckon that officer ought to have the D.S.O.
Source: *Herts. Advertiser, 23rd June 1917.*

Soldiers Corner in the cemetery.

"Sir, - As a frequent visitor to the 'Soldiers Corner in St. Albans Cemetery, I have noticed with great sorrow the number of uncared for graves. Men who have done their duty by fighting for us, are buried there. What I am asking for is this: surely there are some ladies in the town who could, in their spare hours, look after those graves. It seems heartbreaking to think instead of this little spot being a proud addition to the cemetery, it is practically an eyesore.

There is some talk, I believe, of a monument being erected after the war to our heroes who lie buried there. Wouldn't it be better if people acted now, so that after the war, when the time comes for this to be done, the graves will be a credit to St. Albans people? This is a splendid opportunity, to my way of thinking for those who have lost sons in the fighting. If they are buried in one of he cemeteries in France or elsewhere, I am positive that they would like to know hat someone is tending their loved ones grave.

The majority of soldiers' buried in the "Soldiers Corner" are Australians and Canadians. I myself, when there is an overplus of flowers from the grave I tend, put them on these poor fellows graves. The turf is dying for lack of water, and altogether, "Soldiers Corner", with the exception of three graves is in the most deplorable condition.

I ask your readers if they cannot spare a few hours in which to try and rectify this. It costs little, and the loved ones of the heroes who have fought and died for us, and who are buried there, will greatly appreciate this kindly act.

Yours etc.   SYBIL C. GUTTERIDGE   Ivanhoe, St. Albans.
Source: *Herts. Advertiser, 30th June 1917.*

Military Medal for Sergeant Cartmel.

Sergeant Alfred Edward Cartmel, only son of Mr. A. Cartmel, 114 Fishpool street, in 'D' Squadron, Hertfordshire Yeomanry has been awarded the Military Medal, under circumstances outlined in the following report of the Lieut.-Colonel of an Infantry regiment:

I wish to bring to your notice the distinguished services rendered by Sergeant Cartmel and his troop of your squadron which was attached to the battalion under my command from the 24th to 28th March. During the whole period extensive patrolling work had to be done in connection with the southward movement of the Turks, practically the whole troop being employed with very little rest throughout the entire period they were attached to my battalion. Patrols were sent out frequently under heavy rifle fire. They always behaved with the greatest coolness, showing marked courage and determination and bringing back information of the greatest value. On the morning of the 27th March, Sergeant Cartmel with a patrol, pushed forward with great determination to within 300 yards of a Turkish bivouac, north of a village, whence they were heavily fired on, and on the approach of a Turkish cavalry round his flank. He carried out the withdrawal skilfully and suffered no casualties, bringing back information of great value. I consider the work carried out by Sergeant Cartmel and the troop throughout was of the highest order".

Source: *Herts. Advertiser, 30th June 1917.*

'The wonderful tanks'.

Private C.E. Dukes, Bedfordshire Regiment writes to his fiance in St.Albans in a somewhat light-hearted manner about the use of tanks on the Western front:

"You would like a correct description of one of H.M.'s land cruisers. Well here it is: - They can do up prisoners in bundles like straw-binders, and in addition have an adaption of a *Goss printing machine*, which enables them to catch the Huns, fold, count and deliver them in quires, every thirteenth man being thrown out a little farther than the others. The Tanks can truss refractory prisoners like fowls prepared for cooking, while their equipment renders it possible for them to charge into a crowd of Huns, and by shooting out spokes like porcupine quills, carry off an opponent on each. Though 'stuck-up' the prisoners are needless to say, by no means proud of their position.

The cars in question can chew up barbed wire and turn it into munitions. As they run they slash their tails and clear away trees, houses, howitzers and anything else in the vicinity. They turn over on their backs and catch live shells in their caterpillar feet, and they can easily be adapted as submarines. They loop the loop, travel forwards, sideways and backwards, not only with equal speed but at the same time. They spin round like a top, only far more quickly, did themselves in, bury themselves, scoop out a tunnel and come out again ten miles away in half-an-hour. These Tanks can do anything and everything; in fact if there is anything that can't be done, a Tank can do it!
Source: *Herts. Advertiser, 30th June 1917.*

Air raid.

Saurday's air-raid came after due warning, in the brilliant light of a summer's day, and there was considerable suppressed excitement in St. Albans, where the squadron of machines was seen "just like a flock of birds" as one spectator put it - on their return journey, guns having sounded "like heavy distant thunder" while the raiders were operating. As the shells burst around the hostile aerial squadron the while balls of smoke could be distinctly seen from St. Albans, and it was interesting to watch those smoke-clouds as they travelled from the south-east gradually expanding as they approached. From St. Albans the hostile aircraft "looked just like sparrows" and one observer declared that through his binoculars, he distinctly saw an aerial battle in progress. Occupants of a military hospital also had a good view from the upper windows of the building also had a good view of this engagement [over London] to wreck peaceful homes.
Source: *Herts. Advertiser, 14th July 1917.*

The Hertfordshire Regiment prepares for Battle.
Lieutenant F.S. Walthew's notes on the training carried out:
In the latter half of June 1917, the Battalion was billeted in the Houlle-Moule-Serques area, about a kilometre out of St. Omer on the Calais road. In this district a full scale model of the section of the line to

190

be attacked by the *1st Hertfordshires* had been prepared, woods were shown by branches of trees and dummy trenches indicating the German positions etc. Day in and day out the troops were put through the part to be played by them in the attack, advancing first in artillery formation, then extending at a given point which represented the crest of the ridge at the sunken end of *Kitchener Wood* on which was situated the famous *Falkender Redoubt,* and continuing in extended order to the line of the second objective, where in due course the barrage would be picked up.

The plan of the attack was as follows, so far as the *39th Division* was concerned:

The section to be attacked was divided into three separate objectives, roughly the first, second and third German defence systems. There was to be a very thorough artillery preparation for several days previous to the offensive, to be followed by the Infantry advancing in "leapfrog" formation behind an impenetrable barrage. ...

"Pride of place" in the centre of the line had been allotted to the *1st Herts*", said the Brigadier on the day before the offensive was launched. I hoped that this position would not be as strongly held as the first two positions. In order, however, to provide against unforeseen contingencies, four tanks were allotted to the Battalion to assist them when and if necessary, by breaking down uncut wire, etc. etc.

Every man in the Battalion taking part in the attack had firmly impressed upon him that the barrage under cover of which he would advance would be of such intensity that it would be impossible for anything to live in front of him for a depth of 1,000 yards and that consequently no hostile attack would be met for some hours after the capture of the objective. To this end, the Battalion was trained to advance from their jumping off position across the [River] Steenbeck at a steady walk, rifles slung and bayonets fixed, behind the barrage to their objective when they would proceed to consolidate, establish communication with "contact patrol" aeroplanes by means of flares and push out patrols & outposts to the crest of the ridge some 50 to 100 yards further on to obtain observation etc. assisted by Tanks. In the unlikely event of any uncut wire being met with, the Tanks would breach it to enable the Infantry to pass through. Special emphasis was laid on the fact that nothing in the shape of delay on the flanks was to hinder the advance. Additional stress to bear on this point was made at a special corps course on the battle, held two or three weeks prior to the attack. In due time the Battalion reached almost as high a state of perfection as was possible to expect in their training and about the 20th July it, with the remainder of the Brigade, was moved up by motor bus to the camps in the neighbourhood of Watow, preparatory to taking up assembly positions for the battle.

While here, routes to the line were arranged and one officer of each company went up to reconnoitre the assembly positions, which consisted, for the most part, of shell holes behind Hill Top Farm.

On the night of [Monday] 30th July, the Regiment left the bivouacs near Vlamertinghe which they had occupied on the previous day and after a rather trying march across country through desultory shellfire and gas in the pitch black, reached the assembly positions just after midnight without suffering any casualties.

During the night our guns kept up the usual bombardment and at 3.45 a.m. just as dawn was breaking, a burst of flame, along the whole length of the front, ushered in the commencement of the Battle with the most intense barrage put up. The weather, which had been fine practically throughout July had broken on the 28th and during the whole of the 31st, low lying cloud and drizzle rendered co-operation with the R.F.C. almost impossible. In consequence, the state of the ground was such that progress of any sort could only be made with great difficulty and this factor more than anything else led to the comparative failure of the operation.
Source: *Hertfordshire Record Office.*

"Day of Glory".
"Their homes should ring with their story of sacrifice".
The heroism and sacrifice of the "Herts Guards" reported by Mr. W. Beach Thomas, war correspondent with the Daily Mail:

The highest sacrifice in the *Third Battle of Ypres* was perhaps paid by the *Hertfordshire Regiment*, with other Territorials, as gallant as themselves, took St. Julien and pushed forward deep into the enemy's country beyond. I have heard no more splendid or moving tale of gallant men going out to death and glory since the war began, not even the tale of the the *Lancashires*, told the other day. The achievement of some of the same troops in the final capture of Thiepval, St. Pierre Division and the *Schwaben Redoubt* a year ago went almost unrecorded. It would be a double injustice if this second and yet more heroic venture also were left unrecorded, and it is vital to a true history of the war, for the impression has grown that we at one time lost St. Julien. We never lost the whole of it. Some of the gallant who took it always clung to their ring of posts.

We may regard St. Julien as the centre of the battle. We took most prisoners here, nearly one thousand, and most guns - 13 [in all]. In St. Julien itself we inflicted the heaviest losses, and nowhere did the fighting so ebb and flow. Its intricacy was such that the German shelling with 5.9 howitzers grew hotter than most officers had seen, and it had various effects. In front of one knot of men dodging shells under very cool and expert leadership, there broke such an explosion that all believed a land mine had gone up. But in spite of it all, the shock and the continuous bursting of this noisiest of all shells, the men felt quite safe and comfortable in their shell-holes. As one of them said, when they got out of it after the earth had stopped shaking, they found that the land mine was a dump of 5.9 shells exploded by a 5.9 [howitzer].

Losing all the time, but never checked, these troops pushed on a good 1,200 yards to the next line of German trenches. One officer was wounded and set on fire by a fragment of shell which exploded some

S.O.S. lights in his pocket. He put the fire out by rolling over and over in the mud. Disregarding the wound he carried on as before, but without his signals and a good part of his clothing. Such was the conduct of the regiment who were reduced in numbers, but not in spirit.

The men reached the approaches to a trench defended by 400 yards of uncut wire six yards deep and running along a contour swept by machine guns from the left, front and flank. Still they did not stop. Some made their way round, some hacked at the wire and forced a way over it. They took the trench and a good number of prisoners and began to consolidate.

Somewhere about this time the last officers of the *Hertfordshire Regiment* fell, and the Sergeant, himself severely wounded, took command. In front of this occupied trench was a shallow ditch manned by a considerable garrison of the enemy, who now threw up their hands and came forward to give themselves up, when the sound of the machine guns was heard away in the rear of the Territorials, and both German and the British saw more or less what had happened. These regiments had advanced almost alone. A wide space on one flank was occupied by just four men and ground far in the rear was still held by the enemy. Very much the same thing was happening on the other flank.

The surrendering prisoners, suddenly appreciated the position, took up arms again and attempted to fight. The Territorials were more than surrounded, and if I say so, for they were mixed up with the enemy, they fought on. They shot down scores of the enemy in front, especially those who had taken up arms after surrendering, and they dealt with a full dress model counter attack, carried through according to the new German formula, in waves 10 yards apart, and even had time to see some German field guns move forward under the lee of a hill to the right.

At last in the afternoon when it was found that so few of the troops on the flank had got through and machine guns continued to fire from their rear, they decided to fight their way back, and they fought back quite undefeated, though every officer was gone and most non-commissioned officers. Among the men with them was a padre, a chaplain of many fights, who cheered them on and at the end, being the last man to cross a little stream, carried, and when he could no longer carry, dragged a wounded man to safety in the rear. But this was later.

As they struggled back to St. Julien, a group of Germans who had thrust through from their flank held up their hands in surrender and called out for mercy. It happened at the same time that the Germans counter-attacked from the opposite flank, and made some progress, and these men, seeing their fellows surrendering, ruthlessly turned machine guns on their own. If they surrendered, their own men shot them. If they took up arms they proved themselves traitors and were shot down by us. Nor was that all.

About this hour the German artillery had received orders to barrage the whole field and 5.9 shells mixed with some high velocity shells, fell indiscriminately on prisoners, on German counter-attackers and on our own troops fighting homewards. In the worst of the confusion our men kept a clear head, and at last, thanks in great measure to the skilful assistance of their friends in reserve, fighting all the way, but now almost without ammunition, they came through. Some of these supporting companies occupied a small hillock and set up in position as many as 13 machine and Lewis guns. These raked the Germans both left and right and did great havoc. Though our losses were perhaps heavier, there more than at any part of the 15 mile battle front, the enemy's losses were probably on a yet a greater scale.

I write especially of a regiment known to me personally better than any regiment in the Army, and one weighs words with special care in writing of friends. The fight was one of the stoutest fights of the war, worthy of the Guards at the *First Battle of Ypres*. The men were the *Hertfordshire Guards* indeed, and their homes should ring with their

195

story of sacrifice and valour. In the midst of it all, at the very worst, many of the Englishmen among the *Hertfordshires* and their neighbours never lost their native humour. Those who were in the foremost line reached a number of undamaged concrete dugouts with very small bolt-holes, like wigwams, through which you must crawl to enter. From one of these the lurking enemy was loath to come out, so a soldier held out a bomb and said "You'll divide this among you if you don't come out quick"! His language, if not jest, was understood. It was a little farther back, but in a hot place, that the whole contents of a tarpaulin roof, sagged in a thunder-shower, were tipped down a soldier's neck by the agency of a big shell fragment. All he said was "Sergeant can you tell me what it feels like to have sunstroke!"
Source: *Herts Advertiser, 18th August 1917*

A reaction to what happened.

Signaller W.E. Page, Hertfordshire Regiment, writes from Bagthorpe Military Hospital, Nottingham:
I have just arrived back from the severest of fights that our regiment has experienced. We have suffered very heavy casualties but we won the day. I was just behind our famous Colonel when he got killed, and also the Adjutant and Captain. I am afraid we have had a good number taken prisoner, for the Hun counter-attacked and cut some of our men off. The Regiment fought well. I was shot rather badly through both thighs, but I am going on satisfactorily. The remnant of the Regiment is now back at rest.
Source: *Herts. Advertiser, ... August 1917.*

Second Lieutenant R.B. Pawle, writes to Mrs. Page, Crib street, Ware:
I hope you have news of your son. He should be getting on quite well by now. By good luck, I happened to be in charge of some stretcher-bearers, so we took your son down to the dressing station. I assure you that I have never seen such pluck shown. When he found we could not get along the mud, he got off the stretcher and walked. From all accounts he did well in the show. ...
Source: *Hertfordshire Mercury, ... August 1917.*

A popular Hertfordshire officer.

Second Lieutenant R.H. Secretan (22), Hertfordshire Regiment was killed in action on 31st July: The commanding officer wrote:
He was killed instantaneously on 31st July, while leading his platoon against our final objective. His men tell me that nothing could have been more gallant than the way in which he led them. He was always so cheerful and ready to do everything and he was a great favourite with everyone. There is no braver boy in the whole army.

Shot dead during the attack.

Sergeant William James Payne, Hertfordshire Regiment was shot dead during the attack on 31st July. He leaves a widow and young child aged seventeen months, at No.8 Camp View-road, St. Albans.
Sergeant Payne and Quartermaster-Sergeant G.W. Fisher of St. Albans had arranged to write and inform each other's relatives of any untoward event. Accordingly Mrs. Payne received a touching letter from the Quartermaster-Sergeant on 6th August, informing her that her husband was killed on 31st July, adding that a man who was with Sergeant Payne at the time, told him that "Will" who was acting as Company Sergeant-Major, was shot through the head and killed instantly. He has since verified the fact with two other men who saw him fall. As Company Sergeant-Major I have been been working with "Will" and have found him one of the best. He was always cheerful and always ready to do his bit. You have my greatest sympathy.
Source: *Herts. Advertiser, 18th August 1917.*

Two brothers die within days.

Lieutenant L.V. Kent, *South Wales Regiment* died of wounds in France on 31st July; his brother, Second Lieutenant Harold Kent, *South Wales Borderers*, was 4th August. Both were sons of Mr. T. Kent, Holywell House, Holywell Hill, St.Albans.
Source: *Herts. Advertiser, 18th August 1917.*

A tribute to Lieutenant Lake, Hertfordshire Regiment.

A.E.L. writes as follows:
The death of Frank Lake removes a very winning and in many ways a

remarkable personality. His knowledge of natural history was extraordinary, and there was no English flower, bird or fish whose history, name and appearance he did not know. Every hedgerow, field or copse held a special message for him and a Sunday walk in his company seemed to open a new world for his friends. All his mature years were spent in a city office, but his scanty leisure was always at the disposal of any friend with greenhouse or a garden, and with many of the latter in Hertfordshire will in true spring give a silent witness to his loving care. May Mother Earth, who he seemed to understand with a spirit of his own, rest lightly on his unknown grave.
Source: *Herts Advertiser, 9th March 1918.*

Killed in action on 31st July 1917.
Men of the Hertfordshire Regiment
who have no known grave and are list of panels 54 & 56
of the Menin Gate Memorial, Ypres.

This list of 110 names has been compiled from the Memorial Registers held in the Department of Printed Books, Imperial War Museum and from two visits to the Menin Gate Memorial in 1995 and 1998. There are 5 names for which information cannot be found (and these have been omitted). In addition 6 names of men who were killed between 1914 and 1917 are also not included here.

Lance Corporal Joseph Richard Allwood (22), Watford.
Private R.W. Ambrose (23), Hemel Hempstead.
Private Thomas Wallace Arnold (40), Upper Clapton, London.
Corporal J.E. Bilby.
Private B. Blake (41), Newmarket, but married and living in Luton.
Corporal Frederick William Breeze.
Lance Corporal James John Brooks.
Private Bramwell Joseph Brown (34), Hurstpierpoint, Sussex.
Private Percy Buck (26), Hitchin.
Private George Butcher (19), Clacton-on-Sea.
Sergeant George M. Callow, *Military Medal* (26), Luton.
Private George H. Catlin (21), Hertford.
Private Clement Chapman.
Private Walter Charter.

Private George Constantine Clark.
Private Herbert George Clark.
Lance Corporal Henry Beaumont Clarke (20), London.
Lance Corporal John James Coe.
Private John William Percy Conder (22), Baldock.
Lance Corporal William Joseph Cooper (25), Royston.
Private Cecil James Cordell (24), Walkern, Stevenage.
Private Frederick Cox.
Private John Horhan Crouchman.
Private Harold George Crunden (20), Erith, Kent.
Private Bert Culverhouse (19), Watford.
Private Herbert Nicholas Daly (26), Camberwell, London.
Private James Day (22), Tylers Causeway, Hertford.
Private Arthur Dean (22), Letchworth.
Private Percy Edgar Dixey, Petmarsh (sic) (?Pebmarsh), Essex
Private Frederick Doughty (24), Aylsham, Norfolk.
Lance Corporal Sidney Edward Draper (21), Finsbury Park, London.
Private William James Dray (24), Buntingford.
Private Walter J. Duke.
Private George Henry Edwards (28), Walkern, Stevenage.
Private Frederick Fellows.
Private Alfred Finch.
Private Edward William Fitzgibbon.
Private Ernest Folds (23), Coleman Green, Wheathamstead.
Private Albert George Francis.
Private John Stanley Fursdon (21), Chenies, Rickmansworth.
Private Claude Henry Garment (19), St. Albans.
Sergeant Harry Gordon Garrod (23), Stevenage.
Private Albert James Gilbert (22), Whyteleafe, Surrey.
Sergeant Joseph William Gladding, *Distinguished Service Medal*, Ware.
                              married, and living in Norwich
Corporal Frederick Golden.
Private Ernest Gray.
Private C.W. Gurney (21), Watford.
Private Joseph Hagger.
Lance Corporal John Hall (19), Bishops Stortford.

Sergeant Hirim John Hammond (27), Ware.
Private Alfred Henry Herbert Hardy (20), St. Albans.
Private Albert Harrowdell (31), Berkhamstead.
Private Stephen John Hart (20), Hertford.
Private C.R. Harty (36), Ramsgate.
Captain Basil William Head (26), Paignton.
Private George Hoar (26), Berkhamstead.
Lance Corporal Thomas Allan Hughes (21), Letchworth.
Private Frederick Hummerstone (19), Great Hormead.
Corporal Ernest Walter Izzard (31), St. Albans.
Private Charles Javeleau (20), St. Albans.
Private Jabez Juina.
Private William John Kemp (38), Camborne, Cornwall.
Private David King.
Lieutenant Simmonds King (31), Chatham.
Private Cecil Kingsley (23), Stevenage.
Private William George Knight (34).
Lieutenant F.G. Lake.
Private James Leaning (20), Cheshunt.
Lance Corporal Robert Ernest Linge, *Military Medal* (26), Cheshunt.
Captain Sidney Henry Lowry, *Military Cross* (29), Stevenage.
Lieutenant Eric Mackintosh.
Private Arthur Charles Frank Mitchell.
Lance Corporal William Henry Mayer (23), St. Albans.
Captain Alexander Richard Milne (Adjutant)(21), Barnet.
Private William Ivor Mitchell (36), Reading.
Private T.H. Moore.
Private Albert Edward Munt (31), Wheathamstead.
Private Herbert Oakman (19), Waltham Cross.
Lieutenant-Colonel Frank Page, *Distinguished Service Order and Bar*,
(39), Bournemouth.
Private William Pannell (22), Dumbartonshire.
Private Harry Payne (22), Coleman Green, Wheathamsted.
Private William Pettitt (20), Sawbridgeworth.
Private James Plested.
Sergeant Sydney Rand, *mentioned in despatches* (21), Wormley.

Private Ernest George Reed (35).
Sergeant George A. Reynolds, *Military Medal*.
Private Arthur George Rose (21), St. Albans.
Lance Corporal Edwin Ryder (21), Chorley Wood.
Private Charles Henry Salmons (25), Ware.
Private Frank Frederick Sargent.
Lance Corporal Albert Saunder (22), Watford.
Private B.C. Saunders (23), Watford.
Private Percy Austin Scott (37), Ilford, Essex.
Second Lieutenant Reginald Herbert Secretan (22), Bennetts End,
Hemel Hempstead.
Private Alfred William Seager.
Corporal James Henry Sewell (21), Hitchin.
Private Thomas James Simmons.
Private George Henry Skinner (22), Hertford.
Lance Corporal Arthur William Smith (23), Waltham Cross.
Private Ernest Bert Smith (21).
Private Oliver Lewis Smith (36), Hertford.
Private W. Smith (22).
Lance Corporal Ulric Lewis Forester Somerville (23), Chile.
Private Claude James William Sweeney, *Military Medal*, Ware.
Private Frederick Gordon Thompson.
Private James Thomas Walsgrove.
Private Charles Samuel Whittell, Ipswich.
Private Claude Lionel Whittingham (19), Stockwell, London.
Lance Sergeant Arthur Whitman (21), Little Gaddesden.
Private Herbert Wicks (24), Watford.
Sources: Menin Gate Memorial, Ypres & Imperial War Museum, London

Statistics.

The Colonel (Page), ten officers and over 130 men were killed. All the remaining officers and more than 200 men were wounded. 130 or so of the Battalion who were still fit for duty finished the day under the command of the regimental Sergeant-Major, ably asisted by the Padre.
Source: *Sainsbury, J.D. The Hertfordshire Regiment.*

Battle Honours.

Bar to the Military Cross - Revd. A.E. Popham (padre).

Military Cross - Captain J.P. Charles, Second Lieutenants E.W. Marchington and R.I. Edwards.

Distinguished Conduct Medal - Regimental Sergeant Major Tite, Sergeants S. Alibone, S. Osborne, Corporal W. Ashwell and Private F. Bass, Royal Army Medical Corps.

Bar to Military Medal - Lance Corporal W.E. Taylor and Private A.S. Hansford.

Military Medal - Private H. Kent, Lance Corporal S.J. Darby, Corporal R.A.Gough, Private W.C. Smith, Lance Corporal C. Parsloe, Lance Corporal W. Litchfield, Private A.G.Sapsed, Lance Corporal J.R.Cockman, Corporal F.G. Phillips, Private C. Forbes, Private W. Sell, Private H.W. Miles, Corporal J.E. Taylor, Lance Corporal F. Walker, Private E.J. Marshall and Private W. Marshall.
Source: Imperial War Museum.

The Hertfordshires in Battle.
'And how can man die better
Than facing fearful odds,
For the ashes of his fathers,
And the temples of his Gods?   [Macaulay]

The old story is once more repeated,
On the last of the month just gone by,
When the Battalion who'd never been defeated,
Showed the world they knew how to die.

The parapet was left miles behind them
Their aim reached with rifling loss;
But the flanks were no up to mind them
Having a bit stiffer country to cross.

202

The enemy, bent, but unbroken
Very heavily counter-attacked,
But the Herts by the very same token
Held their ground, tho'numbers they lacked.

Mown down by machine gun and rifle
The Colonel and Adjutant fell;
The others, with death but a trifle,
Went down in the murderous hell.

The R.S.M. now commanded,
and the M.O. and he were laid low;
A Sergeant then did as demanded,
Till reserves relieved him from C.O.

And that is the end of the story:-
Eighty alone in the firing line.
The Herts 'held on in their glory,
And fought that honour might shine.

When the history of the war shall be written,
In the book on the knees of the Gods,
Few deeds will come up the telling
How the Herts died facing the odds.

H.D., 8th August 1917.
Source: *Hertfordshire Mercury, an issue in August 1917*

Village welcome for Private Cox V.C.

Dr. F.C. Fisher (Chairman of the Kings Langley Parish Council) congratulated Private Cox, first upon the good recovery he had made from his wounds, and secondly upon having been awarded the greatest military honour a soldier could receive. He recalled that at the recruitment meeting held at Coombe Hill School soon after the war began, Private Cox was one of the first, if not the first to come forward and enlist.

Private Cox had journeyed from Aylesbury reaching Kings Langley by 3.41 train, his arrival signalled by a hearty peal from the bells of All Saint's Church. He was welcomed at the railway station by the Earl of Clarendon and by a large number of spectators who had assembled outside the station. He drove with Lord Clarendon first to the Vicarage and then to the Parish Church, where the Vicar conducted a brief service. Afterwards a presentation was made to Private Cox entitling him to £50 worth of War Loan Stock (which is held in trust by three trustees) and also a gold watch. Presentations were also made to Private Cox's wife and two children.

Source: *Herts Advertiser, 4th August 1917.*

'Everywhere are date-palms'.

Sapper Arthur E. Simms writes to St. Saviour's Parish Magazine of life in Mesopotamia:

The authorities are exceedingly careful of our health, and rush one into hospital on the slightest indication of an undue rise in blood temperature.

Everywhere are date-palms and the fruit is hanging just now in profusion, but it looks very dusty, like large bunches of grapes, very closely packed together. We are fed remarkably well. Yesterday we had plum-duff, and today at breakfast - bacon and tomatoes, which I guess just now are great luxuries in England. Things here are run on very business lines; the profits if the canteen merge into the troop rations; and figures posted up, showing the why and the wherefore of the precautions taken against sunstroke is a wise measure. It is is a crime to be out in the open without a helmet, and one readily accepts the fact and sees the wisdom of it all.

It is a wonderful country and the river is splendid. We see such a mixture of races and it is quite a study finding out who they are and what they are. There are Arabs, Armenians mostly in native dress and a few following European fashions. Trying to get used to the sound and use of different words is bewildering because there are so many.

Source: *Herts. Advertiser, 29th September 1917.*

Ten thousand men arrive at Napsbury Hospital.

Since Napsbury Asylum was converted into a war hospital, the *Herts Volunteer Field Ambulance* have dealt with 68 convoys, numbering ten thousand wounded men from the various fronts. During the past week we have had a very busy time: a convoy arrived on Friday evening with 120 'cots' and 40 'sitters' and on Sunday afternoon the Corps received another call and assisted with the removal of 100 'cot' cases. The same evening the Corps was called out to remove a further 120 'cots' and a few sitters, whilst a further 40 'cots' were taken to another town further north.

The injuries are varied but sufferers from gas effects seem to predominate. The men were all wonderfully cheery and optimistic; and bore their sufferings with much fortitude.

Source: *Herts. Advertiser, 29th September 1917.*

Advertisement Lights Order.

Last winter shopkeepers were permitted to use outside lights, but for the future this is not permissible. The Advertisement Lights Order probihits all sky signs, illuminated signs, facias and advertisements or other lights used at the entrance of any shop of place of amusement for the purposes of advertisement or display.

St. Albans shopkeepers have acted very wisely in endeavouring to arrive at a concerted arrangement in the direction of earlier closing. Drapers, clothiers, boot and shoe retailers have agreed unanimously to close at six o'clock on Mondays, Tuesdays, Wednesdays and Fridays, at one o'clock on Thursdays, and eight o'clock on Saturdays. Grocers are also falling into line and we hope that the purchasing public will so regulate their visits to shops, as as to render it fairly easy for tradespeople to adopt a uniform timetable for closing.

Source: *Herts. Advertiser, 29th September 1917.*

Old friends meet.

Regt. Sgt.-Major Ralph Dunham, an old choirboy of St. Saviour's had a pleasant surprise when another old choir boy came to see him - George Howe, who was looking in the best of health and as happy as possible in these somewhat broody times. Some months ago I was at a concert party and was much impressed by the concert party and by the singing of a tenor whose face I seemed to recognise. I made enquiries and found that he was none-other than Joe Lester, our one time solo boy.

Source: *Herts. Advertiser, 6th October 1917.*

Royal Flying Corps Major receives a decoration.

Major Robert Gregory, M.C. who commands the Training Squadron of the R.F.C. was presented with the French Croix de Chevalier for gallant and meritorious service at a ceremony which took part in Clarence Park, St. Albans.

Addressing the men on parade, Brigadier General Mackenzie spoke of the work of the Flying Corps who has enabled the Army to locate the enemy's position on many occasions and to capture these positions.

Source: *Herts Advertiser, 6th October 1917.*

'Twenty-two months under fire' .

Brigadier-General Henry Page Croft, C.M.G., M.P., who was adjutant of the *Hertfordshire Regiment* when they were sent to fight in Flanders in November 1914, who later commanded the Regiment before being promoted to take charge of a Brigade, is now back in England resuming life as a Member of Parliament. He has written and had published his account of the Regiment between 1914 and 1916. His narrative, written in a breezy and attractive style, is dedicated to his comrades on the battlefield.

Of Lord Cavan, the writer says:

He is one of those exceptional personalities who gives confidence from the first moment you meet them, but unlike the most famous generals and admirals, he makes you feel his friendship at once, and you realise you are dealing with a very human man. ... Pointing to the map he showed us where the enemy had advanced, and then said quite simply: "we will take back this culvert here,

those trenches there, and those brickstacks up to that point" ... The whole description was wonderfully simple, and the orders were given in such a way that not one of us doubted they would prove successful. So it turned out, for a more perfectly conceived and executed little series of operations could not be imagined".
Source: *Herts. Advertiser, 10th November 1917.*

Armourer Staff-Sergeant James Mocock.

On Monday the body of the late Armourer Staff-Sergeant James Mocock was laid to rest in St. Albans Cemetery with full military honours. The coffin was borne on a gun carriage supplied and horsed by the *Royal Army Service Corps* and the team of six horses was driven by Sergeants of the Company riding postillion. The firing party was furnished by the *Queen's Royal West Surrey Regiment* to which the late Staff Sergeant was attached. The bearers were elected from the senior Warrant Officers and Staff Sergeants of the Battalion, while all Warrant Officers and Sergeants who could be spared from military duties were in attendance.

The cortege left 12 Warwick Road, by the great kindness of Mr. and Mrs. Pyne, where the deceased had been billeted last winter. It proceeded by way of St. Peter's Street and Hatfield Road to the cemetery and during the march the drums of the battalion band played the "Dead March in Saul". The service was impressively conducted by the Revd. M. Beadle, Senior Chaplain to the Forces in St. Albans and after the body had been committed to the grave, three volleys were fired over it and the "Last Post" was sounded.

Staff Sergeant James Mocock was a gallant soldier and true patriot and was one of the many old N.C.O.'s who returned to the Colours in the hour it his country's need. As a trained armourer and skilful mechanic, his service were of immense value and to the battalion he served in particular. Although 60 years of age, he was active and unsparing in his devotion to duty and stuck to his post until the last. The funeral arrangements were made by Messrs.W.Goodchild.
Source: *Herts. Advertiser, 10th November 1917.*

207

"Their Majesties King George V and Queen Mary
visiting the battlefields in France, 1917".
Mr Frank O. Salisbury's picture is unveiled.

Sir William Dunn, the Lord Mayor of London asked Mr. Salisbury to paint a panel for the Royal Exchange, London. The panel, 18 feet high by 11 feet wide was to be completed in eight weeks. The next day I had an appointment with Sir William Robertson, Chief of the General Staff who mapped out the King's route. I crossed from Folkestone, having been given the rank of colonel, although I went in mufti. There was a car waiting for me and at my disposal for as long as I was in France. It had no speed limit, and the tremendous pace and the risks it was apparently felt necessary to take in war time did not add to my serenity.
Source: *Portrait and Pageant, by Frank O. Salisbury.*

The painting, unveiled by H.R.H. The Duke of Connaught at the Royal Exchange depicts scenes during the recent visit by the King and Queen to the troops and hospitals. In one picture Sir Douglas Haig is explaining to his Majesty important and highly successful operations; the artist was asked to include many of the generals and visited army headquarters in France to draw them for the the picture. The Prince of Wales gave a sitting within the sound of the guns. In another, the Queen is shown making a hospital visit. Mr. Salisbury's picture contains portraits of many of the army commanders. At the time of unveiling some were incomplete. In the centre above the main scene are painted the Royal Coat of Arms, while the arms of Canada, Australia, India, New Zealand and South Africa surround the panel.
Source: *Herts. Advertiser, 10th November 1917.*

Lord Cavan and Italy, 1917-18.
During November, Lieutenant-General, the tenth Earl of Cavan was summoned and instructed by Sir William Robertson, Chief of Imperial General Staff to go to Italy and take command of the allied forces supporting the Italians, who in the Great War were also part of the allies. His immediate staff, including the Prince of Wales accompanied

him and on his arrival he found a very dispirited army with little discipline. Fresh instructions from London, meant that very soon Lord Cavan relinquished his command to the more senior General, Sir Herbert Plumer, but he remained in Italy during the winter months, 1917-18 as commander of the *XIV Corps* (whom he had commanded since January 1916). Plumer was recalled to France in the Spring 1918 and Cavan became Commanding Officer of the Allied Forces in Italy. An attack was made on the Austrians on the Asiago Plateau (north east of Lake Garda) in June 1918 and in the autumn, the tenth army, comprising allied and Italian forces fought its way across the River Piave (north of Venice) and was instrumental in completely routing the Austrian armies. This led to an armistice being signed in early November 1918 between the Austrian-Hungarian empire and Italy, before the armistice between German and the allies.
Sources: *Compiler's research.*

Flag Day.
Lady Salisbury of Hatfield House wrote to the editor on 12th November 1917 to report that a flag day held all over the county of Hertfordshire during the summer had raised £2,414 10s 3d for comforts for troops serving in Mesopotamia and Egypt (*Hertfordshire Yeomanry*) and Flanders (*Hertfordshire Regiment*).
Source: *Herts. Advertiser, 17th November 1917.*

Separation Allowances: a soldier's wife's complaint.
Sir, - There are hundreds of women whose husbands like mine, are in the Army and in their places we at home have young babies whose ages are from a few weeks to say, eighteen months. We are tied at home looking after and nursing our off-spring. On Monday we go to the post office and pick our allowance up (19s 6d). We go to the grocers, where our sugar card is registered, and buy ¼ lb. tea, 1 lb. of sugar, ½ lb. ½ lb, of margarine, and a tin of food for the baby.

We return home. There is our rent, coal, light, insurance; milk, bread, and food to provide for the baby and the mother for a week, not to mention clothes, soap and a thousand and one more items that are wanted in a home to keep it clean and sweet. Then, Sir, I ask are we to be pestered with people knocking at our door and telling us to economise on food. I think it is being done at the present moment to the bitterest end with hundreds of us. We do not ask pity for ourselves or for our babies, but what we do ask is that the Mayoress and her committee should travel round the better class and ask them to empty their pockets of the surplus coppers, get all the children of from 2½ years to 8 years whose fathers are defending our shores and giving them a jolly good time this Christmas. What, indeed, would better please the little ones, or tend more to gladden their fathers' hearts than to know at least their children were having a good time.

    Yours, etc.   **A 19s 6d per week Receiver.**

Source: *Herts. Advertiser, 8th December 1917.*

Letter from Tidworth Barracks, Wiltshire.

To Viscount Grimston, from Richard N. Maffey:

I am on a draft for Egypt on Friday, 14th December so feel rather doubtful as to whether my application for a Commission will be of any consequence now. As a matter of fact I do not mind as I have always been pretty keen on getting out to the "Holy Land". Although my draft is to be fitted out and ready for the journey by tomorrow, I don't expect I shall be going for another 5 or 6 days.

One unfortunate thing about the affair is that I have not been able to secure leave. I should have very much liked to have seen my parents before going out to Egypt. However I have been fortunate in keeping in the dear old County over 2 years so I certainly must not let this matter dishearten me.

Once again thanking your Lordship for the letter of recommendation and wishing Grimston Tyres the very best of luck.

Source: *Gorhambury Collection. 4th Earl's business correspondence.*

Contents: 1918

The Food Problem in St. Albans.

The general public had been led to believe that there would be a shortage in the supply of meat in the butchers' shops last week-end and consequently there was a tremendous rush on the part of everybody to be early on the scene, with the result that on Friday and Saturday St. Albans witnessed rather unusual, and in many respects extraordinary scenes. People who had money hurried to seize all that could be obtained and thus rendered the prospect of housewives (who did not receive their housekeeping money until Saturday not being able to buy their Sunday joint. The butchers, to their credit, did their level best to make the supplies go round; they had a difficult task with orders to execute from their regular customers and the eager demands of surging crowds to satisfy at the same breath. But the fact remains that many hundreds of people could not get any supplies at all.

There was fortunately a fairly good supply, in the market of the cheaper kind of fish such as fresh herrings, sprats etc. and these were eagerly bought up; and there was a great demand for cooked and tinned meats, "German" sausage and so on. Rabbits, etc. were quite a luxury with the limited supply and the absurdly high prices demanded.

Soon the food resources of the country will have to be strictly economised and it will be absolutely necessary to voluntarily ration supplies or to start a state system of rationing.
Source: *Herts Advertiser, 3rd January 1918.*

Christmas parcel sent in January!

From a letter from Viscount Grimston, Grimston Tyres Ltd to Corporal W. Christmas, of C Company, 4th Bedfordshire Regiment in France:
8 January 1918. - This is to send you our best wishes for 1918 from myself and from the firm. The works are sending you a Christmas parcel which I hope will reach you safely. We thought a parcel sent early in January would come at a more acceptable time than one sent just before Xmas. Here we are keeping busy. We are doing a certain amount of 'spreading' for outside people which makes up for a rather

smaller demand from our own factory for pneumatic tyres of which we are only turning out some 150 tyres a week as against the 200-300 when you were with us. ... Over 140 men have joined up from here, and now as every boy reaches 18 years of age, he goes also.

Source: *Gorhambury Collection. 4th Earl of Verulam's Business Correspondence.*

From the Italian front.

Private F.Archer writes:

We had a grand reception when we arrived. Flowers and fruit were thrown and it seemed to me more like a peace time trip than war. The people are good to us in every way and seem quite interested in the *British Tommy* and his ways. This is a lovely place: the scenery is grand and you can see nothing but mountains for miles and miles. In some places there is snow on the top of them but it is nice and warm down here where we are in the day time, though this is their winter and I don't know what the summer will be like. We shall melt away I expect! I would rather be here than in France as regards buying anything, but we understand that they find it very difficult to get goods to sell.

Source: *Hertfordshire Record Office. St.Saviour's Parish Magazine, St.Albans, January 1918.*

Coping with languages.

Sapper Arthur E. Simms writes from Mesopotamia [later Iraq]:

Doubtless you know that I have been down to India but, as you can see I am now back in Mesopotamia, and fortunately just in time to be detailed to the '*first of the boats*'. Previous to that our party had been doing work not in connection with the special work we came out to do. Oh, yes; the great difficulty one feels is in the languages, but, all things considered, we get on very well - what one can't explain with the tongue one demonstrates either by drawing or gesticulating. Chinese is absolute to everyone. Fortunately some of them speak a sort of English. I think the Indians are delightful chaps and they are just as eager to pick up English as we are to pick up Hindustani - but it is a queer sounding jargon with its '*Dor addammi ack lackory*'. It is quite an apprenticeship watching the natives and the Chinese. The latter are particularly good craftsmen. Their methods are very strange; they use their feet nearly as much as their hands and they want no vice to see their strange-looking benches. It was a real day, the day I got back here, to see the evidence of nice feeling and pleasure the Indians and some of the Chinese at seeing me again. One's heart warmed to them, and especially to one particular Indian whom I had had working as a sort of foreman. He could speak English and he was quite lost for words in trying to express his pleasure at seeing me again. He had been most attentive to me when I lay sick and helpless before I went into hospital. ...

The mornings here now are quite cold and one needs two blankets as well as a top coat to cover one at night, and I am glad to do a run to get a wash. Since I have been out here I have regretted that I never went in for photography; there is the opportunity of a lifetime for it out here. Strange things which we get used to and soon find commonplace would be of immense interest to you at home. ...

Some of our party went for a walk last Sunday evening through a date grove to the Euphrates river. I thought that all the dates had been picked, but we found quite a lot hanging still. Work is speeded up here wonderfully, but of course I cannot give any details. There is some mention of mud in Mesopotamia made in some of the papers, but it hasn't rained since I have been here - only dust, and that in plenty.
Source: *Herts Advertiser, 19th January 1918.*

Christmas on the Western Front, 1917.

Regimental Sergeant-Major Ralph S.Dunham writes:
31st December 1917. - Our Christmas was a huge success. Church Parade was ordered for 9.15 a.m. and everyone joined lustily in the singing of the Christmas hymns. The next event was a football match which was also thoroughly enjoyed. During this match the senior N.C.O.'s, as is the custom in the Army at Christmas time, prepared the billet for the men's dinner. We were fortunate in being in possession of a large barn which enabled us to seat about two hundred men. The villagers lent us plates, glasses and a piano. At one o'clock all was

ready and after a short speech from the Officer Commanding, the men set to to do justice to a meal consisting of beef, pork, vegetables, Christmas pudding, apples, nuts, biscuits and cheese, and last but not least, Tommy's beverage, 'beer'.

From two o'clock until three the men went into the village; visiting their many friends, both military and civil, during which time a stage was erected and the whole place turned into a concert room. At 3.15 our concert troupe, known as the 'Mud Guards' gave an excellent concert, which was repeated the next evening at the Corps, headquarters by request of the staff. The rest of the day the men spent in their own way, whilst the men of the Sergeant's mess commenced their festivities by a dinner with a 'sing-song' afterwards. At eleven o'clock 'lights-out' was ordered and everyone turned in, thoroughly tired out, but nevertheless happy in the thought that their Christmas had been spent in accordance with the traditions of the Army and with 'goodwill towards men' as their motto.

I suppose Christmas in England was rather dull, but probably some of those at home will be able to find a certain amount of satisfaction in knowing that 'Tommy' had a good time, and that the war was, more or less, forgotten by as many men as could be spared from actual work.
Source: *Herts. Advertiser, 19th January 1918.*

"A first, and I hope my only Christmas Day in France".

Private Robert Titmus, formerly steward of the County Club, St. Albans, writes from France:
27th December 1917. - Christmas Day was spent as follows: early service at seven o'clock in a very fine temporary church. Church Parade at ten o'clock and then we had a little time to ourselves until dinner. This consisted of roast-beef, potatoes, swedes, mince tart, plum-pudding, apples, oranges, nuts, cigarettes; so that I think we did very well. Tea consisted of bread and butter, jam and cake, and during the evening various concerts were arranged. We were early to bed, and so ended my first, and I hope my only Christmas Day in France.
Source: *Herts. Advertiser, 19th January 1918.*

Prisoner of war:
he stood by his wounded officer.

Mrs Coker, 2 Oster-terrace, St.Albans receives news from the German Red Cross Society, Frankfurt, that her son - Sergeant John George Coker, Royal Field Artillery who was reported missing on 30th November 1917 is alive and is a prisoner of war. About the same time, she received a letter from an officer in her son's battalion:

3rd January 1918. - The circumstances in which your son was taken prisoner by the Germans are as follows:- "he was on duty on the morning of the 30th November when the Germans broke through our line and breached the battery position at Villers-Gulslain. The battery remained firing until the enemy was close upon them and then one of our officers, Second Lieutenant Annandale, who was second in command was shot through the thigh with a machine gun bullet and was unable to walk. Orders came to abandon the guns and everyone who could walk then retired. Your son, however, with great gallantry, remained with Lieutenant Annandale and, as far as we can know, was taken prisoner with his officer almost immediately. Your son was unwounded. I do not think you need have any fears for his welfare. It will be some months, possibly, before you hear from him, as it is difficult for our prisoners of war to get letters home. Meanwhile I hope that you will find consolation in the splendid way in which he did his duty. I had a high opinion of your son's character and ability.

Sergeant Coker was scoutmaster of the Boy Scouts at St. Saviour's Church, St.Albans. His father, the later Mr. J.G. Coker, who resided at St.Albans for seventeen years was for thirty-five years in the service of Mr. A. Tremayne-Buller, brother of General Sir Redvers Buller. His grandfather was a Troop-Sergeant-Major in the 5th Royal Lancers and served in the East Indies from 1842 to 1846 and gained the star of Maharagpere (1843), the medal for Aliwal (1846), the bar for Sobraon as well as a medal for long service and good conduct. After serving with the Colours for twenty-four years, he retired on a pension and was then associated for a period with the West Kent Yeomanry at Sevenoaks.

Source: *Herts. Advertiser, 19th January 1918.*

Under fire from a submarine.

E.Sharratt, of Temten, Shenley writes of how his cargo ship was off Cape Blanco when it came under fire from a submarine:

21st October 1917. - A cursed submarine started shelling us - 30 shells were fired and everyone missed us. Of course we altered course and went 'hell for leather' and let go with our gun, but the darned thing was not good enough as the submarine was out of range. She stopped shelling us for a time and then started again at intervals. At 3.15 a few more were fired and this time they came too near to be pleasant, and all the time bits of shell were flying about the decks. The ship shook and we thought that she had been hit. So we had orders to leave the ship when we were only about half a mile from the shore. All the time the submarine was firing at us whilst we were getting into the boats and continued as we went ashore. No one was hurt although we took refuge behind some sand dunes. We then marched across the Sahara Desert until we reached a French military post who gave us some food and put us up for the night. The following day the skipper and most of the crew returned and found the ship nearly high and dry. By putting cargo overboard it was hoped to get her back into the water, but this did not work. A passing steamer tried to pull us off but she could not move us and now two coasting steamers are taking the cargo. The ship is half full of water. It is hoped to get another steamer from Gibralter to pump all the water out of the holds.

All the time we were in action I was at the gun loading it (four of us are in the gun crew). We had about a dozen shells all piled up ready for loading and I can tell you that if a shell had struck us on the platform, we should have been no more. I thought I should have done something mad if we had to go into action with a submarine, but when the time came, I was as cool as a cucumber.

Source: *Herts. Advertiser, 26th January 1918.*

Socks very handy in the Trenches.

Private H. Lawrence, 11th Platoon, C Company, 4th Bedfordshire Regiment, British Expeditionary Force in France writes to Viscount Grimston, dated 20th January 1918:

Thank you very much for the parcel which I received whilst in the trenches. It came in very handy especially the socks as it is very muddy out here now and my feet were wet at the time of receiving the parcel.

Well, I don't know when the war is going to end but I know I am fed up and so is everybody else out here. Roll on the time when we can all get back to work. I must close now. Wishing you all the best of luck from a work mate. H.Lawrence.

Source: *Gorhambury Collection. 4th Earl of Verulam's Business Coresspondence.*

An Albanian in Mesopotamia [Iraq].

Gunner Albert E.Siggery, R.F.A. of 66 Culver-road, St. Albans writes to Mr. H.R.Wilton Hall from Mesopotamia:

For the last four weeks we have been travelling by road up country. It was practically an uneventful journey. We certainly had a bit of trouble with some Arabs, but they soon packed up and went off. We stopped for a time at Basra and then went on up to Amarah where we remained for three weeks and then on again till three weeks ago. I have been to Baghdad where there are some 140,000 inhabitants, so you will see that it is a place of considerable size; it is said to be the most civilised town in the East. The temples are splendid and some of their roads are as wide as an average English road, but that is the work of our military. The ordinary roads are very narrow, close and filthy. I see Mr. Arthur Simms (my uncle) has been to the garden of Eden. I have only been within three miles of it but some of our fellows have spriggs of what they were told was the "*Tree of Knowledge*" ... On our way up we passed Ezra's Tomb and the ruins of Old Babylon, so you can see it has been a rather interesting journey.

The ground we have taken over was originally in the hands of the Turks but was taken by our troops. We passed the Sanyat position where the heaviest of the fighting took place and it looked as if it had been 'some' fighting! The Turkish fortifications had been smashed to the ground, and the ground was covered with shells and bombs still unexploded. The Hertfordshire Yeomanry are in this Camp with us,

but I have not met any of them. I have seen some of the fellows who were in the third line of our Artillery but I have not run into Billy Minter yet. We are not yet in the firing line, but it is possible that we shall be there by the time you get this letter. *Later he writes:*
We are now within the sound of the guns, which are little more than five miles away, but it is doubtful whether we shall be there for a few weeks yet as we have a special shooting course to go through first.
Source: *Herts Advertiser, 2nd February 1918.*

An air raid.

After a comparatively long spell of exemption from visits by hostile aeroplanes a considerable number of enemy machines crossed the Kent and Essex coasts on Monday night, and two or three penetrated as far as London. The guns of the anti-aircraft service were very distinctly heard in St. Albans and in the district, but there was nothing to be seen by the many small groups which collected at possible points of vantage. Nor was there the slightest panic.

A lecture was interrupted at the Town Hall by the lights being extinguished, but the lecturer coolly proceeded with his discourse with the aid of a flashlamp for some time, and perhaps nothing could more clearly emphasize St. Albans sense of immunity from, at any rate immediate danger than that scene of a calm and collected audience listening in the dark to a lecture on pig-keeping.

Later the citizens composed themselves to sleep with the sound of protective gunnery still booming on the midnight air, some wondering if the sudden fog, following upon so beautiful a moon-lit night, was in the nature of a providential assurance (as in the case of the tempest and the Spanish Armada), that the righteous shall prevail, as ever.
Source: *Herts. Advertiser, 2nd February 1918.*

A painting is offered to St.Albans Abbey.

An informal Vestry meeting was held at St. Albans Abbey on Friday to discuss a proposed gift of Alderman and Mrs. Faulkner to the Abbey of a painting that they have bought from Mr. Frank O. Salisbury

220

which depicts the funeral procession through St. Albans of Queen Eleanor, wife of King Edward I.

The painting is 17 feet by 6 feet in a frame of gilded oak with coats of arms of the different towns through which the Queen's remains had been taken. Mr Salisbury himself proposed that the painting should hang in the South Transept on the west wall facing east.

A formal Vestry Meeting followed the informal meeting at which members accepted the gift with gratitude and appreciation, subject to permission being given by the Chancellor of the Diocese of St. Albans.
Source: *Herts. Advertiser, 16th February 1918.*

St. Albans bakers agree to using potatoes to make bread.

The Mayor of St. Albans presided over a meeting of bakers of the city and neighbourhood and it was agreed to agree to the proposal put forward by Lord Rhondda and the Ministry of Food that potatoes should be used in the making of bread so as to conserve cereal supplies and release quite a large number of ships from carrying grain and so be able to freight other food necessities.
Source: *Herts. Advertiser, 16th February 1918.*

Lady Wernher helps food production.

The call to landowners to increase the food supply of the country by converting grazing land into tillage has met with a ready response. Lady Wernher, owner of the Luton Hoo Estate has taken steps to promote this object. 84 acres are being ploughed in the park, which is in addition to the acreage being ploughed at the request of the County Committee. Lady Wernher has acquired a motor tractor and will afford its use by tenant farmers for all methods of more intensive cultivation.
Source: *Herts. Advertiser, 16th February 1918.*

A visit to Jerusalem in Palestine.

Corporal J. Hiller, Army Veterinary Corps, who lives at 3 Queen-street, St. Albans writes:
I have made my hoped-for visit to Jerusalem and what a wonderful

place it is. I went with a party conducted by the Senior Chaplain of our Division.

The first place of interest was a palace built on the site of King Herod's palace. Next we visited the church of the Holy Sepulchre, which is built on Calvary. Unfortunately this place is closed to visitors. Then we went to a beautiful mosque built on the site of the Temple. We also went to Bethlehem, the Mount of Olives and the Garden of Gethsemane.

The streets of Jerusalem are very narrow and are built in the form of steps; there is hardly a level street in the place. The streets in the centre are arched over, with just a few places left to let in the light so that it is like walking through lots of tunnels. A number of white donkeys are used out here for dodging about and for carrying messages.

Unfortunately we had to move before the melons were ripe and are now in the hills where, when it rains, it goes on for days without stopping and the mud is awful. We have to be thankful that we are in billets and have our horses with us, so we do not have the worst of the bad weather, for it is very cold.
Source: *Herts. Advertiser, 16th February 1918.*

Wheathamstead soldier returns from a Prison Camp.

Private Arthur Hewson of Wheathamstead was in the 1st Battalion, Bedfordshire Regiment who first went to France in April 1915. He took part in three engagements during the Battle of the Somme, was gassed twice and during the winter of 1916 and early 1917 took part in a number of bombing raids. In April, when the Canadians captured Vimy Ridge, he was struck by a piece of shrapnel and had his left leg shattered. He crawled into a shell hole for shelter and lost consciousness. When he awoke he was picked up by the Germans who took him to a German dug-out, and from there to the town of Douai, where his leg was amputated. He was ill whilst there and for fourteen days had no dressing of the stump. From there he was taken to Tournai and then to Duisberg in the Rhineland where he arrived on

11th May 1917. Though treated reasonably in the hospital, the food received by patients was horrible with three slices of black bread for breakfast at 8 a.m. which was washed down with a wretched concoction called coffee, which tasted like burnt barley. At noon it was black peas and beans in soup and then at 3 p.m. and at 6 o'clock another ration of soup. Had it not been for the parcel from home, few of our brave fellows would have survived.

From Duisberg Hospital he was removed to Dulmen Camp, Westphalia. Here he met Private W.East of Wheathamstead Hill who was taken prisoner about the same time. Both at Duisberg and at Dulmen there were French, Russian, Italian, Romanian and Portuguese prisoners as well as British. Here he remained until 6th January 1918, but the food supply deteriorated. Later he was taken with others to Aachen, the German border town where the Crown Prince visited them. On reaching Rotterdam they were visited by Queen Wilhelmina of Holland. They crossed to England in the ship Koningen Regentes, where concerts were given by both Dutch sailors and the English soldiers just liberated.

On arrival in England, Private Hewson was taken to King George's Hospital, London where he received every attention. What impressed Private Hewson most was the King's message printed on a card which was handed to each of the released prisoners, which read as follows:

The Queen and I send our heartfelt greetings to the prisoners of war of my army on their arrival in England. We have felt keenly for you during your long sufferings, and rejoice that these are ended, and the new year brings you brighter and happier days. - George R.I.
Source: *Herts. Advertiser, 16th February 1918.*

Discharged soldiers.

1,703 soldiers and sailors have been discharged in the County of Hertford. Causes of discharge are as follows: Amputation of the right leg - 21; ditto left leg - 13; ditto right arm - 3; ditto left arm - 6;; ditto both arms and blind - 1; blind - 2; tuberculosis - 62; paralysis - 10;

rheumatism etc. - 61; insanity - 32; shell-shock - 37; wounds - 231; general sickness - 385; dead and removals - 22; no details yet - 115.

Treatment (in-patient): 102 men have received, or are receiving, the treatment ordered; 20 cases are being arranged for, and in 10 cases have refused treatment. Treatment (outpatient): 78 men have been, or are being treated; 56 cases being arranged for, and in 13 cases it has been decided that treatment is not necessary.

118 men have asked for training; 26 cases have been arranged for men to go to bootmaking (6), polytechnics (5), Ministry of Munitions (3), commercial work (3), sundries (6) and completed (3). Twelve cases have been sanctioned by the Ministry of Pensions and are waiting for vacancies; 2 men will start very shortly in motor tractor work.

Several of the men asking for training are not yet fit; two have taken up other employment and one man was unable to go to the Cordwainers' College owing to ill health.
Source: *Herts. Advertiser, 23rd February 1918.*

Last man of the original battalion.
Private Robert Bligh (35), Bedfordshire Regiment of 18 Alma-cottages, St.Albans and son of Mrs Harriet Bligh of 39 Old London-road, St. Albans has died from wounds received in France.

He was the only remaining man of the original battalion of the Bedfordshire Regiment which went to France at the beginning of the war. Like all others, this regiment has been brought up to strength at different times and the original men have naturally dwindled away. For some months he fought side by side with only the other man left of the same battalion and after every engagement it became almost a joke among the men to see them congratulate each other upon their continuous records. Unfortunately, however, the other poor fellow was killed by an unlucky shell about two months ago which left Private Bligh the sole survivor.

He was in the retreat from Mons in 1914, and with the exception of twenty days leave has been in and out of the trenches for the whole three and a half years. During this time he has had marvellous escapes, among the narrowest being a shot that passed through his cap and another later on carved its way through his pack. His rifle was shattered in his hand on two occasions and he was buried alive once by a shell which burst close by. He was seriously wounded on the day when he was told he would be coming home on leave and died on the day on which that leave would have begun.

With all the hardships he endured there was never a grumbling word from him; while he lay wounded his greatest and only trouble seemed to be that as he had lost his right arm his services would not be needed. When on one occasion it was suggested that he had done his bit, he immediately replied: "Don't be absurd, I want to be in at the finish and we are the very men they want for the job. "I never met a man" writes a friend of his, "who fought with a greater sense of duty and as stated, in a letter from the Chaplain on behalf of his friends, comrades, officers and men. "He did his duty bravely, dying as a true soldier and we all honour the memory for his noble example".
Source: *Herts. Advertiser, 2nd March 1918.*

Major Hesketh Prichard.
The son-in-law and husband of Lady Elizabeth, sister of Viscount Grimston of St. Germains, St. Michael's, St. Albans has been mentioned in dispatches a second time for gallant services in France.
Source: *Herts. Advertiser, 9th March 1918.*

St.Albans Artilleryman gains Military Medal.
Driver George Gray (25), Royal Field Artillery, husband of Mrs Gray, 35 Dalton-street, St. Albans has been awarded the Military Medal for his effort, whilst in Palestine in November 1917. Although he became wounded, he carried on driving until the loss of blood forced him to dismount. He was sorely missed when he had gone to hospital as he was always one of the best, with a winning smile on his face. Before the war he was gardener by Messrs. Sander and Son, nurserymen.

Mrs Gray's father, Sapper William Potter, Royal Engineers, of 30 Longmire Road, St. Albans has won both the Distinguished Service Medal and the Military Medal during the present war.
Source: *Herts. Advertiser, 9 March 1918.*

Meat rationing in St. Albans.

On the first day of meat rationing in St. Albans it was found that there was a shortage of 3,346 lbs of meat. During the day, through the Ministry of Food, part of the shortfall was made good
Source: *Herts. Advertiser, 9th March 1918.*

300 acres brought into arable production.

Between February and March 1918, another 300 acres of agricultural land was brought into arable production despite a chronic shortage of labour. Over 12,500 acres have now been ploughed up and only one occupier has refused to co-operate with the *Hertfordshire War Agricultural Committee,* who took him to court and had their case upheld by the magistrates who fined the occupier £100 and costs.
Source: *Herts. Advertiser, 30th March 1918.*

German prisoners of war.

Twelve camps for 600 German prisoners of war have been sanctioned in Hertfordshire. There are camps in Bishop's Stortford, Braughing, Hatfield, Offley, Rickmansworth, St. Albans, Stevenage and Tring.

So far 160 Germans are being used on the land: no more than three prisoners are allocated to any one farm. The farmer is responsible for the safe custody of the prisoners and is required to notify the local police of their arrival. He is responsible for providing them with housing, straw for their palliasses, cooking utensils, crockery and washing facilities. For each prisoner, the farmer pays the camp commandant 25s 0d. minimum a week.
Source: *Herts. Advertiser, 30th March 1918.*

226

"Now boys, change here for 'Blighty' ".

This was a cry of a cheery youth with his head swathed in bandages as the hospital train drew into Napsbury sidings on Tuesday evening. The trains consisted of six wards with 20 cots each and 100 "walking" cases. These latter presented a pitiable appearance as they hobbled out on to the platform. Unshaven, begrimed and tattered, with arms in slings and heads bandaged, and yet cheery withal, they had come from the greatest battle in the world's history. Asked how things were going, the reply was "Oh, we're having a rotten time, but we're winning all right".

About 35 of the *Herts. Medical Volunteer Corps* paraded at 4.50 and though the train was half an hour late, it was cleared by 6.45 and by 7 p.m. the ambulance men were back in their several civilian duties which they had left on receiving the call.
Source: *Herts. Advertiser, 30th March 1918.*

Great Battle in France.

Heavy losses were suffered by the enemy in the latest attacks in France. "Great Battle in France; hostile forces held" epitomised Saturday's news of the offensive. The front extended to 60 miles and the number of men engaged, possibly exceeded 2,000,000 in all, opened on Thursday morning.

On Saturday night Sir Douglas Haig wired that a terrific struggle was going on in the air and that fifty German planes had been brought down. The enemy's massed troops had again offered good targets to our low-flying aeroplanes, and our squadrons had dropped over fourteen hundred tons of bombs on hostile billets and ammunition dumps, and upon the areas in which the enemy's attacking troops were concentrated. All our machines had returned safely.
Source: *Herts. Advertiser, 30th March 1918.*

Feeding the troops.

Private Robert Titmus writes from France to Mr. H.R.Wilton Hall:
15th March. - It was somewhere about the 6th March when the

227

Battalion moved up into the line after a few days rest from the trenches. We left one evening about 8.30 and' reached our dug-out about 9 o'clock. It was quite comfortable and just behind the lines. I had to stay at Headquarters with the cooks to attend to the water supply and see that there was no waste. There I saw how the troops are fed when they are actually in the line and it is a really interesting operation. Carrying parties come down at mealtimes and everything is done to secure that the food shall be kept hot on its way to the men.

During the time that I was in the line I had to sleep with only my greatcoat and a ground sheet to cover me on the ground. Fortunately the weather was warm and only at the dead of night did I feel the cold. Fritz was fairly quiet during the daytime, usually started firing about dusk and kept it up until daybreak. At times I seem to go quite deaf, but that soon wears off.
Source: *Herts. Advertiser, 30th March 1918.*

Death of a prisoner of war taken at Mons, 1914.

The funeral took place in Soldiers' Corner at St. Albans cemetery on Saturday of Sergeant Henry Edmund Angel who died at Napsbury Military Hospital on the previous Wednesday. Military honours were accorded. The body was conveyed to the cemetery on a field gun-carriage, three volleys were fired over the grave by men of the Queen's Regiment. The Revd. W.E. Chadwick, D.D. principal chaplain at Napsbury officiated.

Sergeant Angel, who leaves a widow and a son of eight years, lived at Berkeley-mews, Portman-square, London W. He belonged to the pre-war army, joining the 19th Hussars with whom he served four years. Then he joined the Military Mounted Police, in which corps he served another four years. He served in the South African War, for which he received a medal and two bars. He served six years in the reserve and was called up to rejoin his unit at the outbreak of war. He was severely wounded and taken prisoner at the Battle of Mons in August 1914 and was 3½ years in German prisoner camps. He went through terrible hardships and suffered untold horrors at the hands of

This is to Certify that

Violet Grimston

having completed Five years' service as Nurse of the Voluntary Aid Detachment Herts 38 raised by the British Red Cross Society has been elected by the Council as a Member of the Society and is thereby entitled to wear a Member's Badge for the period that membership of a Detachment is maintained.

Lansdowne

CHAIRMAN OF COUNCIL.

CHAIRMAN OF EXECUTIVE COMMITTEE.

Frank Hastings

SECRETARY.

Date 11 April 1918 M 7289

After five years service as a Voluntary Aid Detachment nurse,
at Bricket House hospital, Violet Grimston was elected
a member of the British Red Cross Society, 1918.

NOTHING is to be written on this side except the date and signature of the sender. Sentences not required may be erased. If anything else is added the post card will be destroyed.

Postage must be prepaid on any letter or post card addressed to the sender of this card.]

I am quite well.

~~I have been admitted into hospital~~

{ sick } and am going on well.
{ wounded } and hope to be discharged soon.

~~I am being sent down to the base.~~

I have received your { ~~letter dated~~ _____
{ ~~telegram~~ ,, _____
{ parcel ,, *11-1-18*

Letter follows at first opportunity.

~~I have received no letter from you~~
{ ~~lately~~
{ ~~for a long time.~~

Signature } *E. a. Taylor*
only

Date *15-1-18*

Wt W3497293. 29246. 6000m. 9716 O. & Co., Grange Mills, S.W

Example of the standard army postcard sent home from the 'front. This (enlarged) card was sent to Grimston Tyres Ltd

through terrible hardships and suffered untold horrors at the hands of his captors, with the result he was repatriated to England in January of this year suffering from mental derangement. His widow, Mrs Angel, his sister and other relatives attended the funeral.
Source: *Herts. Advertiser, 6th April 1918.*

An Irish soldier's funeral.

The interment with military honours took place in Soldiers' Corner on Tuesday of Lance Corporal Michael Moore of the *Royal Munster Fusiliers.* He had been a prisoner of war for some considerable time, which had a serious effect upon him and he was very strange and quiet after his repatriation. The Revd. Dr. Power, Roman Catholic Chaplain at Napsbury officiated. A firing party and buglers took part, the latter sounding the "Last Post".
Source: *Herts. Advertiser, 6th April 1918.*

"Our historic quilt" embroidered at Napsbury.

Transportation from all the turmoil and nerve-racking experiences of the battlefield to the quiet and calm of a military hospital has presented problems that were unanticipated before the war.

As a means of diverting the minds of the men, some ladies hit upon the idea of instructing them in the art of needlework, which could be done while they were still bed-ridden. It cannot be said that the idea at the outset was altogether favourably received. One stalwart fellow openly stated "I'd rather face the Germans than do it". But the ladies could afford to practice patience; and surely enough, the idea was in time assimilated by this stern fighter and one day he remarked somewhat apologetically, "I'll think I'll try a bit". And so he did; and what is more, he became one of the most adept needleworkers in the ward, under the expert instruction of ladies skilled in needlework.

Material with designs stencilled upon it, and a selection of coloured silks were provided, and employed, in the process of training, upon doileys, tea cosies, mats, 'duchesse sets' and so on, and as the men advanced in skill they were entrusted with the more exacting task of

This has led up, by gradual stages to the execution of a very interesting piece of work, which it is hoped, will become a treasured possession of the City of St. Albans. It is composed of a remarkable collection of forty-two regimental badges worked by men in one of the wards at Napsbury Hospital. The base is of Irish linen, the whole being arranged with a suitable border and bearing at the foot the names of the twenty-eight men who have actually accomplished the work. The badges are principally those of the regiments of the men who have been under treatment at Napsbury since its opening, and those included, beside the regiments of the British Isles are those of the Dominions - Canadian, Australian, South African and Newfoundland.

The eagerness with which the men have applied themselves to this task - the ultimate object being to assist the Red Cross Funds in Hertfordshire - has been no less remarkable than the skill displayed by many of them whose previous acquaintance with the use of a needle was practically nil. For instance, a coal-miner and a cobbler, both showed a remarkable aptitude as embroiderers, and an Australian who openly confessed that he had never even so much as sewn on a button before, accomplished work that would be a credit to the most delicate of feminine fingers. A groom, again, proved a most efficient worker. The badge of the Buffs was worked by a man whose right arm was amputated at the shoulder, and that of the King's Own by a sergeant whose right arm was injured in seven places, and he, like his comrades set every one of the delicate stitches with his left hand.

Before being put together, twenty-two badges were sent to H.M. The Queen for inspection, and her Majesty was so much impressed that she sent a letter expressive of warm appreciation of the work. Art needlework experts at South Kensington said that the needlework was unique and could not be reproduced for less than £200.
Source: *Herts Advertiser, 13th April 1918.*

Naval blockade of Zeebrugge and Ostend.

Stokers Petty Officers E.Muskett and A.Wiggens describe the action in which their ship, H.M.S. Sirius was sunk:

We left our base on the 22nd April and proceeded towards Zeebrugge and Ostend [in attempt to blockade the German submarine fleet who were using that part of Belgium as a repair yard for their submarines]. The wind was in our favour and after getting into position, most of the ships' companies left and the remainder carried on to the destination. Everything went favourably until we were getting into Ostend when the wind changed taking the smoke screen away from us and leaving us bare to face the enemy's guns. But having so successfully crept to our position so far, there was no question but to carry on.

We had a very hot time of it. All the batteries were concentrated on us and owing to the intense fire we could not get to our objective, but we did what we could. We were on fire and practically sinking before we got to our place. The first shell had reached us three-quarters of an hour before we got there, and then the Germans began sending barrage and barrage. We had all sorts of fire - star and gas shells, explosive bullets - everything that there was to be had. When we found our ship was grounding the captain gave orders to abandon her. The stokers had to watch the ship for casualties and there being none on the ship he gave the order to get into the boats. Just as we were getting into them one of our motor launches came alongside and took part of the crew off, including ourselves. The motor boat had then to leave owing to the dreadful fire, and when it got a little distance we found we had left some men behind, so the captain of the motor boat proceeded back to the 'Sirius' on the opposite side and took off the Captain, First Lieutenant, and leading torpedo-man. We then had machine guns and searchlights drawn on to us and, altogether, experienced a very warm time. After getting about three miles away it was ascertained that there had still been aboard the 'Sirius' the Engineer Officer and other men, so the Captain hailed another motor boat and told him to go to the 'Sirius' but when he got there he found that he could not get near owing to the intense fire so he gave those on board up for lost. Those of us in the motor boat were then taken to Dunkirk and from there to Dover. On arriving at Dover we heard the glad news that those who were left on the 'Sirius' had got away in one of the ship's boats, and then after pulling for twenty-two miles, they

were picked up by a naval vessel.
Source: *Herts. Advertiser, 6th May 1918.*

Able Seaman C.Yellop on H.M.S.Intrepid tells his story:
We left our base in the *Intrepid* with the remainder of the blockade
vessels, but parted from '*Sirius*' and '*Brilliant*' which had to carry out
their work at Ostend. While we were disembarking the spare hands,
the '*Vindictive*' steamed ahead and arrived at the Mole at Zeebrugge
half an hour before we were due to reach her. But we had a mishap
when the motor launch came alongside to take off our spare hands, as
she got her propellers entangled in the tow ropes and could not come
alongside. It was then too late to make other arrangements to take off
the men who should have left the ship, so we proceeded with them on
board. They formed a gun crew between them and some of the men
stood by the boats ready for lowering when the order was given.

When we were getting near to Zeebrugge we heard the terrible
bombardment of the monitors but could not see anything owing to the
dense clouds of smoke thrown out by the different motor launches.
About ten minutes before we got to our position we could just discern
'*Vindictive*' alongside the Mole. We steamed in, in the following order:
'*Thetis*', '*Intrepid*' and '*Iphigenia*'. The '*Thetis*' rammed the boom
defences, but in doing so got the nets entangled with her propellers
and ran aground, so the other two carried on past. Just as we got past
the '*Thetis*' she received she got a salvo right amidships, but we could
not see what damage was done. As we passed her, her crew sang out
'*Carry on Intrepid*' and '*Good Luck*'. We then proceeded to go into the
channel, firing our guns on either side. When we got into our position
the captain said "Ring the first alarm" - this was to clear the stokeholes
and engine rooms, barring a few men detailed to do the last trick.
When we got into our position the captain gave the orders for
everyone to abandon ship, except two officers and two torpedo men,
detailed to sink her. But with the port engine going full speed astern,
two boats, as they touched the water, were washed away. Although
half full of men, others, myself included, were still on board and had
no boats. I went forward to see if I could get into other boats but not

no boats. I went forward to see if I could get into other boats but not seeing them I returned to see if I could get a raft. Then the ship blew-up. I left all my kit with which we had been issued bar my lifebelt and knife and leaped over the side. I tried to get away from the ship but it was sinking and was drawing me down. Then I received a smack across the head from the oar of a skiff. "Why its young Yellop", said one of the fellows in the skiff and pulled me in and I lay exhausted in the bottom, as I was suffering from being half drowned and from the effects of gas. I was only in the skiff for two minutes when we passed a cutter that was in a whirlpool. Some of those men jumped into the skiff which immediately sank. We were then between the stern of *'Intrepid'* and the wall of the channel. I clambered into the cutter and hung on, though I thought she was going down. Then a motor launch took us aboard which caught fire. Exhausted I burst open a door and found myself in the galley where I got my breath back again. We were then well outside the harbour and went alongside *'H.M.S.Warwick'* and taken aboard. We all had our clothes dried and were given food and wanted nothing. Vice Admiral Roger Keyes, who had commanded this enterprise was on board. Once in Dover we were placed on a depot ship for twelve hours and then we were sent to billets, where local people paid for food out of their own pockets. The following day we were sent to Chatham and were afterwards given leave.

Lieutenant-Commander James Dawburn Young, R.N.V.R. who was killed at Zeebrugge, had lived in Grosvenor-road, St. Albans. He was educated at St. Albans School from 1887 to 1893. A Fellow of the Surveyors' Institution. he then called to the bar.

Lieutenant Alan Cory-Wright of Welwyn who was a lieutenant on the *'Intrepid'* was wounded but reached Dover safely. Aged 22 years he is the third son of Sir Alan Cory-Wright of Ayot-place, near Welwyn.
Source: *Herts. Advertiser, 6th May 1918.*

Sale of Napsbury Hospital needlework.

The Mayor and Mayoress of St. Albans declared open an exhibition and sale of needlework made by wounded soldiers at Napsbury

Military Hospital. On display was the tapestry comprising forty-two regimental badges, which it is hoped can be retained in St. Albans, provided £200 can be raised One donation of £50 was immediately promised.
Source: *Herts. Advertiser, 6th May 1918.*

Frank O. Salisbury painting.

Mr. Salisbury's painting entitled "*Their Majesties the King and Queen visit to the battle districts of France*", which is to be hung in the Royal Exchange, London EC, was on view at the Royal Academy where it was given the place of honour.
Source: *Herts. Advertiser, 11th May 1918.*

Written in a Church Army recreation tent.

Trooper Richard Maffey, Berkshire Yeomanry Base, British Expeditionary Force, Egypt writes to Viscount Grimston, Grimston Tyres Ltd.
16th March 1918. - My Lord, You will probably be surprised to hear that I have arrived in Egypt. We were 13 days on the water. I suppose we ought to congratulate ourselves upon having dodged Fritz in the Mediterranean. It was a very pleasant journey we had. Of course we had our horses to attend to which certainly took up the best part of the time. I was one of the fortunate men who was not troubled with sea-sickness and this added to the pleasures.
Source: *Gorhambury Collection. 4th Earl of Verulam's Business Correspondence.*

Errors of judgement cause two airmen to crash.

An inquest was held into the circumstances in which Second Lieutenant William Ernest Le Feuvre (29) R.A.F. and Cadet William Winslow Wait (21) U.S.A. of the Training Squadron, London Colney, crashed two days before on Thursday in two separate incidents.

Captain Gordon Davis said that he instructed Lieutenant Le Feuvre to take Lieutenant Manning up for instructions in landing. He saw the machine start off, and when at a 150 feet up it did a sharp turn to the left, and then nose-dived and crashed on to the aerodrome. The deceased, who was found with his neck broken and with extensive

234

injuries, had been an experienced pilot. The accident was the result of an error of judgement. He was flying a dual-control machine and it was hard to say how the accident happened. Machines were always overhauled before going up. An American, Lieutenant Wigle said that he had been flying this machine for two hours previously.

In a separate accident, Captain G.W.Allen, M.C. said that he had sent Cadet Wait up to practice firing, and apparently he was flying at low altitude over the Elstree reservoir, when the machine made a steep dive with the engine full on. Cadet Wait had fired three bursts at the target and then tried to pull the machine out diving too quickly. Owing to the fact that the engine was on he attained an enormous speed and in attempting to "feather-out", the wings crumpled-up, resulting in a vertical nose-dive into the reservoir. In this case the Jury returned a verdict of "death from suffocation by drowning", by falling into the Elstree Reservoir, owing to an error of judgement.

The victims of the air crashes were buried with full military honours in the St. Albans cemetery in the presence of one hundred of their late comrades, both officers and men. As the cortege approached the gates two aeroplanes circled overhead, one dipping very low. The Last Post was sounded on bugles, but the third bugler, who provided the solemn echo, had been posted too far away and against the wind, and few heard him.
Source: *Herts. Advertiser, May 1918.*

Cathedral Organist reports for duty.
Mr. W.L. Luttman, M.A. B.Mus. (Cantab) organist of St. Albans Cathedral since 1907 has offered his services to the Admiralty and has been appointed in the anti-submarine department. He reported for duty on Wednesday.
Source: *Herts. Advertiser, 18th May 1918.*

Killed in action etc.
Throughout the Great War, the Hertfordshire Advertiser and St. Albans Times, reported on those who were killed in action, wounded, missing or having become a

prisoner of war. Except in a very few instances, the compiler decided not to list all the casualties. In 1918, the numbers of casualties much increased. Here are some whose names were listed on 18th May.:

Private Walter Cutting, (19) Wheathamsted of *South Staffordshire Regiment* has been missing since 26th October 1917.
Driver Frederick Stone, (25) formerly of Grosvenor-road, St. Albans of *Royal Engineers* was killed in France on 27th April 1918.
Sergeant William Nash, Welwyn of the *Rifle Brigade*, died from wounds received, in France on 22nd April 1918.

Major Charles Clark, M.C. (32), of Thorley, near Bishop's Stortford , R.F.A. was killed on 25th April.
Private Fred. Biggerstaffe of Chipperfield is reported killed in action.
Private F.Bates of Chipperfield is reported killed in action.
Private Archie Biggerstaffe is a prisoner of war in Germany.

Private Lewis Taverner, Sarratt has been wounded for the sixth time.
Private Samuel Draper, Ayot Green of the *Motor Transport, Army Service Corps* was killed in action on 20th April. Another son, Rifleman George Draper was killed in action in October 1916.
Private Horton, Watford who has been missing since 21st March is a prisoner of war in Germany.

Private Cyril Kilby, Watford was killed in a recent battle. His elder brother was killed in the autumn of 1916.
Corporal Frederick W.Waters, of Westbourne-terrace, St. Albans of Hertfordshire Regiment, who has been missing since 31st July 1917 is assumed killed in action. A brother Private Joseph Waters, of *Herts R.F.A.* was killed in Egypt in August 1916.
Private C.Brown, M.G.C., of High Street, Rickmansworth was killed on 6th May 1918.

Private Sidney Sibley (35), Harpenden was killed on 24th April.
Bombardier W.H.Walker (25) of Station-road, Radlett died of wounds on 4th April 1918. His brother was killed on 5th December 1917.

236

Death of Corporal Philip Kingham, M.M.
Former member of Herts. Advertiser "literary" staff.

Corporal Philip Kingham, who shot himself last Sunday morning, died a soldier's death and sacrificed himself for his country as truly as if he had fallen in France. For two years, from November 1914 to November 1916, Philip Kingham served in the ranks of the *Hertfordshire Regiment*, having joined in August 1914, when he was not yet 19 years old. The youngest son of Mr. and Mrs. W.R. Kingham, "Myfanwy", Russell -avenue, St.Albans, he was educated firstly at *Hatfield Road School, St. Albans* from where he obtained a scholarship to the *St. Albans Grammar School*. While there he was attached to the *Officer's Training Corps* where he served as a bugler. He attended *Marlborough-road Wesleyan Church* Sunday School and after he had become proficient in musical studies he became deputy organist.

Upon leaving the Grammar School, he entered the offices of the *Herts Advertiser* as an apprentice journalist and showed marked promise. He was a diligent and studious reader; a youth possessing more than average common sense and self respect and showed many marks of "making good" in the profession he had chosen to adopt.

But when the war broke out his intense patriotism was displayed and he volunteered immediately for service and joined the *Hertfordshire Regiment (Territorial Force)*, accompanied it to Bury St.Edmunds for training and went out to France and Flanders with the regiment on 5th November 1914. He went through two years of the most strenuous work with the *Herts Guards* including several of the great battles of that period, and escaped without a scratch. He was then slightly wounded and sent to the base but soon returned to the firing line and during the *Battle of the Somme* in an important counter-attack, when his lieutenant had fallen and he was practically in charge of his platoon, who were closely following the barrage and where he was somewhat severely wounded in the knee. That was in November 1916, and he was invalided home and since that time had been undergoing treatment with his knee. For his efforts in this battle, he was awarded the Military Medal. He had been in various military hospitals; latterly he had been in hospital at Brighton and was then transferred to a convalescent home at Hove. The trouble with his knee and the obstacle it placed in the way of his return to active service had been a source of considerable dissatisfaction to him; he was, as he put it "fed-up" with a life of inactivity and yearned to get back to the fighting; and when he had last visited St. Albans a month ago and was wishing "good-bye" to his father, he cheerily remarked "I hope soon to be back in France". He was absolutely fed-up with hospital life and frequently requested that he be sent out to the front, but the medical officers would not pass him fit for active service again on account of diseased bone in the knee.

So persistent was he in his request to be doing more useful work and eventually he was transferred to the *Landguard Fort, Felixstowe*. He died as a result of a self-inflicted shot from a rifle and was found in an ablutions block, lying on the floor in a pool of blood. At the inquest, the Jury found that he had committed suicide whilst of unsound mind. It was revealed that he dreaded being discharged.

His body was returned to St. Albans and the funeral was held at Marlborough-road Wesleyan Church and was then buried in the Hatfield-road cemetery, St. Albans (Section E-F) whilst the "Last Post" was sounded by buglers of the training reserve squadron.
Source: *Herts. Advertiser, 25th and 1st June 1918.*

Soldiers' Tapestry.

A proposal, made by Mrs. Chadwick, writing from St. Peter's Church vicarage that the tapestry made by injured soldiers at Napsbury Military Hospital, should be placed on the wall of the Public Free Library opposite the Carnegie window where it would form a very desirable memorial of the war and would prove an object of great interest to a large number of visitors. The St. Albans City Council unanimously agreed to accept the offer and act on the suggestion.
Source: *Herts. Advertiser, 25th May 1918.*

Women's Land Army Rally at St. Albans.

The rally of women workers on the land held on Thursday afternoon was a great success in every way. There was an impressive procession of full-time and part-time workers, with the St. Albans Grammar School Cadet band at its head, and was accompanied by an aeroplane flying overhead, from which were scattered leaflets appealing for recruits.

Source: *Herts. Advertiser, 25th May 1918.*

Private Blow's life as a clerk

Private T.A.Blow attached to the Q.M.G.Branch, G.H.Q., 1st Echelon, B.E.F. France to his former employer, Viscount Grimston, Grimston Tyres Ltd:

13th June 1918. - Your Lordship may remember that I was sent out to France as a shorthand typist. After a few days at Le Havre I was posted to this place, where I am engaged in typing correspondence and long Returns. The work is rather trying and the hours are long. Two other typists are employed in the same office as myself and do similar work. We get to the office soon after 7 a.m. and leave at night at 10 o'clock. During the day we have two hours for recreation, during which time we must do our correspondence and the many little jobs one must do for oneself when away from home.

The newspapers will have informed you that the enemy's aeroplanes are very busy bombing the back areas recently. Because of this, a number of us have been sent to sleep under canvas at a camp some distance away. This makes it necessary for us to rise soon after 6 a.m. and it is about 11 p.m. before we get back to camp and settled down to rest.

Owing to the fact that it is impossible to have a light, you can imagine the confusion that reigns when the ten men are endeavouring to make their beds in the darkness. A rule of the camp is 'no talking'. It is rather hard to obey this command, when, say, one fellow treads on a tender part of another's anatomy. In trying to find a vacant place, one is pulled up short by an exclamation such as, "I say, old man, my face is not a door-mat" or an expression not quite as polite. Until a few days ago I had been sleeping in a hut on bed-boards, i.e. two small trestles and three planks placed on top. I must say I find Mother Earth and

239

leaves make a more comfortable couch than the boards, if there are too many stumps of shrubs, which have been cut to the ground, to make the ground unlevel. Fortunately the weather has been dry and I have not been troubled with rheumatism, a complaint that has troubled me since I have been "up".

The food here is good and well cooked, if not plentiful. But the ration is larger than civilians at home can obtain. Bathing facilities are good and there is no necessity for anyone here to get into a dirty condition.

I am afraid you [may] find this letter very uninteresting. Most of the news I could write, the Censor would be unable to pass. Mrs. Blow informs me you are busier than ever.

Source: *Gorhambury Collection. 4th Earl of Verulam's Business Correspondence.*

Food Rationing.

The possibility of allowing purchasers, on being issued with new ration cards to transfer to other retailers, if they so desire, has been dismissed by the Ministry who say that the matter of transfer is a matter for the *St.Albans City Food Control Committee.*

Source: *Herts. Advertiser, 15th June 1918.*

Call-up notice.

A St. Albans pensioner who is bordering on the sixties has received a calling up notice!

Source: *Herts. Advertiser, 15th June 1918.*

Tins of tripe.

The tins of tripe released from a St. Albans home during the "nervy" period when food hoarding revelations were broadcast are still on exhibition at the Town Clerk's Office. Presenting a ripe and venerable appearance, doubt evidently exists as to whether it would be safe to present them to one of the charitable institutions.

Source: *Herts. Advertiser, 15th June 1918.*

St. Albans Local Tribunal.
Review of the cases of men over 40 years.

Arthur J. Smith (45) married (Grade 2) of College-street, manager of the horticultural , seed and retail department of Messrs. E.Dixon and Son, corn and seed merchants, was granted three months further exemption.

Albert C.F. Fox (43) married (Grade 1) of Kingsbury-avenue, foreman and wood working machinist, etc. employed by Messrs. Miskin and Sons, builders. Application dismissed. To report on 22nd July.

William T. Goodchild (43) married (Grade 1) of Catherine-street, undertaker, informed the tribunal that his brother and partner was already in the Army and the business was the largest of its kind in St. Albans, His aged father was in ill health and took no part in the business. The applicant's son is joining the Army on 18th June. The firm has contracts with Napsbury Hospital, St. Albans Union [Workhouse] and Hill End County Asylum. Application deferred. Three months exemption. Told to join the Police Special Constabulary.

Bertie H. Levin (43) married (Grade 2) of Verulam-road, slaughterman with Mr. H. Patience, Holywell-hill. Levin was the only slaughterman that Mr. Patience had. Mr Patience was asked if butchers were prepared to co-operate with one another. He replied "Yes" and left it to the Tribunal's decision. Levin's application was dismissed and he was ordered to report for service on 8th July 1918.

Frederick Catlin (42) married (Grade 1) master tailor, of George-street, asked for exemption on one-man business grounds. He instructs a Church Lad's Brigade in drilling and band work, and has been a special constable for three years. Mr. Gape (National Service Representative) said that there was no doubt that the applicant had done a lot of good work voluntarily. It seemed as if the only holiday he would get would be in the Army. Appeal dismissed. Told to report on 12th August.

Source: *Herts. Advertiser, 15th June 1918.*

United Service at St. Albans Abbey.

2,500 people participated in the united service of intercession held in the *Cathedral and Abbey Church of St. Alban* on Wednesday evening when the whole of the religious denominations, other than the Roman Catholics were represented. The service was organised by the Dean in association with the Revd. W.H. Allen, representing the nonconformist churches. A Civic Procession was marshalled at the Town Hall and processed to the Cathedral, led by the band of the St. Albans Corps of the Salvation Army. Then came the Herts. Voluntary Medical Corps, Special Constables, St. Albans City Police, City Fire Brigade, City Justices, officials and members of the Corporation. The clergy and ministers processed with the Civic party. A number of V.A.D. nurses from Bricket House Hospital with Lady Thomson at the head joined the procession at the west front of the Cathedral. An invitation to shop keepers and licensed victuallers to close their premises so that their assistants could attend was generally followed. Every seat in the Abbey's Nave, Choir and Transepts was occupied and the service was conducted from the Organ Loft enabling the Ministers to have a commanding influence over both sections of the great assemblage. Never before, probably, has the historic Abbey Church held such a congregation, assembled on behalf of religious thought and a great national cause. Collections taken were donated to the *Herts Prisoners of War Fund* and the *St. Albans and Mid-Herts Hospital*, where the wives and families of those men serving their country are provided for.
Source: *Herts. Advertiser, 15th June 1918.*

Inquest on Flight Lieutenant's death.

The Coroner (Dr. Lovell Drage) held an inquest on Friday on the body of Lieutenant Russell Bruce Dale Whiteside, of the *Highland Light Infantry* who was attached to the *Royal Air Force*, who died as a result of injuries sustained whilst flying.

Edward Clifton, Major, R.A.F. said that on 10th June he was standing outside the sheds when he saw two machines flying towards the sheds, one driven by the deceased, who pulled it out steeply when the engine appeared to stop. He then put his nose down and dived vertically. When about the height of some small trees, the deceased pulled the machine out of the dive, hitting one of the trees and crashing in an adjoining field. The witness proceeded to the spot and found that the pilot had been got out of the machine and had been placed on the wings.

The officer was admitted to *Napsbury Military Hospital* at four o'clock on the afternoon of 10th June where he was operated upon, and from which he appeared to recover. However the following morning he developed signs of compression of the brain and died on the morning of 15th June. The cause of death was compression of the brain consequent upon fracture of the skull.

Before the accident, the officer had been in the air for fifty minutes. The machine had been overhauled prior to the flight.
Source: *Herts. Advertiser, 22nd June 1918.*

National Kitchens Committee.

A report of a *St. Albans City Council* committee has come to the view that the Corn Exchange should be adapted as a National Kitchen and Restaurant. The public will enter the building at the North End, and proceed down a gangway partitioned from the Restaurant, and pass by the Ticket Office towards the service counter, leaving the building by a new exit to be made on the East side. The food stuffs will be delivered to the existing South entrance and the two small rooms at that end of the building will be utilised as Stores. The necessary arrangements will be made for the Staff Cloak Room and Lavatory at the North end. The whole of the equipment proposed, as suggested by the Central Kitchens Branch of the *Ministry of Food*, who have examined the plan and approve of the general arrangements. The cost of structural alterations, fittings, drainage, equipment and contingencies will amount to £650 0s 0d. The Committee recommends that the plan and scheme be approved. It is understood that the Treasury will advance the whole cost, free of interest, such loan to be repaid by the Local Authority in ten yearly instalments.
Source: *Hertfordshire Record Office. St. Albans City Archives. (25th June 1918)*

Garden Fête raises funds for local hospitals.

Viscountess Grimston judged efforts by local schools to turn a penny into a shilling. *St. Albans High School* raised £31 1s 4¼d; *Alma-road Girls School* £14 8s 8½d; and *Fleetville County Council School* £9 12s 1d, whilst an open class resulted in £6 7s 8¼d, in all a total of £62 9s 2d. These trading competitions were intended to arouse a very real interest in the art of war philanthropy, on the basis that it may be easy for a wealthy man to sign a generous cheque, but not so easy for a small child to accumulate in more modest and humble fashion a substantial sum.

£500 has been raised from the garden fête which was held at Kitchener's Meads for the benefit of the *Bricket House V.A.D. Hospital* and other war-time organisations.

Source: *Herts. Advertiser, 6th and 13th July 1918.*

Ambulance men inspected.

Lord Clarendon inspected the *Hertfordshire Royal Army Medical Voluntary Corps* under the command of Major T.P. Grosart Wells at Birklands, St. Albans on Sunday morning, an event which was held in brilliant sunlight and with a aeroplane from the *R.A.F.Training Squadron* flying in the sky above. About sixty officers and men were on parade.

Source: *Herts Advertiser, 13th July 1918.*

Field Marshal, H.R.H. The Duke of Connaught
St. Albans School Officer Training Corps inspection.

On Tuesday afternoon, the *St.Albans School Officer Training Corps* paraded on the School field at Belmont Hill where they were inspected by H.R.H. The Duke of Connaught. 270 Cadets were on parade, headed by their bugle band (under Sergeant Drummer Johnson).

In the present war, 63 former cadets have been killed or have died from wounds; and 301 have been wounded. Commissions have been taken up by 325 and the following honours have been awarded: Distinguished Service Order, 4; Military Cross, 11; Military Medal, 4;

244

Distinguished Service Medal,1; Croix de Chevalier; while a large number have been mentioned in despatches.

A military display took place which commenced with a march-past. The Corps was in two companies and the "Eyes-right" movement as each passed the Field-Marshal was particularly pleasing, as was the acknowledgement of the soldier-like figure on the platform. Company and platoon drill followed, during which the Duke strolled about the field watching the various movements with careful observation. Later, two instructors - Company Sergeant-Major Rose and Sergeant Instructor Gray of the *Army Gymnastic Staff* attached to the *Queen's Regiment*, stepped into the arena, the signal for physical exercises to commence. Whilst the Duke conversed with them, the boys divested themselves of cap and tunic. The Corps was divided into two squadrons for the drill, C.S.M. Rose taking the seniors, whilst Instructor Gray drilled the juniors.

H.R.H. then addressed the cadets paying tributes to them and their headmaster, Major Montague Jones, who had, himself, been on active service in the war. After the Corps had marched away, the Duke talked with five wounded soldiers who were among the crowds at the entrance to the field. Informing the Headmaster of his feelings of satisfaction at the military display given by the Cadets, H.R.H. promised that he would sign a special copy of the War Office report on the inspection, so that it might be kept among the records of the school.
Source: *Herts. Advertiser, 13th July 1918.*

In Italy.

Sergeant F.C.Keightley of St.Albans writes from Italy, where Lord Cavan commands the allied armies in the fight against the Austrians:
Just a line to say that there are still a few of the old *Herts. Regiment* in Italy and although we belong to different battalions that is still the regiment we consider the best. We nearly always get the *Herts Advertiser* about a week old and then it is: "Did you see so and so is wounded?" or old ---------- has got the military medal", and we are

sorry to see many of the boys reported missing. Well, I expect some of you will be wondering what we are doing out here.

For a small portion of the time we are down on the plains, but even then we start training at 5 o'clock in the morning and keep on till 11 o'clock and then we have a 'silent period' as on the plains it is much too hot after 11 o'clock to do anything, so we have an enforced three and half hours' quietness and then tea and keep in till the cool of the evening. But when we are up in the mountains we are nearly always about 25 per cent short of men who are down with mountain fever, a kind of bad influenza. Well, we were holding the line in this sort of condition up here a few days ago and the Austrians took it into their head to give us a strafing one morning. They sent over gas and shrapnel and *whizz bangs* and we had a bad five hours. Then they managed to gain a place in our line owing to one of our posts being scuppered by their artillery and we had to fight for it, but they had come to stay and they were pouring men into the trenches wholesale. We were not strong enough to force them out at once so we blocked the trench and made it uncomfortable for them with bombs and I tell you we executed many of them.

Well, the day was fairly peaceful, although we all had some good practice at sniping and some good success as well. At night they brought up reserves but we did the same and next morning we counter-attacked and put the wind up them properly, and after some hours of pretty stiff fighting they cried 'enough'. We got plenty of prisoners and we also found heaps of dead. Our losses were few, so I fancy they paid a very high price for holding our line for twenty-four hours. We lost our two best officers and two were wounded.

In close fighting and with bomb, rifle and bayonet, or Lewis gun we are a match for about five times our own strength, and the odds on that Sunday were much greater than that and their losses and ours, counting killed, wounded and missing are at about 10 to 1. We are now waiting to come out for a week or so for a rest.
Source: *Herts. Advertiser, 23rd July 1918.*

246

Mentioned in despatches.

First class mechanic, *Royal Air Force,* Arthur J. Allen, son of Mr. J. Allen of Oswald road, St. Albans has been mentioned in despatches by General, Sir Henry Plumer, who considers this soldier's distinguished and gallant service, and devotion to duty, deserving of special mention.

Source: *Herts. Advertiser, 23rd July 1918.*

Note: General Plumer replaced Lord Cavan as Commander of the British Forces in Italy in November 1917 but returned to France and the Western Front in April 1918. During that period, Lord Cavan reverted to being Comander of the XIVth Corps in Italy. In April he succeeded Plumer and commanded the allied forces at the Battles of Asiago (June) and Vittorio Veneto (November). This later battle, which involved the crossing of the River Piave, north of Venice in full flood, was instrumental in bringing about an Armistice between the Austrians and the Allies in early November, one week before the Armistice was declared on the Western Front.

We arrive in Baghdad.

From a letter to his wife from Gunner J.J. Jackson, Royal Field Artillery of St. Albans who was a member of the old Herts. Artillery Battery:

Just before we reached Baghdad we had to cross the river Diala. On each side of this river are several British graves of soldiers who had the misfortune to drop whilst crossing the river. No better graves can be wished for as miniature gardens surround them.

During our stay, the majority of us had a good look round the place. It is 500 hundred miles from Basra by the river route and half that distance by land. Its population is about 140,000 of whom 55,000 are Jews. They wear a bright red fez and many have adopted European dress. They ask for double the price they want and if you are not as sharp as they are they do a good deal. The Armenians are equally as bad; if it was not for a government price list they would do us down thick and thin.

The main street of Baghdad is about the only street of any consequence: all other parts seem to be very dirty and narrow. All I

247

saw in Baghdad which was any good to look at were three mosaic towers which are very prominent for miles around. We are now in camp eighty miles north and lord knows where the 'Johnnie' [the Turks] are.

We went through the Persian hills after him and were in the hope of giving him something for our trouble, but as soon as we opened fire on him, he was glad to hop it and we were greatly disappointed.
Source: *Herts. Advertiser, 23rd July 1918.*

Proposed Memorial to the Kent family.
A special vestry was held on Thursday and it agreed that a faculty be sought from the *Chancellor of St.Albans diocese* to erect a memorial window to Mr. Thomas Kent, who had been a churchwarden at St. Albans Abbey for forty-five years, his wife, and two sons who fell on 1st and 4th August 1917 in the third Battle of Ypres.
Source: *Herts. Advertiser, 7th September 1918.*

Prisoners of War escape.
A hue and cry was raised throughout Hertfordshire on Friday night and during the weekend at the news of the escape of a German prisoner from the labour camp at Marsh Moor, North Mymms. Four prisoners attempted to escape but two were failed in the attempt. A third was quickly recaptured. Johann Tietzik (22) managed to get away and remained at large until Sunday evening, when he was re-taken at North Mymms, not far from the camp.
Source: *Herts. Advertiser, 7th September 1918.*

Hertfordshire Regiment in great offensive.
On 23rd August they joined in an attack [in France] and the operation was a great one, the objective, a very hard one, being taken as arranged. Records show that the men were magnificent when the order was given to attack and the Huns were greatly demoralised, literally hundreds of them surrendering. Two officers & 30 men were killed, 20 men are missing and 15 are wounded.
Source: *Herts. Advertiser, 7th September 1918.*

248

Flying fatality.

Alfred Seddon, a flying cadet, aged 18, of Bolton met with a sudden death by crashing his machine on 24th August near St. Albans. On the day of the fatality, Second Lieutenant Walker of the R.A.F. said he saw the machine driven by Seddon at 200 feet engaged in very flat gliding turns, and then at about 80 feet the machine stalled and began to spin, coming to earth in a vertical nose dive. A verdict of death by misadventure was announced by the Coroner.

Source: *Herts. Advertiser, 2nd November 1918.*

St. Albans National Kitchen opens.

The day before the new *Model National Kitchen* opened to citizens of St. Albans the Mayor and Corporation sampled a war-time luncheon at the Corn Exchange. The menu consists - Tomato soup, fish, mock goose and apple sauce, potatoes, French beans, pastries, lemon pudding and sauce, blanc- mange, rice pudding, ginger cake, and a cup of tea or coffee, from which it is possible to pick items to the cost of eighteen pence or a shilling. There were a few teething troubles but these were sorted out in a few days. On Tuesday food gave out and there were no teas served, although 400 suppers were either carried away or consumed on the premises.

Source: *Herts. Advertiser, 2nd November 1918.*

Napsbury Military Hospital.

On 5th November 1918, 94 injured soldiers arrived by sick convoy. 41 had gunshot wounds, 5 had influenza or bronchitus and 7 had been gassed. The remainder had various causes including debility, burns, varicose veins, mental instability and insanity.

16 were discharged in November (within a month of admission), 17 in December and 2 in February 1919. 22 were transferred to other hospitals. The shortest stay in hospital was 9 days and longest stay was 267 days.

Source: *Public Record Office. Napsbury Military Hospital records.*

Influenza epidemic.

The number of deaths in St. Albans in the first week of the epidemic was nine; last week the number increased to twenty (half military and half civilian) and there have been a number of deaths this week.

Though it is believed the outbreak is on the wane, the *Medical Officer of Health* has advised people to live in the open air as far as possible and to keep rooms well ventilated and full of fresh air. He also advised that the churches close their Sunday Schools. Day schools which had been closed for ten days reassembled the following day, but there was only 50 or 60 per cent. attendance, and at the request of the Medical Officer, they were closed for another week.

The nursing staff at *Napsbury Military Hospital* has suffered severely from the epidemic. There have been many cases among the staff, some of which have proved fatal, and a special ward has had to be set apart for them. Yesterday, there were still fifty of the staff "off duty", but we are assured that the epidemic is "on the wane" and the number of patients is decreasing.

At *Bricket House V.A.D. Hospital* the nursing staff have been sorely taxed by the influx of serious cases. Several have proved fatal. In order to give relief to the overworked nurses, members of the *Volunteer R.A.M.Corps* have been taking night duty and their assistance has proved of great value , especially in dealing with some of the more troublesome cases of delirium.

During the week-end, several members of the *National Kitchen*, St. Albans contracted influenza, with the result that on Monday morning the Management were faced with the position of being unable to open.
Source: *Herts. Advertiser, 9th November 1918.*

V.A.D. Nurse's Military Funeral.

Full military honours were paid at the interment [in Soldiers' Corner] of V.A.D. Nurse Hilda Florence Chadwick, aged 20, who died on 2nd November. She had nursed at *Napsbury War Hospital* since July, and had endeared herself to patients, sister-nurses and principals. The principal mourners were her mother, brother, sister and brother-in-law, all from Portsmouth and the officiating clergyman was the Revd. A. Thompson, a personal friend of the family.

The Countess of Verulam represented Bricket House, but the prevailing influenza epidemic prevented the nursing staff at Bricket House being represented. A firing party were present and three buglers sounded the 'Last Post'. The wreaths included tributes from the Matron, patients and nursing staff at Napsbury, the N.C.O.'s and men of the 9th Company, R.A.M.C., and from Col.Rolleston. Messrs. W. Goodchild & Sons, of Catherine-street, were the undertakers.
Source: *Herts. Advertiser, 9th November 1918.*

The Armistice is signed.

Captain H.N.G. Bushby, Royal Defence Corps, 1916-1919 of Wormleybury, Hertfordshire writes:
Monday, 11th November 1918. - To Hertford by 10.8 a.m. train from Broxbourne. It arrived at Hertford about 10.30 a.m. and the engine exploded 6 fog signals, the first intimation I had of the signing of the armistice. To Orderly Room [6 Maidenhead-street, Hertford] and noticed many flags hung out. At 11.10 a.m., QMS Howard told us, Lieutenant Evans and myself, that it was officially announced that the armistice was signed. Then the church bells were pealed.

I finished the morning's work, gave the Orderly Room staff a peace offering and on the way back saw Fore-street already gay with flags. Most men were subdued. Many women were weeping. A half company of soldiers marched by singing. There seemed little excitement.
Source: *Hertfordshire Record Office. Deposit D/EBuf1.*

Peace - Thank God!

Between Saturday and Monday, 9th to 11th November 1918, the German Kaiser abdicated together with the Crown Prince. During this time there was a rapid advance by the Allied armies including the taking of 18,000 German prisoners. In Germany revolution spread as the army joined the population in revolt. The Armistice, it was arranged was to come into force at the eleventh hour of the eleventh day of the eleventh month of 1918 and was signed to last for thirty-five days.

Source: *Herts. Advertiser, 16th November 1918.*

Herts. Advertiser first with the news in St.Albans.

The first intimations of peace were given in announcements which appeared outside the *Herts. Advertiser* offices, that the Armistice had been signed at 5 o'clock, to come into force at eleven o'clock.

Source: *Herts Advertiser, 16th November 1918.*

Hertfordshire County Council suspends meeting.

A sitting of the *County Council* in *St. Albans Town Hall* was suspended by the Chairman, the Right Honourable T.F. Halsey and he and members of the council proceeded to the balcony overlooking the Market-square. After announcing the cessation of hostilities, the assembled crowds waved flags and spontaneously burst into singing the National Anthem.

Source: *Herts. Advertiser, 16th November 1918.*

Reaction to the news.

Huge flags were quickly flying from roofs and church towers, the air-raid siren shrieked out in delight, church bells rang out and soon shops and houses, even in the remotest streets became beflagged with apparently every man, woman and child carrying a flag. In the afternoon local troops paraded through the streets. Local school children were given a day's holiday, having had it explained to them that a cessation of hostilities had occurred. Numerous thanksgiving services were held in the churches of many religious denominations. By Tuesday, Gabriel, the curfew bell in the city's Clock Tower was heard striking the hour, as in pre-war times.

Shortly after the announcement from the Town Hall balcony, an aeroplane was seen flying over the city, firing rockets. During the afternoon several hundred of the local troops paraded through the streets. A huge crowd gathered in the Market-square during the evening and the *City Band* played popular airs, and there was much singing, dancing and flag-waving. It was also refreshing to see the lamps alight again.

Local churches including *St.Paul's Church, St.Albans,* the joint congregations of *Trinity Congregational Church* and *Dagnall-street Baptist Church, Marlborough-road Wesleyan Church* held special services and special Masses were held in the Roman Catholic churches.
Source: *Herts. Advertiser, 16th November 1918.*

Local communities respond to the News.

School children were already on holiday in **Harpenden** because of the influenza outbreak and they and other people hurried into the streets when the church bells rang out about mid-day announcing the Armistice. Church services were held at night with silent prayers for the heroes who had laid down their lives for their country.

Flags were soon flying in **Hatfield**, but celebrations took place on Tuesday when the munitions workers at *Messrs. Waters & Sons* were given time off. Tradesmen closed their shops at mid-day for several hours and farmers gave their workpeople time off. A procession formed, led by the Rector and church officials which included uniformed nurses from the V.A.D. hospital and several wounded soldiers and discharged soldiers and sailors. A simple service was held in front of Hatfield House with addresses and a moment's silence. The Rector said "In honour of the Navy, I ask you to sing "Rule, Britannia". The first verse was then sung, and afterwards the three verses of the "National Anthem". Afterwards the gathering dispersed.

People "let themselves go" in **Watford**. Hooters and aircraft guns filled the air with a pandemonium of noise. Flags were hoisted on churches and public buildings, business premises and private houses and even pet dogs and cats were decked out in national colours. Impromptu dancing soon filled the streets and the following day the police report not a single occurrence of drunkenness the previous night.

Immense relief and thankfulness was felt at **Radlett** when people heard the news and special thanksgiving services were held in the Parish and Congregational Churches.

Immediately the glad tidings were heard in **Elstree**, the Rector held a special service of thanksgiving and another service was held the same evening. Children on holiday because of the influenza outbreak found it a special opportunity for a demonstration of joy, waving flags, dancing and singing. The rejoicings were restrained but sincere.

The inhabitants of **Welwyn** were not behind in showing their great joy at the Armistice. Immediately the people began to hang out flags and bunting and the whole place was full of animation. Patriotic songs were lustily sung and were the order of the day, and the Boy Scouts paraded the streets in the evening with their bugle band.

Work was suspended in **Codicote** when the news became known. The principal shops were closed and the large school flag was run up and school children were supplied with flags and marched round the village, accompanied by the Headmaster and the teachers, singing patriotic songs, and then assembled on the Hill and heartily sang the National Anthem. They then went to the school playground and saluted the flag and gave hearty cheers. In the village a large quantity of flags and bunting was displayed and in the evening the church bells rang out merrily.

Knebworth celebrated and the Boy Scouts bugle band led an enthusiastic crowd round the village and marched to *St. Martin's church* for a service of thanksgiving. The church remained open and lighted until 10 o'clock so that any who could not attend the service could go and offer up thanks privately. The V.A.D. hospital staff and patients lit a large bonfire.

The good news was received at **Kimpton** soon after eleven o'clock with joyousness prevailed that had not been known for years. To give additional brightness to the dull, rainy day, the church bells range out a merry peal.

The armistice celebrations at **North Mymms** included much flag waving and display of bunting, the ringing of bells, and the parading of the village by singing and joyous children. On Tuesday an unusually large congregation attended a special service of thanksgiving at the church.

Source: *Herts. Advertiser, 16th November 1918.*

Roman Catholic Chaplain awarded the V.C.

The Revd. Father Edward McGrath who for twelve months was an assistant priest at Beaconsfield-road, St.Albans Roman Catholic Church was awarded the Victoria Cross for services rendered whilst an Army Chaplain in Mesopotamia and France.

Source: *Herts. Advertiser, 16th November 1918.*

Hertfordshire Regiment to march into Germany.

An announcement has been made that the *Hertfordshire Regiment,* which has been at the front since November 1914 is to march into Germany flying the regimental colours which were deposited in Hertford Church before they left for France.

Source: *Herts. Advertiser, 7th December 1918.*

Bishop of St. Albans writes:

We seem to have lived years in the last few weeks. The entire collapse of the Central Powers of Europe - Bulgaria, Turkey, Austria and finally Germany; the acceptance by each of them of terms of armistice which would make any renewal of the war impossible, has caused great nations to thank God in a way beyond anything in the experience of most of us.

There will be problems enough for statesmen and for people during the weeks that are to follow. We shall meet them, I hope, with courage and firmness, and as our unity has been preserved during the more than four years that are past, we need not be ashamed to commit to God's keeping in private and public prayer the difficulties that are yet to be met.

Source: *St. Albans Diocesan Gazette, December 1918.*

Death of Miss Charlotte Day, W.R.A.F.

A fortnight ago last Tuesday, Miss Day, daughter of Mr. and Mrs. George Day, of 30 Marlborough-road left St. Albans bright, well, and happy, to join the Women's Royal Air Force at Salisbury. She caught cold at Salisbury and was taken to Blandford Camp suffering from influenza and was subsequently removed to Weymouth Royal Hospital, where she died from double pneumonia on Saturday.

The news has caused intense regret among a wide circle of friends. Miss Day who was 34 years of age, was a Sunday School teacher and a member of St. Saviour's Church and a member of the English Church Union. For some years she had been an assistant with Mr. H.A. Richardson, bookseller, High-street, but she was exceedingly anxious to take up war-work and for a considerable time before joining the W.R.A.F. she was an inspector at a munitions factory at Woolwich.

She leaves three sisters and three brothers. The funeral took place at St. Albans Cemetery on Thursday and was preceded by a service at St. Saviour's Church. An officer and twenty members of the W.R.A.F. from Shenley headed the cortege and were followed by a bugle party.

Source: *Herts. Advertiser, 7th December 1918.*

Civilian prisoner of war: a golfer's experience.

Mr. Arthur Andrews, golf professional of 28 Heath-road, St.Albans has returned home after four years spent as a civilian prisoner of war in the Ruhleben Camp, near Berlin. Mr. Andrews, who had been going to Germany in the summer months in the previous five years, and in during the summer 1914 had gone to lay out a golf course for Prince Henry of Prussia and others at Hanover. He became concerned at the outbreak of hostilities and suggested that he should return to England but the Prince ordered him to proceed with his contract. The Prince

256

said that he would be all right and would not be arrested and would be given safe escort home. Like many other Prussian promises this was destined to be broken and in November 1914 he was thrown into gaol for two days and then marched to the railway station through a jeering and derisive crowd en-route for Ruhleben Prison Camp. When we were ordered by the guards to work, we refused as we were civilians and I survived by conforming to the rules. We made life in the camp bearable and had an Arts and Science Union, a garden. We lived in daily hope of release. When the revolution finally came in Germany, the guards disappeared and we were allowed out where we pleased. I was among those who went to visit Berlin. There were many lively scenes and all the military buildings were seized and the officers were summarily relieved of their epaulettes by the Soldiers and Workers' Council, whom the guards from our camp promptly joined. At our camp the red flag was raised. Yes, my nerves are pretty bad, but this Christmas will be a very different season of "peace and goodwill" to the four Christmases which have preceded it for me, and for thousands of other ex-prisoners.

Source: *Herts. Advertiser, 14th December 1918.*

St. Albans "Thanksgiving Week".

£135,000 has been raised for the St. Albans Thanksgiving Week.

Source: *Herts. Advertiser, 14th December 1918.*

Lieutenant Frank Young, V.C.

Second Lieutenant Frank Young, late *1st Battalion, Hertfordshire Regiment (T.F.)* of Hitchin, joined up as a 14½ years old bugler. He was mobilised in his 19th year and served in France with his father, then a Sergeant-Major in the Battalion. Both father and son received commissions which were gazetted in 1917. Posted to his old Regiment, in the action of 18th September 1918, he bombed an enemy trench, clearing it single-handed, before he fell mortally wounded he was seen knocking out several of the enemy with his fists. Throughout four hours of intense hand-to-hand fighting, Second Lieutenant Young displayed utmost valour and devotion to duty.

Source: *Herts. Advertiser, 21st December 1918.*

Colours of the Bedfordshire Regiment.

Colours of the *1st Battalion, Bedfordshire Regiment* were handed over at St. Paul's Church, Bedford on Tuesday afternoon to an escort from France which included Sergeant Arthur Faulder, M.M. and bar, of St. Albans and Lieutenant Sheldrake, also of St. Albans. The colours are to be taken to the regiment.

Source: *Herts. Advertiser, 21st December 1918.*

Thomas Cook's representative returns from Austria.
The experiences of a St. Albans civilian.

As a representative of the tourist agents - Thomas Cook and Son, Mr. Ernest O'Dell, son of Mr. J. O'Dell of Victoria-street and St. Peter's-street, was in Austria in August 1914 at Karlsbad along with 170 other British people who were "taking the cure". At the outbreak of hostilities he was informed that he must consider himself a prisoner of war. Eventually all but six people and Mr O'Dell were released and these seven remained at Karlsbad until 1915. During that period they lived in the town but were not permitted to go to the theatre, were required to be within doors by 8 p.m. and to report to the police on a weekly basis. Their letters were opened and their money was retained, only just sufficient for their immediate requirements being doled out to them, for fear that they would escape by train. From October 1915 until March 1916 they were sent to a small village three miles away and then they were transferred to a general camp at Drosendorf, near Vienna, but there, too, they were allowed to live in the village and not in the camp which had Italian, French, Serbian, Russian and some British prisoners. They had their own club and were allowed to play football, but were restricted to the village, and allowed to be out until 11 p.m. "Regards treatment, I have nothing to complain of" said Mr. O'Dell. The food was bad so we welcomed the food parcels which came from Prisoners' Aid Society. Otherwise things would have been very bad. I was a prisoner from September 1914 until 1st November 1918 and I got off lightly compared with other poor wretches. We were allowed twenty cigarettes a month or five cigars and I was used to smoking twenty cigarettes a day! Whilst the French prisoners were repatriated long before us, by up to two years in some cases, we were left eating our hearts out with longing for home, wife and bairns. We only had German and Austrian newspapers to read and the occasional English newspaper, perhaps one in six months got through to us and we were often amused to read that our enemies were never defeated, their line was never and could never be broken through, and that they only made strategic retreats.

Some days before the Armistice we knew that the day of deliverance was approaching. When the great day did arrive we were not permitted to come home via Switzerland, as the Swiss refused to sign our passports, so we had to come via Trieste, Venice, Padua, Milan, Turin, Paris and Le Havre to Southampton. Now I am making up some leeway in the matter of good wholesome food. Out there we read that London was in ruins and the English were starving! I am glad that the reports in the German and Austrian papers were all lies. I never again want to see either Germany or Austria. My firm has been consistently good to me, and now I am going to indulge in a little rest and recuperation.
Source: *Herts. Advertiser, 21st December 1918.*

Another Airman is killed.

Last Thursday afternoon, Second Lieutenant James Lionel Andrews of the *Royal Air Force* was executing a number of stunts in the air and it appears that the deceased was unable to get his machine into a horizontal position before diving to the ground. He was killed instantly and the machine was wrecked. He was 31 years old, married and leaves a widow and two children. He and they had been living in Radlett. The Jury, at the Coroner's Court, returned a verdict of "Death from misadventure".

On Monday, his funeral took place at St. Albans Cemetery where he was accorded full Military honours. The service was conducted by the Revd. W.E.Chadwick, Vicar of St. Peter's, St. Albans and Chaplain at Napsbury Military Hospital.
Source: *Herts. Advertiser, 21st December 1918.*

Peace arrives in France and Belgium.

From two letters sent to St. Saviour's, St. Albans by Sergeant Folkes and Sapper Morley:

Sergeant Folkes writes, - We witnessed rather a touching scene a few days ago. It chanced to be that we were the first troops to enter a fairly large town, until recently occupied by the Hun. He left sooner than he intended to, and of course we took possession. Plenty of civilian inhabitants were left and the reception we received was grand. Little children who for four years hardly knew what daylight was, came running out to cheer their deliverers. Old men, women alike, the beast of a Hun had been giving them a bad time. You may picture their delight on seeing a different soldier than the one just left.

Sapper Morley writes, - There are a fair number of civilians here and they were all excited in the first few weeks of their liberation. Flags and garlands were hung from their houses and for days they looked hardly able to realize what had happened, and whether perhaps, it was but a dream.

In the early days of the war, six unknown English soldiers were killed here and are buried in the cemetery. The people have erected a fine monument to them, and flowers have been placed upon the graves much to the displeasure of the Germans who fined any they found doing so. They say that their life was very irksome under German rule. They were continually having to pay fines and penalties for trifling restrictions. In addition to being badly used, the Germans took away all the men and the young women capable of working. A few, however managed to escape, or hide until our advance parties arrived. On the first Sunday of our arrival they had a Thanksgiving *Te Deum* and went in procession to the English graves which they decorated with flowers and garlands and special orations were given. This village is in a lace and tapestry district but all their machinery has either been taken away or destroyed. Many roads and houses, also nearly all the churches were mined, but fortunately, in nearly all cases the-charges were removed in time.

Source: *Hertfordshire Record Office. St. Saviour's Parish Magazine, Dec. 1918*

Christmas 1918.

For the first time for five years, the hearts of the people were attuned to the joyous festival of Yuletide, and they were able to fix their thoughts on the Nativity, undisturbed by "war's discordant voices"

Holly and mistletoe were displayed in profusion, and there appeared in many houses multi-coloured paper and other decorations. The Food Controller still retained a certain grip on food stuffs, but with the philosophy borne of four and a half years of a "do without" policy, that fact was not allowed to perturb us. All things considered, Christmas dinner was quite luxurious. It was a "kiddies' Christmas" and once again the "long stocking" made its appearance on the bedrail to be filled by Santa Claus.

Services were well attended commencing with Choral communion and finishing with evensong at 3.30 p.m. The Cathedral was decorated with flowers, and the rood screen had the flags of the allies placed there, to celebrate the great victory. This presented a very striking effect.

The inmates at St. Albans Hospital had a very pleasing Christmas and dinner was provided by the Mayor who sent turkey and crackers, so that Christmas dinner was all right. The Dean and the choir boys from the Abbey sang carols on Christmas afternoon. The wards were gaily decorated at Bricket House V.A.D. Hospital. There was a short service on Christmas morning and the dinner was the best served in the history of the hospital. Gifts were distributed to each of the patients from ladies in America.

At Napsbury Military Hospital there was no mistaking the thoroughness of Christmas celebrations. A plentiful supply of plum puddings had been bought in London. A real old-fashioned Christmas dinner of roast beef was provided. Services of Holy Communion and Morning Prayer were held and the ladies of the vicinity saw that the 1,150 wounded patients had a jolly Christmas.
Source: *Herts. Advertiser, 28th December 1918.*

In Memoriam

Bombardier A. Crawley

died in hospital in Belgium, 11th December 1918.

He sleeps besides his comrades
In a hallowed grave unknown:
But his name is written in letters of love
In hearts he left at home.

Mother, brothers and sisters, 14 Warwick Road, St. Albans.

Source: *Herts. Advertiser, December 1918. This entry represents all the notices published at that time.*

A Memorial in St. Albans Abbey.

A ironwork grille in front of a recess, where for many years the Toc H lamp was displayed. Now the lamp has been placed on the window ledge in the War Memorial chapel. The recess is cut into the south-east pillar of the central tower, facing into the South Transept. and is now used to display a flower arrangement. The inscription on a brass plate reads:

This grille is in Memory of Harold J. Cunningham, Capt. Adj. 6th Beds. Regt. killed in action 4th Oct. 1917 and of Robin A.W. Williams, Lieut. 2nd. K.O.Y.L.I. killed in action on Hill 60, 18 April 1915.

Given by their Mothers.

Contents 1919

Scapa Flow, Scotland

At the Armistice, German navy ships were impounded at Scapa Flow. After the Versailles Treaty which ended the war, the German scuttled some battleships. A St.Albans 'lad' writes from H.M.S.Revenge at Christmas 1918:

I have had the honour or (misfortune) of spending Christmas at that most popular 'seaside resort' of Scapa Flow, which is situated north of Scotland.

We have our German devils nicely bottled up here. They look lovely. I'd like to take them to sea and use them as a target for our 15 inch midgets; what we were all itching to do when we escorted them across the North Sea to their, or our "little home in the North". They are not allowed to lower any boats of any sorts.

There are four St. Albans lads on my ship, and we are all looking forward to ten days' leave, which we have been promised some time this year.

> Many thousands of miles we have travelled
> > Keeping the Huns at bay,
> And although their Fleet has surrendered.
> > We are guarding them even to-day.

Source: *Herts. Advertiser, 4th January 1919.*

Award of the Royal Red Cross.

Miss Sylvia Glossop,who was mentioned in despatches by Sir Douglas Haig last year, has now been awarded the *Associate Royal Red Cross*. She is eldest daughter of the Revd. Canon G.H.P. & Mrs Glossop, St. Albans and has been in France, cooking for the troops, for four years.

Source: *Herts. Advertiser, 11th January 1919.*

In Germany.

Lieutenant-Colonel, the Revd. F.H. Wheeler, Chaplain of the Forces, formerly pastor of Trinity Congregational Church, St. Albans, writes from Cologne, Germany:

We arrived in Cologne two or three days ago. Our journey through Belgium - passing Ypres, Courtrai, Brussels and Liege was a triumphal march, with flags, arches and streamers over the roads, with many an address of welcome and countless tokens of joy and gratitude. Then we came to the German frontier and the flags and rejoicings stopped abruptly. Instead of smiles we got scowls and sour looks, though for the most part the people affected a sullen indifference, or a gaze of grudging curiosity as we passed.

We arrived in Cologne without incident and billeted ourselves, requisitioning whatever accommodation we required. The people do not like it, but they have to make the best of it. We go about the streets safely, but are required to be armed, and not go alone. Stern proclamations are posted in the streets. The people do not look starved, though no doubt there is a considerable shortage of food, and they do not wear paper clothes. At first they seemed inclined to treat us a new sort of tourist, but the proclamations posted today will change all that. They will taste some of the severities and humiliations they have inflicted on others. We have got to cross the River Rhine and hold the country thirty miles beyond.

Source: *Herts. Advertiser, 11th January 1919.*

Brutality of German Doctors.

Private Joseph Charles, 13th East Surrey Regiment, son of Mr. Charles Tuck, 168 Hatfield-road, St.Albans tells us of his experiences as a prisoner of war in Germany:
He spent nine months in various camps but was treated only by German doctors, who cut and hacked him about unmercifully when they removed a piece of shrapnel from his cheekbone, without an anaesthetic. The called him a "dirty English" when he made too much noise during the operation.

Whilst a prisoner, the Germans loaned him and others to a firm of contractors who were building bridges at some very large iron smelting works. They worked seven days a week, and worked harder on Sunday than the other days.

After the Armistice was signed they were still badly treated and were nearly starved whilst in an isolation camp, having refused to work any more. When that camp was broken up, 500 men marched several miles to an N.C.O.'s camp where there were plenty of provisions. Having partaken of very necessary food, they set out on a five days' march towards Holland. Many fell out by the way, though none was left behind. Private Tuck marched all 130 kilometres. Then conveyances were hired and then men, now 700, were carried the rest of the way. At last they arrived in Rotterdam where they were medically examined, had a bath and an entire change of clothes. Then a good meal was much enjoyed and they crossed by boat to Hull and were taken to Ripon camp, Yorkshire for repatriation.

Source: *Herts. Advertiser, 25th January 1919.*

Freedom of the City of St.Albans.
Lord Cavan's return from Italy.

General, the Right Honourable the Earl of Cavan, Knight of St.Patrick (K.P.), Knight Commander of the Order of the Bath (K.C.B.), Member of the Victorian Order (M.V.O.), Commander of His Majesty's Forces in the Italian Campaign (1918), honoured St. Albans with a visit accompanied by the Countess of Cavan, and received a presentation of the Honorary Freedom of the City of St. Alban, also an Illuminated Address from the members and supporters of the Hertfordshire Hunt and farmers of the county as marks of appreciation of his distinguished service to the country and the [British] Empire.

The event which was organised at short notice, was a complete and unqualified success. Thousands lined the streets and there was much bunting, flags of the allies and the flag of Italy displayed in honour of Lord Cavan.

The Earl and Countess of Cavan drove from their home in Wheathamstead, through Sandridge and along Sandridge-road, St. Albans to Stonecross, where is situated The Cricketers Public House. Here they were invited to change from a motor car to a carriage which was drawn, not by horses, but by huntsmen and farmers of the Hertfordshire Hunt down St. Peter's-street to St.Albans Town Hall and the general gaiety of the scene was enhanced by the ringing of the bells of St. Peter's Church and the Abbey. At St. Peter's Church, the Earl of

Cavan was vastly pleased to find the Band of the Grenadier Guards awaiting him. The instrumentalists then headed the procession. The cheering was general on all sides and in the Market Place, the crush and enthusiasm was very great. Handkerchiefs were waved by the ladies, orders were shouted to the troops lined up. The Earl stepped quickly across the road to inspect the Guard of Honour provided by the Queen's Westminsters, before entering the Town Hall for the conferring of the Freedom in the first floor Assembly Room.

A large and distinguished gathering was seated in the room where this extraordinary meeting of the City Council was held. The Mayor of St. Albans (Alderman A.Faulkner) proposed the resolution that Lord Cavan be admitted to the Honorary Freedom of the City "for his splendid work on the Western Front, and for the crowning glory of his achievements in North Italy". To General Lord Cavan we may apply Tasso's eulogy of Godfrey, the deliverer of Jerusalem in the first crusade:-   *I sing the illustrious chief*
Who much in council, much in field sustained,
Till just success, his glorious labours gained.

The resolution was then put and carried with enthusiasm, whereupon Lord Cavan was presented with an illuminated address embodying the certificate of Freedom. In reply, Lord Cavan returned thanks to the Council, and said that they had done him a very great honour, so great that it was impossible for him to adequately express his thanks. He could only obey the order of the great French General, Marshal Foch, "Soyez, fier", (Be Proud), and say how very proud he was to receive the freedom.

He spoke of the 600 Irish Guards that he lost one day and 200 to 300 Grenadiers the same day, and how his forces had become practically negligible but for the great hearts of the remaining Guardsmen, when Lord French (another Hertfordshire man) at that critical moment sent him the Hertfordshire Regiment. He went to see Lord Hampden (their Commanding Officer) in the field where they were - and which was dirtier than any field they could imagine - and there he found the

Herts. Regiment as happy and bright as to-day. He told Lord Hampden how serious was the position, which it was his duty to do, and that he must have half the battalion sent up into the line that night, and that line must be held at all costs. This was done, and there the men of Hertfordshire stood ranged along the hill-side opposite the enormous German army, and never gave one yard until they were relieved by the French. It was solely because of great men like that he stood there to be so honoured that day.

Three cheers for Lady Cavan were then given enthusiastically. Another speech was then made by the Marquess of Salisbury on behalf of the Hertfordshire Hunt. The proceedings then came to a close and Lord and Lady Cavan returned to Wheathamstead, though not before he stopped to talk to members of the Band of the Grenadier Guards (with whom he had served for thirty years before the war).
Source: *Herts. Advertiser, 25th January 1919.*

Lord Cavan's welcome in Wheathamstead.

On Tuesday, in spite of the inclemency of the weather, a whole-hearted, spontaneous, and enthusiastic reception was accorded General the Earl of Cavan on his arrival home. The welcome was deep and true, and expressive of the deep appreciation the people of Wheathamstead feel for his lordship, and to the younger generation who vociferously cheered him on his arrival and subsequently all down the village and in the station yard.

The main street presented quite a festive appearance. Streamers crossed the route and hundreds of flags adorned houses and telegraph poles on either side of the High-street and Station-road. At the entrance to the village was one large banner with the words "Welcome Home" upon it. "Hearty Welcome" was the motto of another stretching across the centre of the village; and still another appeared in front of *May Cottages* bearing the inscription "Welcome Home".

At 4 p.m. motors began to arrive and at 4.15 p.m. the bells of St.Helens Church began to peal. Scouts took up their position by the Lych Gate

In January 1919, the City of St. Albans conferred the Freedom of the City on the Rt. Hon. the Earl of Cavan, who had only recently returned from Italy, where he had been Commander in Chief of the allied forces.

On his arrival in St. Albans from Wheathamstead he and Lady Cavan transferred from a car to an open carriage which was drawn to the Town Hall by huntsmen and farmers of the Hertfordshire Hunt.

General Lord Cavan with the Mayor of St. Albans, Alderman A. Faulkner after the Freedom ceremony on the steps of the Town Hall.

Temporary war memorial built in front of the
Clock Tower, St. Albans, 1919-20

Unveiling the War Memorial, St. Peter's-green, St. Albans, May 1921.
by General, the 10th Earl of Cavan.

of the Parish Church. Two hundred children, the scouts, returned soldiers, representatives from the Clubs and the Village Fire Brigade came next, then the tradesmen and Parish Councillors brought up the rear. Punctually at 4.30 p.m. the hum of his lordship's motor car was heard and in a few seconds arrived.

Lady Maud Barrett and Lady Ellen Lambart (sisters of Lord Cavan) were among those who gave him his first personal welcome. The procession gathered in the station yard and the square near the Great Northern Railway Station. Mr. Whately, chairman of the Parish Council welcomed his lordship and ended with these words "We welcome you back, for there is no county so good as Hertfordshire, and there is no place like home. I sincerely congratulate you upon your safe return to Wheathamstead.

In response, Lord Cavan thanked the children and my dear old fiends and neighbours. He recounted some of the achievements that he had taken part in during the war. "I am pleased to be safe home once more in Wheathamstead: it was here that my mother taught me the goodness of Almighty God, and secondly, because during the war, I have learned to put absolute confidence in the English soldier. Then the National Anthem was sung and cheers were given as Lord and Lady Cavan rode away.
Source: *Herts. Advertiser, 25th January 1919.*

Welcome to General Lord Cavan and Rear Admiral Sir Lionel Halsey
by Hertfordshire County Council.

At the Shire Hall, Hertford, the chairman of the County Council - Mr. T.F. Halsey presented addresses of welcome to Lord Cavan and Sir Lionel Halsey for their services during the recent war. Later, the two Hertfordshire fighters and other guests were entertained to lunch by the County Council.
Source: *The Times, 4th February 1919.*

National Kitchen, St. Albans.

From the Committee's report of the working of the Kitchen from October to December 1918:

After three weeks had run it became evident to the Committee that the management left much to be desired, particularly as the weekly trading account had not been kept by the supervisor. It was shown that there was a considerable loss. The Supervisor was relieved of her position and the matter reported to the Ministry of Food. A Miss Ivy Gordon was sent as Supervisor and after a brief period of closure, the National Kitchen re-opened on Monday, 11th November. At the time of the closure, the accounts now reveal that there was a total deficiency of £117. Since then there has been a growing profit and by the end of January 1919, the profits made are such that the deficit is well on the way to being cleared.

Under Miss Gordon's management, the National Kitchen is open for mid-day dinners and teas, but not suppers. This has been found to be much more satisfactory, for both staffing and general management.

Source: *Hertfordshire Record Office. St. Albans City Archives.*

Club for Ex-Service Men.

28th January. - A club for ex-servicemen is to be established in temporary premises at the Abbey Institute for ex-servicemen. In January a provisional committee was elected and it proposes to entertain to supper any returned prisoners of war on 10th February to be followed by a social meeting at 8 p.m. at which ex-servicemen will be welcomed, and each is invited to bring a lady friend.

Source: *Herts. Advertiser, 1st February 1919.*

"The little Corporal".

Napoleon has gone down to posterity as the "little Corporal". Corporal W. Dean, *7th Bedfordshire Regt.* is also small in stature and on Tuesday morning he received the Military Medal in front of St. Albans Town Hall where a full parade of *Queen's Royal West Surrey Regt.* stood ankle deep in snow to witness the presentation, made by Major Devereux. At the end of the parade, Corporal Dean who is one-armed, took the

salute as the troops marched past. In giving him the medal, Major Devereux said that: "at Thiepval, on the 26th and 27th September 1916 during the battle of the Somme, when the platoon seargeant had become a casualty, Corporal Dean, in a splendid manner rallied the platoon and led them forward to the attack, although himself severely wounded, under heavy shell fire and machine-gun fire. His example of coolness largely added to the successful capture of the town. Here is a man, who, only wearing a corporal's stripes, was able to take command of his platoon and carry out the duties of a soldier just as well as any trained officer. He did it, and you can do it when your turn comes, if it ever does. It is a great pleasure to me on these parades to give medals of this kind, because it is a proud thing for the whole British Army, which brings men like Corporal Dean up before youngsters, and it is a grand example to you, and the ones you have to follow if ever the need comes".
Source: *Herts. Advertiser, 1st February 1919.*

Bricket House is closing down.

The few remaining patients at the 31st January 1919 have now been transferred to other hospitals and there only remain the discharged soldier out-patients who attend daily for massage treatment.

Bricket House was not a convalescent hospital but a hospital for the treatment of acute cases. At first it was used as a field hospital by *6th Field Ambulance* then in St. Albans. Members of the British Red Cross *Voluntary Aid Detachment [V.A.D]* were asked to provide help on a daily basis. In December 1914 the hospital was mobilised by the War Office and has not been empty for a day since. A total of 2,298 patients have been received including 52 transferred from *Napsbury Military Hospital.* Although the nursing and household staff have been provided by *Detachment 38 V.A.D.* there has been a resident-sister-in charge and two two trained nurses, one for day and the other for night duty. Mrs. Boy has been the Commandant. Since 1916, Major Grosart Wells has been responsible for surgical and medical care supported by R.A.M.C. officers stationed in St. Albans.
Source: *Herts Advertiser, 8th February 1919.*

271

Massacre of Armenian Priests.

A photograph sent to the *Herts. Advertiser* by Company-Sergeant W.H.Brazier, musketry instructor of the *1st Garrison Battalion, Bedfordshire Regiment* arrived with a letter which explains how he came into possession of it: "I came across a fellow in Delhi [India] from Mesopotamia belonging to the Australian Forces, who stated that during an advance he captured a Turkish prisoner, and seeing that he had in his possession a camera, took it away from him. On examining it, he noticed that the film had been used, and on developing it, found that it contained the photograph of five Armenian priests being hung with Turkish soldiers posing for the camera"!

Source: *Herts. Advertiser, 15th February 1919.*

Naval experience in the Baltic.

Gunner Harold Farrar, A.B., H.M.S. Calypso, of Lemsford-road, St. Albans writes:
Moving eastward, in December, we used our guns on the coast of Estonia which was then occupied by the Bolsheviks, and for some days reconnoitred and patrolled this inhospitable shore. On Boxing Day we sighted a Bolshevik destroyer and promptly made her haul down her flag by shooting off her propellers, and put her in tow of our own destroyers, but she sank on arriving in harbour. The next day we met another enemy ship and made her "useless for present evil". We took allied refugees from Reval to Helsingfors and in one night became frozen in, but an icebreaker made us a way to the open [sea].

Early in January we had the welcome news that we were to be relieved, and we reached Rosyth via Copenhagen on 8th January, where we received the still more welcome news that we were to proceed to our home port - Chatham and "pay-off". We arrived in Sheerness in due order, unshipped our ammunition and then into dock in the Medway, where presently our temporary home, H.M.S. "Calypso" is to proceed to a milder climate. My naval days are nearly ended, as I bid good-bye to a rich experience over some years in varied ships of the most useful peacemaker in the world - Britain's fleet.

Source: *Herts. Advertiser, 15th February 1919.*

In Russia.

Private Walter Welch, Royal Sussex Regiment, of St. Albans and formerly a porter on the Midland Railway writes to chums on the railway:

7th February. - We used to hear in England that the winter is the healthiest weather, but the weather here is sometimes too healthy, especially when it gets a few degrees under zero. I have seen icicles before, but never on my moustache, and my breath seemed to freeze as it issued from the mouth.

I have been in Russia since August 1918 and we had a rough time out here the first two months, but on 21st October we had an accident on the way to Kandbaska when the engine left the track and three carriages piled on top of one another, and although the officers were thrown about not one suffered a hurt. There were five deaths and thirty-six injured in two covered vans which contained two companies of men. I was lucky, and I dressed injuries as we had no doctor and two stretcher bearers there.

I am now at Murmansk doing guard to the General. I shall not be sorry to leave here as we really do not know who is who and some are a bit desperate. We had some trouble higher up the line as the 'Bolsheviks' were blowing the bridges up, but nothing has happened lately, only train accidents, but that is a common thing here.

Source: *Herts. Advertiser, 25th February 1919.*

Boy Scout heroes.

All seven St. Albans troops of Boy Scouts and the five packs of "Cubs" paraded in St. Peter's-street and attended a Memorial Service for the Scouts who fell during the War in St. Albans Abbey. 300 scouts and 120 cubs occupied the centre Nave. The drum and bugle band, under Bandmaster Warwick, lent spirit to the occasion. Their colours were received by the Dean of St. Albans who laid them on the altar rails. Commissioner Charles Dymoke Green accompanied by Colonel de Burgh, District Commissoner H. Salwey and Mr. H.S. Martin, O.B.E. occupied front positions in the choir stalls whilst facing them were the Mayor and Mayoress of St. Albans.

The service, which lasted about an hour began with the singing of the National Anthem. The Dean then read out the names of the scouts who had fallen - Frederick Clark; Cedric Edwards; Harold Dent Smith; Walter R.W.Bell; James R.Mealing; Harold E.Reece; Walter Stockdale; Lewin Card; Claud H. Garment; Leonard Garment; Reginald V. Hunt; Frank W.Wilks; E.Butler; W.R.S.Payne; Fank Wilkinson and Leonard Rowley.

Mr. T.H.Coxall, the Deputy Organist played the *Dead March* then Bandleader Betts and Bandmaster Warwick sounded Reveillé.

A Public Rally was held during the weekend and Colonel Ulrich de Burgh, C.B. told those present that at the outbreak of war, nobody was ready - but the Scouts were ready. They were drawn on by the Post Office, War Office and the Admiralty for all sorts of curious tasks, but in forty-eight hours they occupied the coastline of England, and from that moment until the end of the war the coast-guard service from John O'Groats to Land's End had been carried out by Boy-Scouts under the supervision of the Admiralty. No less than 25,000 boys, aged 15 to 18 had taken part in this coast-guard service. Some had served three continuous years, others for three and a half years and some for four years. During that time there had been no cases of cowardice or treachery and only eight minor cases involving morals had occurred.

God bless the parents who allowed them to go; they had done magnificent service, but they had reaped their reward. Weakling boys with thin faces returned magnificent young men able to hold any other position in other places.
Source: *Herts Advertiser, 1st March 1919.*

Prisoners of War Help Committee.
Private C.H. White, 1st Bedfordshire Regiment of Park-lane, Colney Heath writes:
9th March. - I wish to thank the *[Hertfordshire Regiments' Prisoners of War Help] Committee* for your kindness to me during the time I was a prisoner of war in Germany. The fact that I have arrived home and in good health is proof that I received the bulk of goods sent to me. But

for the great work of these Committees, not many of us would have returned; the kind friends and contributors can never realise the feelings of these men out there in the camps, when opening a parcel from home. Simple though the words, "received with thanks", those moments of heartfelt gratitude will live for ever in our memories.

I was taken prisoner at La Bassée on 13th October 1914 and was repatriated on 1st January 1919.
Source: *Herts. Advertiser, 15th March 1919.*

Police Constable receives Italian Decoration.
St. Albans Police Constable Charles Hallett, who served in the Military Mounted Police from December 1915 served for two years in England and then went out to Italy. For his strenuous work in regulating traffic and evacuating prisoners during the Italian advance into Austria in November, he received the Italian *Croce Merito di Guerra*, and was presented the decoration from an Italian General.
Source: *Herts. Advertiser, 22nd March 1919.*

St. Albans Scouts at Buckingham Palace.
Seven St. Albans Scouts - Patrol Leaders T. Norman; D. Wilson; G. Foxlee; W. Martin and E. Hester, with Seconds V. Stanton and A. Hester were honoured to be invited to do duty at Buckingham Palace on the occasion of 20th March at the Military Investiture. There were large numbers present and so the duties were arduous, but were well carried out. The King, on learning that Patrol Leader Norman had served for two years during the war in the Royal Navy, commanded that he should be presented to him, and questioned him as to the ships he had served on and as to how he liked the life.
Source: *Herts. Advertiser, 29th March 1919.*

St. Albans Scouts Roll of Honour.
167 have served or are serving in H.M. Forces; 18 have lost their lives; one has won the R.F.C, four the M.M. and two have had mentions in despatches.
Source: *Herts. Advertiser, 29th March 1919.*

London welcome to The Guards.

After four and and a-half years of fighting with many successes and many disappointment, victory was celebrated with a great military pageant in the the capital which had witnessed the departure of the "contemptible little Army" in August 1914.

The parade marched from Buckingham Gate to Hyde Park Corner by way of Buckingham Palace, The Mall, Trafalgar Square, The Strand, Fleet Street, St.Paul's Cathedral, Mansion House, Cheapside, Holborn, Shaftesbury Avenue and Piccadilly Circus.

Lord Cavan, the first General to command the *Guards Division* when it was constituted, rode proudly by, his hand ever and again at the salute. Cavan, the resolute leader of men who saved the day, with his Guardsmen, at Gheluvelt, in the first battle of Ypres - Cavan, who helped so stoutly to pull the metal out of the fire for our Italian friends on the Piave; who was given command of the Italian army, one of the incidents which made this war just past unlike all other wars in our history. Very young he looked to have borne such a part - very young, very smiling, very pleased with the way the people received him and recognised the part he had played. ...
Source: *Observer, 23rd March 1919.*

From St. Albans to Germany.

The whole of the *53rd Queens Westminster Regiment* have left St. Albans for Dover before embarking on the "Antrim" to Dunkirk, where they were taken to a rest camp before journeying on to Germany to join the Army of Occupation. The Queen's was a training battalion, but most of the 'Boys' who have left St. Albans have been here since September 1918. Lieutenant-Colonel Purnell was in command, and Major Devereux was second-in-command.
Source: *Herts. Advertiser, 12th April 1919.*

Hatfield Road School, St. Albans.

This school which earlier in the war had seen two of its former pupils awarded the highest honour (posthumously) - the Victoria Cross:

Private Warner and Lieutenant Smith is again the centre of attention.

Lance-Corporal Frank Reginald Gough, *Hertfordshire Regiment,* formerly of St. Albans and now of Canonbury is being presented with his Military Medal by the Headmaster, Mr. John Roe. Corporal Gough might have been presented with the medal by his Majesty the King, but made it clear that he wished to have it presented at his old school from his old master. The whole of the school was paraded.

He won his distinction in the Hindenburg line near Havrincourt at three o'clock on 18th September 1918. In the same engagement, Lieutenant Young, *Hertfordshire Regiment,* was killed and the posthumous award of the Victoria Cross was bestowed on this heroic officer.
Source: *Herts. Advertiser, ... April 1919.*

War Memorial for Park Street.
An obelisk monument is to be erected at Park Street, near St. Albans, to the honour of the men who joined the Army, Navy or Air Force - not from the civil parish of St. Stephens.
Source: *Herts. Advertiser, 30th May 1919.*

In the next few years every Hertfordshire town, village, church and chapel erected monuments to commemorate those who died in the Great War. In many places, General Lord Cavan was invited to unveil the memorials.

Peace Night in St. Albans
After seven months of suspense and acute anxiety, came the signing of the *Versailles Treaty,* and with it came the unspeakable relief to the whole civilised world. When the Peace was finally announced in London, news reached St. Albans by way of the evening papers. Plans to sound a siren at the Town Hall came to nothing. The people of St. Albans were not slow to celebrate the news and later in the evening fun reigned fast and furious in the streets of the city and until after midnight.

The bells of St. Albans Abbey, which had been in readiness for ringing as soon as the news was announced now pealed forth and the bells of neighbouring churches followed suit. The following day (Sunday) all the churches held services of thanksgiving.

Source: *Herts. Advertiser, 5th July 1919.*

Victory Loan Week: Objective £250,000.

The Mayor of St. Albans has set a target of £250,000 to be raised in Victory Loan Week. There are eight reasons why Victory Loan should be bought:

(1) to maintain our reputation as a business nation;

(2) to put national finances on a secure basis for Peace;

(3) to develop a greater feeling of confidence in the business world;

(4) to enable our banks to transfer to trade the financial support they now give to the Government;

(5) to clear the way for a development of our industry and commerce;

(6) to create employment for our demobilised soldiers, sailors and war-workers;

(7) to bring down the cost of living;

(8) to improve the conditions of our foreign trade.

Within days £80,000 had been raised and the Mayor was heard to comment that Radlett, which had set out to raise £78,000 new money had, in reality raised £119,429!

In reply to a telegram received from the Chancellor of the Exchequer, the Mayor replied "hope to raise over ten pounds per head of population by Saturday night". ALDERMAN FAULKNER (Mayor).

Military Funerals at St. Albans Cemetery.

Driver Frederick William Gates (26), Hertfordshire Artillery, son of Mr. and Mrs. F.W.Gates, 5 Heath-road, St. Albans died at Purfleet Military Hospital on his return to England, from three years in Egypt, from dysentery and pneumonia.

He died on 9th July. Driver Gates was educated at Bernards Heath School and had been a member of St. Saviour's Church Sunday School. For six years he had been an assistant in Freeman, Hardy and Willis,

278

High Street as a boots salesman.

Driver Gates had been ill for some eighteen months and would have left the Army had it not been for several bouts of malaria. His remains arrived from Purfleet on Saturday and the funeral took place the following Tuesday with the first part of the burial service read at St. Saviour's Church. The coffin, wrapped in a Union Jack was then rested on a gun carriage and accompanied by former St. Albans comrades and an officer and firing party from the *Middlesex Regiment*, Mill Hill, and was taken to St. Albans Cemetery where the burial took place. The rifle party fired three volleys over the open grave and the ceremonial concluded with the sounding of the Last Post.

The mourners included his parents, brother, sister, step-brother and the Managers of the St. Albans and Harpenden branches of Freeman, Hardy and Willis.
Source: *Herts. Advertiser, 19th July 1919.*

Private Sidney Lea (21), Hertfordshire Regiment, formerly of Hemel Hempstead, but who since the age of 14 years had resided with his mother at Mr. Richardson's, 19 Church-street died at St.Albans Hospital after a stay of one year and ten months, and this followed five months at King George Hospital.
Private Lea, who prior to his enlistment had been employed at the Model Dairy, was a member of the Abbey Church Lads Brigade and was confirmed whilst on active service. He had been injured by shrapnel in the spine at Ypres, which resulted in paralysis of the legs. He had a wonderful spirit and courage and was often pushed about the streets in an invalid chair by a score of his late comrades.

The body was taken on a gun carriage covered with the Union Jack provided by the *Transport Company of the Royal Army Service Corps* who are stationed in Clarence Park. At the Cemetery his remains were buried and at the close of the impressive service, the Last Post was sounded.
The principal mourners were his mother and uncle, Mr.Richardson and family. A large number of wreaths were sent.
Source: *Herts. Advertiser, 16th August 1919.*

279

St. Albans Drumhead Memorial Service.

The St. Albans branch of the National Federation of Discharged and Demobilised Sailors and Soldiers organised a Drumhead Memorial Service on the Abbey Orchard. A procession from the Market Place was led by the Salvation Army Band, the Combined Choirs, officers and members with the banner of the Federation, other ex-servicemen, serving soldiers and sailors, boys scouts, officiating ministers and clergy, the City Band, the police, the fire brigade, the Corporation of St.Albans and The Mayor.

In front of the Clock Tower a plinth, surmounted by a plain ash cross similar to those erected over the graves in Belgium and France, was placed. Offerings of flowers received on Sunday morning remained there until after the service, when they were removed to Soldiers' Corner in St. Albans Cemetery. A party of Boy Scouts guarded the Memorial.

Lieutenant-Colonel Wheeler (former pastor of Trinity Congregational Church), St. Albans said he was afraid he could not hope to make the whole of such a large company hear his voice, but he would do his best. They were assembled to do their best to pay fitting tribute and honour, and to remember with tenderness and pride those whom they had loved and lost. Don't make your service one of grief and tears. Rather be thankful that we were at the place where duty called us, and that death found us ready and loyal to the last. Be thankful that the cause for which we have fought and died has triumphed.

After hymns and prayers, the St. Albans Silver Band played the Dead March and the service terminated with the Benediction, the Last Post and Reveillé (sounded by four buglers), and a verse of the National Anthem.

Source: *Herts. Advertiser, 23rd August 1919.*

The Passing of Queen Eleanor. -
Alderman and Mrs Faulkner's magnificent gift unveiled.

The magnificent Academy picture by Mr. Frank O. Salisbury, entitled

"The passing of Queen Eleanor" and depicting the funeral cortége of the beloved wife of Edward I, passing through St. Albans on its way to Westminster Abbey, which has been generously given by Alderman and Mrs. Faulkner, of St. Albans, was unveiled and dedicated at a fitting and impressive service on Monday evening attended by a large congregation.

At the request of the Dean, Mrs. Faulkner unveiled the painting and Alderman Faulkner then said: "We offer this picture in thanksgiving to Almighty God for the deliverance of Jerusalem to British arms and for the devotion of the men of Hertfordshire who have so nobly offered their lives for their King and country in the great war which we pray may [result] in a righteous and abiding peace".
Source: *Herts. Advertiser, 17th September 1919.*

Note: In October 1973, this large canvas, which had been part of the ornamentation of St. Albans Abbey since 1919, was cut from its frame in a burglary, which also saw other ornaments stolen. It has never been seen since that date. A small reproduction copy was given to the Abbey subsequently on behalf of Mr. Salisbury's estate, signed by the artist.

A Memorable Anniversary.
Hertfordshire Regiment.
5th November is a day that will live in the memories of many Hertfordshire homes. Five years ago on that day, the *1st Hertfordshire Regiment,* 1000 Hertfordshire men under the present Lord Lieutenant of the county, Colonel Lord Hampden - left England for their great adventure in the war. Viscount French of Ypres, writes, thus ...

"The call came upon them like a bolt from the blue. No warning had been given. Father and son, husband and brother left families, homes, the work and business of their lives almost at a moment's notice to go on active service abroad. It seems to me that we have never realised what it was these men were asked to do. They were quite different to the professional soldiers who are kept and paid through years of peace for this particular purpose of war, who spend their lives practising their profession and gaining promotion and distinction, and who, on

281

being confronted with the enemy, fulfil the ambition of their lives. ... I say, without the slightest hesitation that without the assistance which the Territorials afforded between October 1914, and June 1915, it would have been impossible to have held the line in France and Belgium, or to have prevented the enemy from reaching his goal - the Channel seaboard".
Source: *Herts. Advertiser, 8th November 1919.*

Hertfordshire Yeomanry.

A meeting was held in London with the purpose to form an Old Comrades Association and to make arrangements for a re-union of all Yeomen who served at any time in the Regiment at a smoking concert.
Source: *Herts. Advertiser, 8th November 1919.*

Armistice Day, 1919.

On Tuesday all movement ceased at "the eleventh hour of the eleventh day of the eleventh month" in commemoration of the hour when the Armistice came into force.

At the psychological moment the siren on the Town Hall sent forth its weird shriek, Union Jacks fell to half-mast, soldiers stood to attention and two ladies in the centre of the Square did not speak for two minutes. Citizens stood in groups with heads bared, all vehicular traffic ceased, and one man about to bite an apple stood petrified. What was remarkable was the intense silence. There was no civic formality in carrying out His Majesty's beautiful idea, each man stood at his post, and it was unquestionably the most intense two minutes contemplative silence in the life of the City and nation. Thus was the victory for Right and Freedom solemnised at St. Albans. Elsewhere in Hertfordshire and throughout the nation similar scenes took place. At Boreham Wood a train came to a standstill!
Source: *Herts. Advertiser, 15th November 1919.*

A Gruesome task.

29th November. - Sir, In consequence of an accident to the car during our recent tour of the Battlefields we perforce became the guests of the officers of the *723rd Labour Company*, whose camp is on the well-known Passchendaele Ridge, and from them we received the utmost kindness, hospitality and attention.

In the course of conversation we were informed that part of their duty consisted of searching the battlefields, exhuming bodies of British soldiers, identifying them as far as possible from discs and papers, and re-interring them in the Military Cemetery.

When I mention the fact that the "padre" stated that he had identified 26 bodies that day and he had 300 more to go through the following day, some idea of their merciful but gruesome task can be gathered. I need hardly point out that the work this Company is doing results in great relief to many sorrowing families, the fate of whose relatives is unknown only that they are posted as "missing" without any knowledge of where or how they made the great sacrifice.

E.W.Lewis, *The Cantlings, Redbourn, Herts.*
Source: *Herts. Advertiser, 6th December 1919.*

John George Coleman

During the final stages in preparing this anthology for print, I found a space on the St. Albanson cemetery plan I had produced. A visit gave me the name - J.G.Coleman, but his name does not appear on the CWGC list. The cemetery office were able to tell me that he was a drummer, of Kings-road. Beryl Carrington looked him up on the *St. Albans Roll of Honour* (published by Gibbs & Bamforth) It revealed that J.G. Coleman was of the Bedfordshire Training depot, established in 1914 by Herbrand, 11th Duke of Bedford, who had previously served in the *Grenadier Guards*. After the Military Service Act, 1916 was passed, it became a command depot, and the Duke the colonel-commandant. Coleman died in the V.A.D. hospital, Ampthill, on 24 October 1918 at the age of 16 years old.

Sources: *St. Albans cemetery office; Beryl Carrington; St. Albans Roll of Honour; Ann Mitchell, Archivist, Woburn Abbey; Dictionary of National Biography.*

Contents 1920-1925

Stone plaque above a front door in Letchmore-heath, near Radlett.

Sopwell Lane memorial in the St. Albans Abbey Parish.
One of ten that were erected after the war. They are believed to be unique.
Two plaques have been re-instated, November 2002. (*see page 286*)

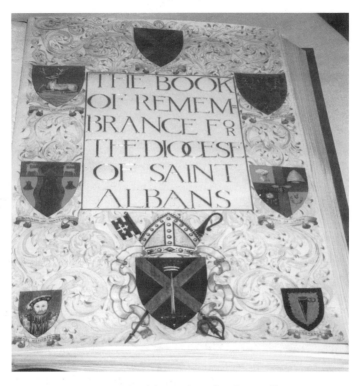

Cathedral and Abbey Church of St. Alban
St. Albans Diocesan War Memorial Chapel

Title page of one of the three Books of Remembrance
and kept in a specially designed lectern.

Entries are arranged by location: here is that of
Edward Warner, V.C. *Bedfordshire Regiment* and other men.

Edward Warner. V.C.	Private.	Bedfordshire Regiment.
Frederick Thomas Warren.	Corporal.	King's Royal Rifle Corps.
Frank Warwick.	Private.	Bedfordshire Regiment.
William Walter Warwick.	Rifleman.	Rifle Brigade.
Frederick Wilson Waters. (M.M)	Corporal.	Hertfordshire Regiment.

Cross of Sacrifice.

In the central avenue of St. Albans Cemetery stands a "Cross of Sacrifice" similar to many such crosses found in British war cemeteries in Europe and beyond. By the time this memorial was dedicated, the permanent headstones had been placed in position in Soldiers' Corner, the area of the cemetery set aside for the graves of servicemen. Yet around the cemetery lie other graves, some with headstones carved by the Imperial (later Commonwealth) War Graves Commission, and some which have individual headstones, placed there by their own families. The Cross was dedicated on Sunday, 24th October 1920.

St. Albans War Memorial.

General, the tenth Earl of Cavan was invited to unveil the City of St. Albans' War Memorial which was built on St. Peter's Green at a cost of £372 in 1921. In addition the St. Albans Corporation paid out an equivalent sum on landscaping the area, which included a memorial garden. The architect was Sir Edgar Wigram and the stone mason, Charles Alderton, of Harpenden.

Names of those who died in World War II were added to the memorial In 2001, some names, missing from the memorial, were added.

Street Memorials within the Abbey Parish.

100 men from the Parish of St. Albans Abbey died in the Great War. Ten memorials were carved on plaques which were affixed to buildings in the streets around the Abbey in Albert-street, Bardwell-road, Pageant-road and Sopwell-lane to the east; Holywell-hill and Orchard-street* to the south; Fishpool-street to the west; High-street Lower Dagnall Street* and Verulam-road to the north. It is believed that in England, they are unique. All but the plaque in High-street are on the walls of private houses. The Abbey's archives, shows that the department store of Selfridges, London were the owners of the High-street building.

Over forty years later the *St. Albans City Council* reached agreement with all but one of the owners on whose propérty the memorials are situated, whereby the Council undertakes future maintenance. Agreement was not reached with the owner in Lower Dagnall-street*, where the plaque is blank and in Orchard-street*, off Abbey Mill-lane, where the tablet had been missing for some considerable time.
Source: *The Street Memorials of St. Albans Abbey Parish, by Alice Goodman. Published by the St. Albans and Hertfordshire Architectural and Archaeological Society. 1987. ISBN 0-901194-08-5. [available from bookshops and the Society].*

*On Sunday, 24th November 2002, memorials in Orchard-street and Lower Dagnall-street were reinstated. Graham Lyndon-Jones, the Dean of St. Albans and St. Albans and Hertfordshire Architectural and Archaeological Society have been involved in securing funds to undertake this work.

St. Albans Diocesan War Memorial.

On Tuesday, 16th June, 1925 the dedication of the St.Albans Diocesan War Memorial took place in the Cathedral and Abbey Church of St. Alban. The Bishop of St. Albans dedicated the stained glass in the Great West Window, which had been designed by Mr J. Ninian Comper.

In addition, three books of Remembrance were dedicated which contain the names, with their regiments of the 12,778 men and women of the Diocese of St. Albans "who suffered death when they were serving in the cause of their country in that great war which begun on the fourth day of August in the year of the Lord MDCCCCXIIII".
Source: *Compiler.*

War Memorial chapel, St. Albans Abbey

In 1995, the memorials which had been placed upon the north wall of the Nave were re-organised and brought together in a new Memorial chapel. Here are held the banners of Veterans' organisations, the Royal British Legion, plaques recording the conflicts of the 20th century including the lectern which holds the three books recording the names of those men and women who died in the Great War. After completion there were found to be some whose names were missing and these have been added subsequently. The pages of these three books are changed periodically.

On the window ledge to the north of the Altar, is placed the Toc H lamp, which once was kept in the recess behind a grille in the South Transept.

Nearby, behind the Nave Altar is the Spanish Crystal Cross, given by the Glossop family in memory of two of their sons who died in the war.

St. Albans Roll of Honour.

In the later stages of the war, the *Herts. Advertiser* announced publication of a *Roll of Honour*. Names of those who lived in the St. Albans Abbey parish are recorded (see above). Elsewhere in the City there may have been illuminated panels erected in streets where many men were in the army. These individual *Rolls of Honour* may all have perished, because they were not intended to be permanent.
Source: Gibbs & Bamforth. St. Albans Roll of Honour.

Dividing St. Albans into four quarters shows where the greatest number of deaths occurred. In the **North-west** (west of St.Peter's-street & Harpenden-road and north of Verulam-road), those roads with the highest incidence of deaths are Kimberley-road (13), Church-street (12), Bernard street (9), and Cannon-street (9), Catherine-street (8) and Dalton-street (8). Fewer deaths were listed in 27 other roads.

North-east (east of St.Peter's-street etc. and north of London-road). Roads with the highest recorded deaths notified: Alexandra-road (14) , Hatfield-road (14), Castle-road (11), Sandpit-lane (11), Arthur-road (10), Culver-road (9), Upper Culver-road (8), Heath-road (8), Upper Heath-road (8). Fewer deaths were listed in 58 other roads.

South-east (south of London-road; east of Holywell-hill). London-road

(14), Albert-street (12), Sopwell-lane (11) plus Park-corner (5). Park-corner is on the bend between the *White Lion* public house and Keyfield-terrace; Longmire-road (8). Fewer deaths in 15 other roads.

South-west (west of Holywell-hill; south of Verulam-road). Fishpool-street (18), King's-road (13), Holywell-hill (10), Verulam-road (9), Gorhambury-estate (8). Fewer deaths reported in 28 other roads. There were 41 names on the *Roll of Honour*, for whom their address was not recorded. Names of some who lived outside St. Albans-city were listed on nearby estates, farms and farm cottages. Streets with high number of deaths reflect the most densely populated areas.
Source: *Compiler from Roll of Honour.*

"Guard our sailors and soldiers".

As part of the research carried out by the committee who have enabled the Orchard-street and Lower Dagnall-street memorials to be replaced in-situ, an illuminated roll for Abbey Mill-lane and Orchard-street has been found in a person's loft. 25 names were listed. A copy of a *Roll of Honour* has been found which lists men who went to war from Cannon-street, West View-road and Ashwell-street. 48 names are listed.
Source: *Brian Moody, Hon.Secretary, St.Albans & Hertfordshire Architectural and Archaeological Society.*

Diocesan War Memorial Window

At the **head of the window** and in the **main rose** of the tracery are the shields of Great Britain, England, Scotland, Ireland, Wales, America, France, Italy and Belgium, enclosing the shields of the six Boroughs within the Diocese of St. Albans and the Badges of the Hertfordshire and the Hertfordshire and Bedfordshire Regiments. The **left hand rose** contains the shields of Russia, Serbia, Romania, Montenegro, Greece and Portugal; and the **right hand rose,** the Star of India, Newfoundland, Canada, Australia, New Zealand and South Africa.

Above them are the **shields** of St. Alban and St. George under smaller **shields** of St. Edward the Confessor, the older Patron of England, and the lilies of St. Louis of France. Between them are scrolls with the words *Glory to God on high and on earth peace to men of good will* [from the Gloria in Excelsis].

Immediately beneath, at the **head of the nine lights**, is the nine-fold choir of the heavenly host which look down on the great soldier saints which are [left] *St. Martin* [France]; *St. Alban* [England]; *St. Michael* [the heavenly warrior]; [right] *St. George* [England] with the slain dragon at his feet; *St. Joan of Arc* [France]; *St. Quintyn* [Flanders]. With the exception of St. Joan and St.Michael, which are clothed in medieval armour, the others are in Roman military dress. St. Alban holds a sword as well as the "Alban [round-headed] Cross".

Above these lights is the youthful figure of Jesus Christ, 7ft 6in. tall and a soldier and a sailor. They are surrounded by a historical group which consists of Mary, Mother of Jesus and the other women behind the sailor, St. Mary Magdalen (centre light) and St. John and the centurion (right).

In the background are horsemen who carry the flags of the Allied Nations. The figures stand on a green "sward" strewn with poppies and in front of the architectural base are the badges of the Air Force and the Artillery.

Source: *St. Albans Abbey. Order of Service, Tuesday, 16th June 1925.*

St. Albans Cemetery, Hatfield Road.

	L	K	J	I	H	G
6	Pte.A.W.Stolton (34) Bedfordshire Rgt 17 May 19	Pte.J.A.McLellan(24) 13bn Canadian Inf. d.7 Oct.16	Pte.J.E.Pollard 1bn Canadian Inf. d15 Dec.16	Cpl. A.Cosgrove 7bn.Canadian Inf. d.2 Oct.16	Dvr.F.W.Gates(26) Royal Field Artillery d.7 Jul.19	Pnr.W.Catlin(48) Royal Engineers d.29 Dec.19
5	Pte. W.Fennell (43) 4 South African Inf. Rgt. d.1 Apr.19	Spr.J.T.Sharp (38) Royal Engineers d.25 Dec.18 Pte.H.W.Warren (21) Suffolk Rgt. + d.17 Dec.18	Pte. H. Beesley (20) 85bn Canadian Inf. d.10 Nov.18	Nurse H. Chadwick Vol. Aid Detachment d.2 Nov.18	Pte.C.W.Mabbott(19) Canada Mch.Gun.C. d.23 Oct.18	Pte.J.Strickland(35) 51bn Australian Inf. d.2 Oct.18
4	Ft/Cdt.J.B.Hebley (29)Royal Air Force & Ldn.Rifle Brigade d.14 Feb.19	Pte.J.V.O'Toole 30bn Australian Inf. d.27 Oct.16	Pte.M.J.Quinn (27) The Queens d.9 Nov.18 Pte.J.H.Knapp(34) R.A.S.C. d.7 Nov.18	Pte.P.G.Keegan(20) Inns of Court OTC d.3 Nov.18 Pte.F.J.Fennell (43) R.A.M.C. d.1 Apr.19	Boy Mech.W.Fennel (16) R.A.F. d.20 Jul.18 Pte.E.Jones Devonshire Rgt. d.20 Jul.18	Pte.R.J.Weaver (21) 18th Hussars d.25 May 18
3	Pte. A. Izzard (24) Bedfordshire Rgt. d.30 Jan.19	Pte.E.Ellerbeck (27) 5bn Canadian Inf. d.13 Dec.18	Pte.C.H.Beard Middlesex Rgt. d.8 Nov.18 Spr.A.Thorpe (27) Royal Engineers d.6 Mar.18	J.G.Coleman (16) d.24 Oct.18	Cpl.L.Mackenzie(21 3rd London Rgt. d.14 Jul.18 Pte.G.Pudsey Lincolnshire Rgt. d.30 Jun.18	Pte.A.Sturgess (26) 22bn Australian Inf. d.5 Dec.17
2	A.M.II H.J.Field (41) R.A.F. d.15 Jan.19 Pte.J.Quinn (45) Loyal N.Lancs.Rgt. d.16 Feb.19	Pte.W.J. Dean 20bn Rifle Bde. d.12 Nov.18 Pte.S.A.H.Piper(40) R.A.S.C. d.26 Nov.18	A.M.III. W.Harrison Royal Air Force d.3 Nov.18 Pte.H.C.Bassett(18) The Queens d.1 Nov.18	Pte.E.N.Bates 24bn Canadian Inf. d.24 Oct.18	Pte.A.W.Brooker(41) 53bn The Queens d.19 Jun.18 Pte.D.Hennessey(58) R.A.M.C. d.16 Jun.18	Pte.A.Reading 12bn Australian Inf. 13 Oct.17
1	Pte.W.M.Gillin 22bn.Australian Inf. d. 22 Aug.16 *headstone date incorrect. Was buried August 1916. Remains were exhumed & rebuied here.1918..*	Pte.A.Winsall (25) 39bn Australian Inf. d.9 Nov.18	Pte.G.J.Walton (22) R.A.M.C. d.1 Nov.18 Cpl.H.Rackett (27) Royal Engineers d.30 Oct.18	Pte.G.C.Hibberd R.A.M.C. d.27 Oct.18 Pte.II. W.R.Bennett Royal Air Force d.21 Aug.18	Pte.R.Millen (36) 34bn Australian Inf. d.25 Apr.18	Gnr.W.Martin (34) Royal Garrison Art. d.20 Dec.17 Pte.T.Hingley R. Berkshire Rgt. d.15 Aug.17

Soldiers' Corner Graves

	1	2	3	4	5	6	7
F	Pte.W.H.Simpson 3 Rgt S.African Inf. d.22 Apr.18	L/Sgt.C.I.McKay 54bn Canadian Inf. d.20 Aug.18	Sgt.L.J.Fox. StA Anti Aircraft Defence Royal Garr. Artillery d.18 Apr.18	Rfm.W.F.Crawford (24)2 Kg.R.Rifle Cor. d.15 Nov.17	L/Cpl.R.Simmonds The Queens d.15 Aug.17	Pte.H.Heath (32) 26 Training Reserve Bn. d.8 Aug.17 / Pte.W.McGregor (30) R.A.S.C. d.21 Sep.17	Pte.T.Tortoishell 3 Austrian Pioneers d.8 Jun.17
E	Pte.W.Taylor (45) Bedfordshire Rgt. d.15 Jul.20	Spr.L.Loureiro(36) known as Spr.Vasco Australian Engineer. d.3 Aug.18	Pte.H.G.Hill(28) Bedfordshire Rgt. d.13 Apr.18 / Dvr.C.Wakeling Royal Field Artillery 4 Apr.18	Pte.A.D.G.Crook(25) 78bn Canadian Inf. d.31 May 17		Sgt.R.J.Arnott (29) R.A.S.C. d.18 May 17 / Pte. B. Miller Suffolk Rgt. d.12 May 17	Pte.L.Whittingham 40bn Australian Inf. d.14 May 17
D		Lt.J.S.Hobbs(43) Royal Field Artillery d.3 Aug.18	L/Cpl.H.E.Angel(36) Military Police Corp. d.27 Mar.18 / L/Cpl.M.Moore(32) Royal Munster Fus. d.27 Mar.18	Pte.J.J.Baynes 16bn Australian Inf. d.5 May 17		Pte.W.J.Wilkinson Suffolk Rgt. 29 Dec.16 / Pte.F.J.Flint (34) Middlesex Rgt. d.31 Dec.16	Pte.J.B.Needham E.Yorkshire Rgt. 29 Dec.16 / Pte.G.Halsey (39) Bedfordshire Rgt. d.27 Dec.16
C		Pte.A.H.Poole (44) 12bn Australian Inf. d.22 May 18	L/Cpl.T.McGrath(23) Australian A.S.C. d.18 Mar.18	Pte. H. Marshall (19) 44bn Australian Inf. d.2 Apr.17		Pte. A. Ross (43) R.A.S.C. d.13 Dec.16	Pte. A. Cable Bedfordshire Rgt. d.4 Dec.16 / Pte.J.O'Keefe R.Irish Fusiliers d.24 Nov.16
B		Pte.H.Paterson(29) 16bn Australian Inf. d.17 May.18	Pte.D.C.MacNiven 25bn Australian Inf. d.6 Feb.18	Pte.M.Rose 13bn Durham L.Inf. d.18 Apr.17	Pte.A.F.Welsh (31) R.Inniskilling Fus. d.18 Mar.17	Pte.J. Lee (47) Royal Air Force d.19 Mar.19 / Pte.L.Somers (49) Irish Guards d.28 Oct.16	Pte.J.B.Eyles (39) The Queen's d.3 Oct.16
A		Pte.J.W.E.Burns(21) 49bn.Australian Inf. d.22 Apr.18	C.Sgt.Maj.W.Oakes (34) Middlesex Rgt. d.5 Dec.17	Cpl.J.L.P.Gifford Hon.Artillery Com. d.11 Mar.17 / CQMR Sgt.A.How (37)Middlesex Rgt. d.11 Mar.17		Dvr.J.T.Rippard Royal Engineers d.6 Oct.16	Pte.ll. W. Evans Royal Air Force d.30 Dec.18 / Pte.W.A.Winter Hampshire Rgt. d.7 Jul.16

St. Albans Cemetery, Hatfield-road.

Chapel

C

B

A

CEMETERY

B.Z46
BJ48 BJ49
BF48
BE48
BD47
BC47
BB47
BB47
BB46
EB48
EF51

E
F

E
F

**Soldiers' Corner
Graves, 1916-20**

**Graves along
Eastern edge**

Graves of those not interred in
Soldiers' Corner, St. Albans Cemetery, Hatfield Road.
A list of burials and their location in the Albans cemetery. For each is given their surname, rank, initials, regiment, date of death and the section of the cemetery in which their grave can be found plus the row and grave number.

Adams, Pte. D.J. *2bn Bedfordshire Rgt. d.29 Jul.16.* [E.F12]
Andrew, 2/Lt. J.L. *Royal Flying Corps. d.13 Dec.17* [E.C24]
Angel, L/Cpl. H.E. *Military Mounted Police Corps d.27 Mar.18* [D.4A]
Atkins, Sgt. P.A. *Herts Yeomanry d.23 Nov.15* [C. A22]
Baker Burrows, L/Cpl. *1bn King's Royal Rifle Corps d.28 Jun.18* [E.Z34]
Barker, Pte. S.T. 5bn Royal Fusiliers *d.3 Feb.15* [B.J48]
Beirne, 2/Lt. W. *89th Sqdn. Royal Air Force d.18 Aug.18* [E.N19]
Blatherwick, 2/Lt. W.G. *56th Training Sqdn.R.A.F. d.19 May.18* [E.I24]
Brazier, Pte.D. *S.Staffordshire Regt. d.2 Apr.16* [B.B47]
Callen, Pte. W. *MT Royal Army Service Corps d.20 Aug.19* [E.F51]
Chieza, Pte. A. *4bn Bedfordshire Regt d.14 Feb.20* [A.26/37]
Clark, Pte. H.J. *MT Royal Army Service Corps d.4 Mar.19* [B.Z/A3]
Cloutte, Pte. J.R. *Canadian Army Service Corps d.17 May 17,* [A.T18]
Cole-Hamilton, Capt. C.W.E. *2bn Royal Scots/R.F.C.d.2 Jul.17* [E.A24]
Constable, Pte.J.R. *Herts Regt. trans. to Labour Corps d.30 Jun.19* [C.Y29]
Curnow, Pte. H.J. *Royal Welch Fusiliers, d.28 Feb.19* [A.B21]
Day, (Miss) C. *RAF.Records(Blandford),W.R.A.F. d.30 Nov.18* [E.I25]
Doherty, Pte. P. *66th Field Bakery, R.A.S.C. d.9 Apr.16* [B.Z46]
Fenwick, F/0. H.E. *24Sqdn. R.A.F. d.4 Nov.20* [A ZA33]
Finn, Pte P. *Royal Munster Fusiliers, d.29 Oct.15* [B.C47]
Ford, Spr. G.F. *2Ldn.Field Coy, Royal Engineers d.13 Apr.15* [A.A38]
Fox, Pte. R. *27bn Durham Light Infantry d.11 Apr.17* [E.O11]
Gathard, L/Cpl. A. *8bn Bedfordshire Regt. d.31 Jan 16* [C.J32]
Goodfellow, Pte. H. *2bn Coldstream Gds. d.29 Apr 19* [B.Z/C2]
Graham, Pte. E. *Royal Army Service Corps, d.3 Sept. 15* [B.E48]   [E.K24]
Graham, Flt.Cdt.V.W. *41st Training Depot (Denham), RAF, d.16 Jul 18*
Greathead, 2/Lt. J.H. *Royal Flying Corps, d.11 Jan 18* [E.D24]
Harvey, Pte. A. *Depot, Bedfordshire Regt. d.31 Aug.17* [E.Q8]

Hiskett, Pt. F.J. *1/5bn Suffolk Regt 4 Sept.19* [E.S18]
Hope, Pte. B. *7bn Bedfordshire Regt/Labour Corps d.31 Aug.20* [E.I30]
Kingham, Cpl. P.E. [MM] *Hertfordshire Regt. d.19 May 18* [E.S20]
Lawford, Pte. R.R. *South Staffordshire Regt. d8 Aug.15* [B.D47]
Lawrence, Pte G. *3bn Bedfordshire Regt. d.20 Dec.15* [B.B46]
Lea, Pte. S. *Hertfordshire Regt. d.9 Aug.19* [E.F30]
Le Feuvre, Lt. W.E. *27th Training Sqdn. R.A.F. d.9 May 18* [E.H24]
Lewis, Pte.II. G.W. *R.A.F. d.28 Nov.18* [E.F26]
Lynes, Pte. P.J. *M.T.Royal Army Service Corps d.4 Oct.15* [B.F48]
Mackey, Lt. E.R. *Royal Flying Corps d.15 Mar.17* [B.F48]
Manktellow, Pte. C, *5bn Royal Sussex Regt. d.5 Jan.16* [B.J49]
Markwell, Cpl. F.H. *Hertfordshire Regt. d.8 Dec.16* [E.H19]
Martin, Pte. H. *20bn London Regt. d.13 Apr.15* [A.F37]
Meadway, Lt. B.W. *7bn Northamptonshire Regt. & 56 Training Sqdn. R.A.F. d.4 Jun.18* [E.J24]
Millard, Dvr. D.D. *Royal Army Service Corps d.6 Dec.18* [E.O18]
Miller, Lt. C.T. *76bn Canadian Infantry & Royal Flying Corps d.8 Dec.16* [F.H1]
Mocock, Armourer St/Sgt. J.A. *Royal Army Ordnance Corps d.1 Nov.17* [E.R11]
Muskett, Skr P.O. E.W. *H.M.S.Pembroke, R.N. d.23 Feb.20* [B.Zc41]
Penfold,Pte. C. *2/1bn Hertfordshire Regt. d.13 Apr.16* [E.E16]
Smith, Pte A. *Iniskilling Dragoons d.30 Dec.17* [E.R6]
Smith, Pte. J. *3bn Hampshire Regt. d.8 Sept.17* [E.B48]
Stone, Pte. A.C. *3bn Bedfordshire Regt. d.7 Jul.15* [E.A16]
Swinnerton, Pte. A.C. *3bn Bedfordshire Regt. d.2 Feb.16* [B.B47]
Warwick, Rfn. W.W. *Post Office Rifles d.28 Oct.18* [E.D28]
Watson, Pte. G.F. *6Ldn. Field Ambul. R.A.M.C. d.29 Mar.15* [A.D35]
Wheeler, Skr. P.O. C.E. *H.M.S.Victory, R.N. d.20 Sept.18* [E.Y5]
Wilson, Pte. H. *2bn Middlesex Regt. d.9 Dec.18* [E.Z12]
Woodman, Pte. T.F. *Herts. Yeomanry d.29 Nov.16* [F.C1]

List of other graves, by section and year of burial.

Section A
Chieza, Pte (1920)
Cloutte, Pte (1917)
Curnow, Pte (1919)
Fenwick, FO (1920)
Ford, Spr (1915)
Martin, Pte (1915)
Watson, Pte (1915)

Section B
Brazier, Pte (1916)
Clark, Pte (1919)
Goodfellow, Pte (1919)
Graham, Pte (1915)
Muskett, Skr.P.O. (1920)

Section C
Atkins, Sgt (1915)
Constable Pte (1919)
Gathard, L/Cpl (1916)

Section D
Angel, L/Cpl (1918)

Section E
Adams, Pte (1916)
Andrew, 2/Lt (1917)
Baker Burrows, L/Cpl (1918)
Beirne, 2/Lt (1918)
Blatherwick, 2/Lt (1918)
Cole-Hamilton, Capt. (1917)
Day, Miss (1918)
Fox, Pte (1917)
Graham, Flt/Cdt (1916)
Greathead, 2/Lt. (1918)
Harvey, Pte (1917)
Hiskett, Pte (1919)

Section E (continued)
Hope, Pte (1920)
Kingham, Pte (1918)
Lea, Pte (1919)
Le Feuvre, Lt. (1918)
Lewis Pte.ll (1918)
Markwell, Cpl (1916)
Meadway, Lt (1918)
Millard, Dvr (1918)
Mocock, Armourer S/Sgt (1917)
Penfold, Pte (1916)
Smith, Pte J. (1915)
Stone, Pte. (1915)
Warwick, Rfn (1918)
Wheeler , Skr P.O. (1918)
Wilson, Pte (1918)

Section F
Mackey, Lt (1917)
Miller, Lt. (1916)
Woodman, Pte (1916)

Eastern edge of cemetery
Barker, Pte (1915)
Callen, Pte (1919)
Doherty, Pte (1916)
Finn, Pte (1915)
Graham, Pte (1915)
Lawford, Pte (1915)
Lawrence, Pte (1915)
Lynes, Pte (1915)
Manktellow, Pte (1916)
Smith, Pte A. (1917)
Swinnerton, Pte (1916)

Great War graves elsewhere in Hertfordshire.

Abbots Langley [9 graves]
Aldbury (St.Mary) [1]
Aldenham [1]
Apsley End [6]
Ardley [1]
Ashwell (Congregation) [1]
Ashwell New [1]
Ashwell (St.Mary) [3]

Baldock District [2]
Barnet (Christ Church) [9]
Barley Churchyard [1]
   (St.Mary) [1]
   (St.Margaret) [2]
Bayford [2]
Bengeo [3]
Benington [1]
Bishops Stortford [2]
Bourne End [2]
Braughing [3]
Breachwood Green Baptist [1]
Broxbourne (St.Augustine) [1]
Buckland [1]
Bushey (St.James's} [15]

Cheshunt Burial Ground [24]
Chipperfield [2]
Chipping Barnet (St.John) [19]
Chorley Wood (Christ Church)[6]
Codicote [2]

Flamstead [4]

East Barnet Great Northern [104]
2 Belgian, 52 German, 12 Austrian
Elstree (St.Nicholas) [3]

Frogmore (Holy Trinity) [4]

Graveley [1]
Great Amwell [1]
Great Berkhamsted [14]

Harpenden (St.Nicholas) [10]
Hatfield Cemetery [10] and
   1 German prisoner
Hatfield Hyde [1]
Hemel Hempstead, Heath La. [15]
Hertford (All Saints) [9]
Hertford District [5] and
   1 Belgian soldier
Hertford (St.Andrew) [6]
Hertingfordbury [4]
Hinkworth [1]
High Wych (St.James} [2]
Hitchin District [29]
Hockerill [1]
Hoddesdon District [9]
Holwell [1]
Hunsdon [2]

Ickleford [1]

King's Walden [1]
Kings Langley [2]

Knebworth (St.Martin) [3]
Knebworth (St.Mary) [3]
Kimpton [2]

Langleybury [1]
Lemsford [1]
Lilley [2 graves]
Little Amwell [3]
Little Gaddesdon [3]
Little Munden (All Saints)
    28 German civilians
Little Wymondley [1]
London Colney [1]
Long Marston [1]

Markyate New [7]
Much Hadham [3]

Northchurch Baptist [1]
Northchurch (St.Mary) [1]
Norton, Letchworth [1] and
    4 Belgian graves

Offley [1]

Pirton [1]
Ponsbourne (St.Mary) [1]
Potton End [1]
Radlett [2]
Radwell [1]
Redbourn (St.Mary) [5]
Rickmansworth District [18]
Royston [1]
Royston Noncomformist [1]

St.Albans (Hill End Hospital
    Cemetery) 1 Austrian civilian
St. Albans (St.Michael's) [1]
St.Ippolyts's [2]
St.Paul's Walden [2]
Sandon [2]
Sandridge [2]
Sawbridgeworth [5]
Shenley (St.Botolph) [5]
Shephall [1]
Standon [1]
Standon, Old Hall Green RC
    churchyard 1 German civilian
Stanstead Abbots [2]
Stapleford [1]
Stevenage (St.Nicholas) [11]

Tewin [3]
Therfield [2]
Thorley [2]
Thundridge [2]
Tring [16]

Walkern [2]
Ware New Cemetery [15]
Ware Old Cemetery [1]
Wareside (Holy Trinity) [3]
Watford Cemetery [57]
Watton-on-Stone [1]
Welwyn Cemetery [2]
Westmill [2]
Wheathamstead (St.Helen) [4]
Willian [1]
Wilston, Tring [2]
Wormley [1]

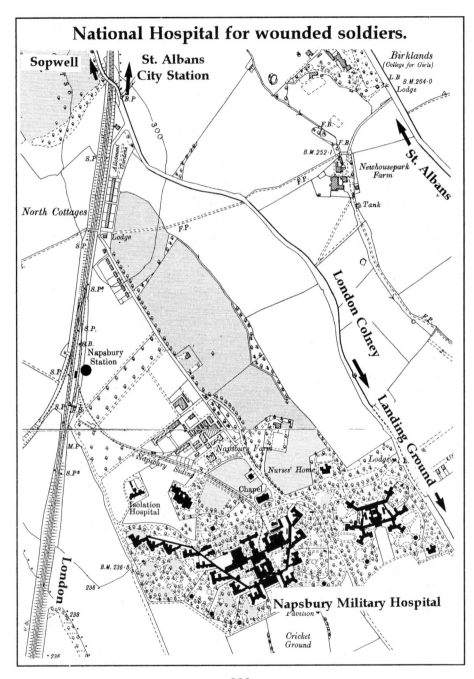

National Hospital for wounded soldiers.

London Colney Landing Ground.

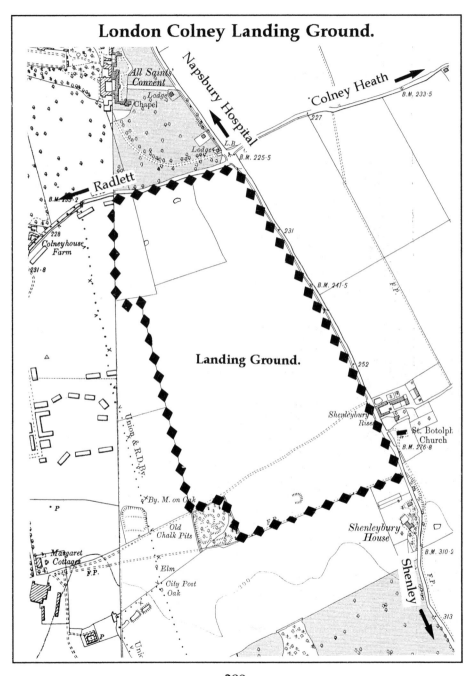

All Saints Convent

Lodge
Chapel

Napsbury Hospital

Colney Heath
B.M. 233·5

227

Lodge

L.B.

B.M. 225·5

Radlett

B.M. 233·2

228

Colneyhouse
Farm

231·8

231

B.M. 241·5

F.P.

252

Landing Ground.

Union & R.D. By.

Shenleybury
Rise

St. Botolph
Church
B.M. 276·8

By. M. on Oak

Old Chalk Pits

F.P.

Shenleybury
House

B.M. 310·2

P

Margaret
Cottages

F.P.

Elm

City Post
Oak

300

Shenley

F.P.

313

P

Union

299

Bibliography

Bedfordshire Regiment. War Diary, 1914-1919.

Clayton, P.B. Letters from Flanders: war time letters to his mother.

Croft, Henry Page
    My life of strife. 1949.
    Twenty two months under fire. 1917.

Gibbs & Bamforth Ltd. St. Albans Roll of Honour.

Goodman, Alice. Street Memorials of St. Albans Abbey Parish. 1987.

Herts. Advertiser and St. Albans Times.

Hertfordshire Mercury.

Hertfordshire Regiment. War Diary, 1914-18.

Imperial War Graves Commission Annual Reports, 1925-28.

Imperial War Graves Commission Memorial Registers of Cemeteries.
  (in Imperial War Museum Library).

Lever, Tresham. Clayton of Toc H. 1971.

Sainsbury, J.B. The Hertfordshire Regiment. 1988.

Salisbury, Frank O. Portrait and Pageant. 1944.

Salisbury, Frank O. Sarum Chase. 1953.

Sources of information

Bedfordshire Record Office, Bedford.

Cavan Archive.

Gorhambury Collection, St. Albans.

Hertfordshire Archives and Local Studies, Hertford.

Hertfordshire Libraries - Central Resources, Hatfield and
 - St.Albans Central Library.

Guildhall Library, London.

Imperial War Museum Library, London

London Library

Luton Central Library

Luton Museum Service

Museum of St. Albans

Public Record Office, Kew

St.Albans City and District Archives

Toc H., Wendover, Buckinghamshire.